Lecture Notes in Artificial Intelligence 2307

Subseries of Lecture Notes in Computer Science
Edited by J. G. Carbonell and J. Siekmann

Lecture Notes in Computer Science
Edited by G. Goos, J. Hartmanis, and J. van Leeuwen

Springer

Berlin
Heidelberg
New York
Barcelona
Hong Kong
London
Milan
Paris
Tokyo

Chengqi Zhang   Shichao Zhang

Association
Rule Mining

Models and Algorithms

 Springer

Series Editors

Jaime G. Carbonell, Carnegie Mellon University, Pittsburgh, PA, USA
Jörg Siekmann, University of Saarland, Saarbrücken, Germany

Authors

Chengqi Zhang
Shichao Zhang
University of Technology, Sydney, Faculty of Information Technology
P.O. Box 123 Broadway, Sydney, NSW 2007 Australia
E-mail: {chengqi,zhangsc}@it.uts.edu.au

Cataloging-in-Publication Data applied for

Die Deutsche Bibliothek - CIP Einheitsaufnahme

Zhang, Chengqi:
Association rule mining : models and algorithms / Chengqi Zhang ;
Shichao Zhang. - Berlin ; Heidelberg ; New York ; Barcelona ; Hong Kong ;
London ; Milan ; Paris ; Tokyo : Springer, 2002
  (Lecture notes in computer science ; Vol. 2307 : Lecture notes in
artificial intelligence)
  ISBN 3-540-43533-6

CR Subject Classification (1998): I.2.6, I.2, H.2.8, H.2, H.3, F.2.2

ISSN 0302-9743
ISBN 3-540-43533-6 Springer-Verlag Berlin Heidelberg New York

Springer-Verlag Berlin Heidelberg New York
a member of BertelsmannSpringer Science+Business Media GmbH

http://www.springer.de

© Springer-Verlag Berlin Heidelberg 2002
Printed in Germany

Typesetting: Camera-ready by author, data conversion by Boller Mediendesign
Printed on acid-free paper   SPIN: 10846539   06/3142   5 4 3 2 1 0

Preface

Association rule mining is receiving increasing attention. Its appeal is due, not only to the popularity of its parent topic 'knowledge discovery in databases and data mining', but also to its neat representation and understandability. The development of association rule mining has been encouraged by active discussion among communities of users and researchers. All have contributed to the formation of the technique with a fertile exchange of ideas at important forums or conferences, including SIGMOD, SIGKDD, AAAI, IJCAI, and VLDB. Thus association rule mining has advanced into a mature stage, supporting diverse applications such as data analysis and predictive decisions.

There has been considerable progress made recently on mining in such areas as quantitative association rules, causal rules, exceptional rules, negative association rules, association rules in multi-databases, and association rules in small databases. These continue to be future topics of interest concerning association rule mining. Though the association rule constitutes an important pattern within databases, to date there has been no specilized monograph produced in this area. Hence this book focuses on these interesting topics.

The book is intended for researchers and students in data mining, data analysis, machine learning, knowledge discovery in databases, and anyone else who is interested in association rule mining. It is also appropriate for use as a text supplement for broader courses that might also involve knowledge discovery in databases and data mining.

The book consists of eight chapters, with bibliographies after each chapter. Chapters 1 and 2 lay a common foundation for subsequent material. This includes the preliminaries on data mining and identifying association rules, as well as necessary concepts, previous efforts, and applications. The later chapters are essentially self-contained and may be read selectively, and in any order. Chapters 3, 4, and 5 develop techniques for discovering hidden patterns, including negative association rules and causal rules. Chapter 6 presents techniques for mining very large databases, based on instance selection. Chapter 7 develops a new technique for mining association rules in databases which utilizes external knowledge, and Chapter 8 presents a summary of the previous chapters and demonstrates some open problems.

Beginners should read Chapters 1 and 2 before selectively reading other chapters. Although the open problems are very important, techniques in other chapters may be helpful for experienced readers who want to attack these problems.

January 2002   *Chengqi Zhang and Shichao Zhang*

Acknowledgments

We are deeply indebted to many colleagues for the advice and support they gave during the writing of this book. We are especially grateful to Alfred Hofmann for his efforts in publishing this book with Springer-Verlag. And we thank the anonymous reviewers for their detailed constructive comments on the proposal of this work.

For many suggested improvements and discussions on the material, we thank Professor Geoffrey Webb, Mr. Zili Zhang, and Ms. Li Liu from Deakin University; Professor Huan Liu from Arizona State University, Professor Xindong Wu from Vermont University, Professor Bengchin Ooi and Dr. Kianlee Tan from the National University of Singapore, Dr. Hong Liang and Mr. Xiaowei Yan from Guangxi Normal University, Professor Xiaopei Luo from the Chinese Academy of Sciences, and Professor Guoxi Fan from the Education Bureau of Quanzhou.

Contents

1. Introduction

Association rule mining is an important topic in data mining. Our work in this book focuses on this topic. To briefly clarify the background of association rule mining in this chapter, we will concentrate on introducing data mining techniques.

In Section 1.1 we begin with explaining what data mining is. In Section 1.2 we argue as to why data mining is needed. In Section 1.3 we recall the process of knowledge discovery in databases (KDD). In Section 1.4 we demonstrate data mining tasks and faced data types. Section 1.5 introduces some basic data mining techniques. Section 1.6 presents data mining and marketing. In Section 1.7, we show some examples where data mining is applied to real-world problems. And, finally in Section 1.8 we discuss future work involving data mining.

1.1 What Is Data Mining?

First, let us consider transactions (market baskets) that are obtained from a supermarket. This involves spelling out the attribute values (goods or items purchased by a customer) for each transaction, separated by commas. Parts of interest in three of the transactions are listed as follows.

Smith milk, Sunshine bread, GIS sugar
Pauls milk, Franklin bread, Sunshine biscuit
Yeung milk, B&G bread, Sunshine chocolate.

The first customer bought Smith milk, Sunshine bread, and GIS sugar; and so on. Each data (item) consists of brand and product. For example, 'Smith milk' consists of brand 'Smith' and product 'milk'.

In the past, the most experienced decision-makers of the supermarket may have summarized patterns such as 'when a customer buys milk, he/she also buys bread' (this may have been used to predict customer behaviour) and, 'customers like to buy Sunshine products' (may have been used to estimate the sales of a new product). These decision-makers could draw upon years of general knowledge and knowledge about specific associations to form effective selections on the data.

Data mining can be used to discover useful information from data like 'when a customer buys milk, he/she also buys Bread' and 'customers like to buy Sunshine products'.

> Strictly speaking, *data mining is a process of discovering valuable information from large amounts of data stored in databases, data warehouses, or other information repositories.* This valuable information can be such as patterns, associations, changes, anomalies and significant structures [Fayyad-Piatetsky-Smyth 1996, Frawley 1992]. That is, data mining attempts to extract potentially useful knowledge from data.

Data mining differs from traditional statistics in that formal statistical inference is assumption-driven in the sense that a hypothesis is formed and validated against the data. Data mining, in contrast, is discovery-driven in the sense that patterns and hypotheses are automatically extracted from data. In other words, data mining is data driven while statistics is human driven.

One of the important areas in data mining is association rule mining. Since its introduction in 1993 [Agrawal-Imielinski-Swami 1993] the area of association rule mining has received a great deal of attention. Association rule mining has been mainly developed to identify the relationships strongly associated among itemsets that have high-frequency and strong-correlation. Association rules enable us to detect the items that frequently occur together in an application. The aim of this book is to present some techniques for mining association rules in databases.

1.2 Why Do We Need Data Mining?

There are two main reasons why data mining is needed.

(1) The task of finding really useful patterns as described above can be discouraging for inexperienced decision-makers due to the fact that the potential patterns in the three transactions are not often apparent.

(2) The amount of data in most applications is too large for manual analysis.

First, the most experienced decision-makers are able to wrap data such as "Smith milk, Pauls milk, and Yeung milk" into "milk" and "B&G bread, Franklin bread, Sunshine bread" into "bread" for the mining pattern "when a customer buys milk, he/she also buys Bread". In this way, the above data in Section 1.1 can be changed to

milk, bread, sugar
milk, bread, biscuit
milk, bread, chocolate.

Then the potential association becomes clear. Also, data such as "Smith milk" is divided into "Smith" and "milk" for the mining pattern "customers like to buy Sunshine products" for predicting the possible amount sold of a new product. A set of parts of the above data in Section 1.1 is listed below.

Smith, Sunshine, GIS
Pauls, Franklin, Sunshine
Yeung, B&G, Sunshine.

The pattern "customers like to buy Sunshine products" can be mined.

As will be seen shortly, there are also some useful patterns, such as negative associations and causality, that are hidden in the data (see Chapters 3, 4, and 5). The most experienced decision-makers may also find it very difficult to discovering hidden patterns in databases because there is too much information for a human to handle manually. Data mining is used to develop techniques and tools for assisting experienced and inexperienced decision-makers to analyze and process data for application purposes.

On the other hand, the pressure of enhancing corporate profitability has caused companies to spend more time identifying diverse opportunities such as sales and investments. To this end huge amounts of data are collected in their databases for decision-support purposes. The short list of examples below should be enough to place the current situation into perspective [Prodromidis 2000]:

- NASA's Earth Observing System (EOS) for orbiting satellites and other space-borne instruments send one terabyte of data to receiving stations each day.
- By the year 2000 a typical Fortune 500 company was projected to possess more than 400 trillion characters in their electronic databases, requiring 400 terabytes of mass storage.

With the increasing use of databases the need to be able to digest the large volumes of data being generated is now critical. It is estimated that only 5-10% of commercial databases have ever been analyzed [Fayyad-Simoudis 1997]. As Massey and Newing [Massey-Newing 1994] indicated, database technology was successful in recording and managing data but failed in the sense of moving from data processing to making it a key strategic weapon for enhancing business competition. The large volume and high dimensionality of databases leads to a breakdown in traditional human analysis.

Data mining incorporates technologies for analyzing data in very large databases and can identify potentially useful patterns in the data. Also, data mining has become very important in information industry, due to the wide availability of huge amounts of data in electronic forms and the imminent need for turning such data into useful information and knowledge for broad applications including market analysis, business management, and decision support.

1.3 Knowledge Discovery in Databases (KDD)

Data mining has been popularly treated as a synonym for *knowledge discovery in database*, although some researchers view data mining as an essential part (or step towards) of knowledge discovery.

The emergence of data mining and knowledge discovery in databases as a new technology has occurred because of the fast development and wide application of information and database technologies. Data mining and KDD are aimed at developing methodologies and tools which can automate the data analysis process and create useful information and knowledge from data to help in decision making. A widely accepted definition is given by Fayyad et al. [Fayyad-Piatetsky-Smyth 1996] in which KDD is defined as the non-trivial process of identifying valid, novel, potentially useful, and ultimately understandable patterns in data. This definition points to KDD as a complicated process comprising a number of steps. Data mining is one step in the process.

The scope of data mining and KDD is very broad and can be described as a multitude of fields of study related to data analysis. Statistical research has been focused on this area of study for over a century. Other fields related to data analysis, including statistics, data warehousing, pattern recognition, artificial intelligence and computer visualization. Data mining and KDD draws upon methods, algorithms and technologies from these diverse fields, and the common goal is extracting knowledge from data [Chen-Han-Yu 1996].

Over the last ten years data mining and KDD have been developed at a dramatic rate. In *Information Week*'s 1996 survey of 500 leading information technology user organizations in the US, data mining came second only to the Internet and intranets as having the greatest potential for innovation in information technology [Fayyad-Simoudis 1997]. Rapid progress is reflected, not only in the establishment of research groups on data mining and KDD in many international companies, but also in the investment area of banking, in telecommunication and in marketing sectors.

1.3.1 Processing Steps of KDD

In general, the process of knowledge discovery in databases consists of an iterative sequence of the following steps [Han-Huang-Cercone-Fu 1996, Han 1999, Liu-Motoda 1998, Wu 1995, Zhang 1989]:

- *Defining the problem.* The goals of the knowledge discovery project must be identified. The goals must be verified as actionable. For example, if the goals are met, a business can then put newly discovered knowledge to use. The data to be used must also be identified.
- *Data preprocessing.* Including data collecting, data cleaning, data selection, and data transformation.
  Data collecting. Obtaining necessary data from various internal and external sources; resolving representation and encoding differences; joining data from various tables to create a homogeneous source.

Data cleaning. Checking and resolving data conflicts, outliers (unusual or exceptional values), noisy or erroneous, missing data, and ambiguity; using conversions and combinations to generate new data fields such as ratios or rolled-up summaries. These steps require considerable effort often as much as 70 percent or more of the total data mining effort.

Data selection. Data relevant to an analysis task is selected from a given database. In other words, a data set is selected, or else attention is focused on a subset of variables or data samples, on which discovery is to be performed.

Data transformation. Data are transformed or consolidated into forms appropriate for mining by performing summary or aggregation operations.

– *Data mining.* An essential process, where intelligent methods are applied in order to extract data patterns. Patterns of interest in a particular representational form, or a set of such representations are searched for, including classification rules or trees, regression, clustering, sequence modeling, dependency, and so forth. The user can significantly aid the data mining method by correctly performing the preceding steps.

– *Post data mining.* Including pattern evaluation, deploying the model, maintenance, and knowledge presentation.

Pattern evaluation. It Identifies the truly interesting patterns representing knowledge, based on some *interesting measures*; tests the model for accuracy on an independent dataset one that has not been used to create the model. Assesses the sensitivity of a model; and pilot tests the model for usability. For example, if using a model to predict customer response, then a prediction can be made and a test mailing done to a subset to check how closely the responses match your predictions.

Deploying the model. For a predictive model, the model is used to predict results for new cases. Then the prediction is used to alter organizational behavior. Deployment may require building computerized systems that capture the appropriate data and generate a prediction in real time so that a decision maker can apply the prediction. For example, a model can determine if a credit card transaction is likely to be fraudulent.

Maintaining. Whatever is being modeled, it is likely to change over time. The economy changes, competitors introduce new products, or the news media finds a new hot topic. Any of these forces can alter customer behavior. So the model that was correct yesterday may no longer be good for tomorrow. Maintaining models requires constant revalidation of the model, with new data to assess if it is still appropriate.

Knowledge presentation. Visualization and knowledge representation techniques are used to present mined knowledge to users.

The knowledge discovery process is iterative. For example, while cleaning and preparing data you might discover that data from a certain source is unusable, or that data from a previously unidentified source is required to be merged with the other data under consideration. Often, the first time through, the data mining step will reveal that additional data cleaning is required.

With widely available relational database systems and data warehouses, the data preprocessing (i.e. data collecting, data cleaning, data selection, and data transformation) can be performed by constructing data warehouses and carrying out some OLAP (OnLine Analytical Processing) operations on the constructed data warehouses. The steps (data mining, pattern evaluation, and knowledge presentation processes) are sometimes integrated into one (possibly iterative) process, referred to as data mining. Patterns maintenance is often taken as the last step if required.

1.3.2 Feature Selection

Data preprocessing [Fayyad-Simoudis 1997] may be more time consuming and presents more challenges than data mining. Data often contains noise and erroneous components, and has missing values. There is also the possibility that redundant or irrelevant variables are recorded, while important features are missing. Data preprocessing includes provision for correcting inaccuracies, removing anomalies and eliminating duplicate records. It also includes provision for filling holes in the data and checking entries for consistency. Preprocessing is required to make the necessary transformation of the original into a format suitable for processing by data mining tools.

The other important requirement concerning the KDD process is 'feature selection' [Liu-Motoda 1998, Wu 2000]. KDD is a complicated task and usually depends on correct selection of features. Feature selection is the process of choosing features which are necessary and sufficient to represent the data. There are several issues influencing feature selection, such as masking variables, the number of variables employed in the analysis and relevancy of the variables.

Masking variables is a technique which hides or disguises patterns in data. Numerous studies have shown that inclusion of irrelevant variables can hide real clustering of the data so only those variables which help discriminate the clustering should be included in the analysis.

The number of variables used in data mining is also an important consideration. There is generally a tendency to use more variables than perhaps necessary. However, increased dimensionality has an adverse effect because, for a fixed number of data patterns, it makes the multi-dimensional data space sparse.

However, failing to include relevant variables can also cause failure in identifying the clusters. A practical difficulty in mining some industrial data is knowing whether all important variables have been included in the data records.

Prior knowledge should be used if it is available. Otherwise, mathematical approaches need to be employed. Feature extraction shares many approaches with data mining. For example, principal component analysis, which is a useful tool in data mining, is also very useful for reducing the dimension. However, this is only suitable for dealing with real-valued attributes. Mining association rules is also an effective approach in identifying the links between variables which take only categorical values. Sensitivity studies using feed-forward neural networks are also an effective way of identifying important and less important variables. Jain, Murty and Flynn [Jain-Murty-Flynn 1999] have reviewed a number of clustering techniques which identify discriminating variables in data.

1.3.3 Applications of Knowledge Discovery in Databases

Data mining and KDD is potentially valuable in virtually any industrial and business sectors where database and information technology are used. Below are some reported applications [Fayyad-Simoudis 1997, Piatetsky-Matheus 1992].

- Fraud detection: identifying fraudulent transactions.
- Loan approval: establishing credit worthiness of a customer requesting a loan.
- Investment analysis: predicting a portfolio's return on investment.
- Portfolio trading: trading a portfolio of financial instruments by maximizing returns and minimizing risks.
- Marketing and sales data analysis: identifying potential customers; establishing the effectiveness of a sale campaign.
- Manufacturing process analysis: identifying the causes of manufacturing problems.
- Experiment result analysis: summarizing experiment results and predictive models.
- Scientific data analysis.
- Intelligent agents and WWW navigation.

1.4 Data Mining Task

In general, data mining tasks can be classified into two categories: *descriptive data mining* and *predictive data mining*. The former describes the data set in a concise and summary manner and presents interesting general properties of the data; whereas the latter constructs one, or a set of, models, performs inference on the available set of data, and attempts to predict the behavior of new data sets [Chen-Han-Yu 1996, Fayyad-Simoudis 1997, Han 1999, Piatetsky-Matheus 1992, Wu 2000].

A data mining system may accomplish one or more of the following data mining tasks.

(1) **Class description**. Class description provides a concise and succinct summarization of a collection of data and distinguishes it from other data. The summarization of a collection of data is known as 'class characterization'; whereas the comparison between two or more collections of data is called 'class comparison' or 'discrimination'. Class description should cover its summary properties on data dispersion, such as variance, quartiles, etc. For example, class description can be used to compare European versus Asian sales of a company, identify important factors which discriminate the two classes, and present a summarized overview.

(2) **Association**. Association is the discovery of association relationships or correlations among a set of items. They are often expressed in the rule form showing attribute-value conditions that occur frequently together in a given set of data. An association rule in the form of $X \rightarrow Y$ is interpreted as 'database tuples that satisfy X are likely to satisfy Y'. Association analysis is widely used in transaction data analysis for direct marketing, catalog design, and other business decision making process.

Substantial research has been performed recently on association analysis with efficient algorithms proposed, including the level-wise Apriori search, mining multiple-level, multi-dimensional associations, mining associations for numerical, categorical, and interval data, meta-pattern directed or constraint-based mining, and mining correlations.

(3) **Classification**. Classification analyzes a set of training data (i.e., a set of objects whose class label is known) and constructs a model for each class, based on the features in the data. A decision tree, or a set of classification rules, is generated by such a classification process which can be used for better understanding of each class in the database and for classification of future data. For example, diseases can be classified based on the symptoms of patients.

There have been many classification methods developed such as in the fields of machine learning, statistics, databases, neural networks and rough sets. Classification has been used in customer segmentation, business modeling, and credit analysis.

(4) **Prediction**. This mining function predicts the possible values of certain missing data, or the value distribution of certain attributes in a set of objects. It involves the finding of the set of attributes relevant to the attribute of interest (e.g., by statistical analysis) and predicting the value distribution based on the set of data similar to the selected objects. For example, an employee's potential salary can be predicted based on the salary distribution of similar employees in the company. Up until now, regression analysis, generalized linear model, correlation analysis and decision trees have been useful tools in quality prediction. Genetic algorithms and neural network models have also been popularly used in this regard.

(5) **Clustering**. Clustering analysis identifies clusters embedded in the data, where a cluster is a collection of data objects that are "similar" to one an-

other. Similarity can be expressed by distance functions, specified by users
or experts. A good clustering method produces high quality clusters to ensure that the inter-cluster similarity is low and the intra-cluster similarity
is high. For example, one may cluster houses in an area according to their
house category, floor area, and geographical location.

To date data mining research has concentrated on high quality and scalable
clustering methods for large databases and multidimensional data warehouses.

(6) **Time-series analysis**. Time-series analysis analyzes large set of time
series data to determine certain regularity and interesting characteristics.
This includes searching for similar sequences or subsequences, and mining
sequential patterns, periodicities, trends and deviations. For example, one
may predict the trend of the stock values for a company based on its
stock history, business situation, competitors' performance, and the current
market.

There are also other data mining tasks, such as outlier analysis, etc. An
interesting research topic is the identification of new data mining tasks which
make better use of the collected data itself.

1.5 Data Mining Techniques

Data mining methods and tools can be categorized in different ways [Fayyad-
Simoudis 1997, Fayyad-Piatetsky-Smyth 1996]. They can be classified as clustering, classification, dependency modeling, summarization, regression, case-
based learning, and mining time-series data, according to functions and application purposes. Some methods are traditional and established, while some
are relatively new. Below we briefly review the techniques.

1.5.1 Clustering

Clustering is the unsupervised classification of patterns (observations, data
items, or feature vectors) into groups (clusters). The clustering problem has
been addressed in many contexts and by researchers in many disciplines;
this interest reflects its broad appeal and usefulness as one of the steps in
exploratory data analysis. Typical pattern clustering activity involves the
following steps:

(1) pattern representation (optionally including feature extraction and/or
selection);
(2) definition of a pattern proximity measure appropriate to the data domain;
(3) clustering or grouping;
(4) data abstraction (if needed); and
(5) assessment of output (if needed).

Given a number of data patterns [1] as shown in Table 1.1, each of which is described by a set of attributes, clustering [2] aims to devise a classification scheme for grouping the objects into a number of classes such that instances within a class are similar, in some respects, but distinct from those from other classes. This involves determining the number, as well as the descriptions, of classes. Grouping often depends on calculating a similarity or distance measure. Grouping multi-variate data into clusters according to similarity or dissimilarity measures is the goal of some applications. It is also a useful way to look at the data before further analysis is carried out. The methods can be further categorized according to requirement on prior knowledge of the data. Some methods require the number of classes to be an input, although the descriptions of the classes and assignments of individual data cases can be unknown. For example, the Kohonen neural network is designed for this purpose. In some other methods, neither the number nor descriptions of classes need to be known. The task is to determine the number and descriptions of classes as well as the assignment of data patterns. For example, the Bayesian automatic classification system-AutoClass and the adaptive resonance theory (ART2) [Jain-Murty-Flynn 1999] are designed for this purpose.

Table 1.1. An example of data structure

Instances	Attributes					
	1	2	$\cdots$	j	$\cdots$	m
x_1	x_{11}	x_{12}		x_{1j}		x_{1m}
x_2	x_{21}	x_{22}		x_{2j}		x_{2m}
.						
x_i	x_{i1}	x_{i2}		x_{ij}		x_{im}
.						
x_m	x_{m1}	x_{m2}		x_{mj}		x_{mm}

As a branch of statistics, clustering analysis has been studied extensively for many years. Research has mainly focused on distance-based clustering analysis, such as occurs when Euclidean distance is used. There are many textbooks on this topic. Notable progress in clustering has been made in unsupervised neural networks, including the self-organizing Kohonen neural network and the adaptive resonance theory (ART). There have been many reports on the application in operational state identification and fault diagnosis within process industries.

1.5.2 Classification

If the number and descriptions of classes, as well as the assignment of individual data patterns, are known for a given number of data patterns, such as

---

[1] sometimes called instances, cases, observations, samples, objects, or individuals
[2] also called unsupervised machine leaning

those shown in Table 1.1, then the task classification is to assign unknown data patterns to the established classes. The most widely used classification approach is based on feed-forward neural networks. Classification is also known as supervised machine learning because it always requires data patterns with known class assignments to train a model. This model is then used for predicting the class assignment of new data patterns [Wu 1995]. Some popular methods for classification are introduced in a simple way as follows.

Decision Tree Based Classification

When a business executive needs to make a decision based on several factors, a decision tree can help identify which factors to consider and can indicate how each factor has historically been associated with different outcomes of the decision. For example, in a credit risk case study, there might be data for each applicant's debt, income, and marital status. A decision tree creates a model as either a graphical tree or a set of text rules that can predict (classify) each applicant as a good or bad credit risk.

A decision tree is a model that is both predictive and descriptive. It is called a decision tree because the resulting model is presented as a tree-like structure. The visual presentation makes a decision tree model very easy to understand and assimilate. As a result, the decision tree has become a very popular data mining technique. Decision trees are most commonly used for classification (i.e., for predicting what group a case belongs to), but can also be used for regression (predicting a specific value).

The decision tree method encompasses a number of specific algorithms, including Classification and Regression Trees, Chi-squared Automatic Interaction Detection, C4.5 and C5.0 (J. Ross Quinlan, www.rulequest.com).

Decision trees graphically display the relationships found in data. Most products also translate the tree-to-text rules such as 'If (Income = High and Years on job > 5) Then (Credit risk = Good)'. In fact, decision tree algorithms are very similar to rule induction algorithms, which produce rule sets without a decision tree.

The primary output of a decision tree algorithm is the tree itself. The training process that creates the decision tree is usually called induction. Induction requires a small number of passes (generally far fewer than 100) through the training dataset. This makes the algorithm somewhat less efficient than *Naive-Bayes algorithms*, which require only one pass (See Naive-Bayes and Nearest Neighbor in next subsection). However, this algorithm is significantly more efficient than neural nets, which typically require a large number of passes, sometimes numbering in the thousands. To be more precise, the number of passes required to build a decision tree is no more than the number of levels in the tree. There is no predetermined limit to the number of levels, although the complexity of the tree, as measured by the depth and breadth of the tree, generally increases as the number of independent variables increases.

Naive-Bayes Based Classification

Naive-Bayes is named after Thomas Bayes (1702-1761), a British minister whose theory of probability was first published posthumously in 1764. Bayes' Theorem is used in the Naive-Bayes technique to compute the probabilities that are used to make predictions.

Naive-Bayes is a classification technique that is both predictive and descriptive. It analyzes the relationship between each independent variable and the dependent variable to derive a conditional probability for each relationship. When a new case is analyzed, a prediction is made by combining the effects of the independent variables on the dependent variable (the outcome that is predicted). In theory, a Naive-Bayes prediction will only be correct if all the independent variables are statistically independent of each other, which is frequently not true. For example, data about people will usually contain multiple attributes (such as weight, education, income, and so forth) that are all correlated with age. In such a case, the use of Naive-Bayes would be expected to overemphasize the effect of age. Notwithstanding these limitations, practice has shown that Naive-Bayes produces good results, and its simplicity and speed make it an ideal tool for modeling and investigating simple relationships.

Naive-Bayes requires only one pass through the training set to generate a classification model. This makes it the most efficient data mining technique. However, Naive-Bayes does not handle continuous data, so any independent or dependent variables that contain continuous values must be binned or bracketed. For instance, if one of the independent variables is 'age', the values must be transformed from the specific value into ranges such as 'less than 20 years', '21 to 30 years', '31 to 40 years', and so on. Binning is technically simple, and most algorithms automate it, but the selection of the ranges can have a dramatic impact on the quality of the model produced.

Using Naive-Bayes for classification is a fairly simple process. During training, the probability of each outcome (dependent variable value) is computed by counting how many times it occurs in the training dataset. This is called the prior probability. For example, if the Good Risk outcome occurs twice in a total of 5 cases, then the prior probability for Good Risk is 0.4. The prior probability can be thought of in the following way: "If I know nothing about a loan applicant, there is a 0.4 probability that the applicant is a Good Risk". In addition the prior probabilities, Naive-Bayes also computes how frequently each independent variable value occurs in combination with each dependent (output) variable value. These frequencies are then used to compute conditional probabilities that are combined with the prior probability to make the predictions. In essence, Naive-Bayes uses conditional probabilities to modify prior probabilities.

Nearest Neighbor Based Classification

Nearest Neighbor (more precisely k-nearest neighbor, also k-NN) is a predictive technique suitable for classification models.

Unlike other predictive algorithms, the training data is not scanned or processed to create the model. Instead, the training data *is* the model. When a new case or instance is presented to the model, the algorithm looks at all the data to find a subset of cases that are most similar to it. It then uses them to predict the outcome.

There are two principal drivers in the k-NN algorithm: the number of nearest cases to be used (k) and a metric to measure what is meant by nearest.

Each use of the k-NN algorithm requires that we specify a positive integer value for k. This determines how many existing cases are looked at when predicting a new case. k-NN refers to a family of algorithms that we could denote as 1-NN, 2-NN, 3-NN, and so forth. For example, 4-NN indicates that the algorithm will use the four nearest cases to predict the outcome of a new case.

As the term 'nearest' implies, k-NN is based on a concept of distance. This requires a metric to determine distances. All metrics must result in a specific number for the purpose of comparison. Whatever metric is used, it is both arbitrary and extremely important. It is arbitrary because there is no preset definition of what constitutes a 'good' metric. It is important because the choice of a metric greatly affects the predictions. Different metrics, used on the same training data, can result in completely different predictions. This means that a business expert is needed to help determine a good metric.

To classify a new case, the algorithm computes the distance from the new case to each case (row) in the training data. The new case is predicted to have the same outcome as the predominant outcome in the k closest cases in the training data.

Neural Networks Based Classification

Have you ever made an extraordinary purchase on one of your credit cards and been somewhat embarrassed when the charge wasn't authorized, or been surprised when a credit card representative has asked to speak to you? Somehow your transaction was flagged as possibly being fraudulent. Well, it wasn't the person you spoke to who picked your transaction out of the millions per hour that are being processed. It was, more than likely, a neural net.

How did the neural net recognize that your transaction was unusual? By having previously looked at the transactions of millions of other people, including transactions that turned out to be fraudulent, the neural net formed a model that allowed it to separate good transactions from bad. Of course, the neural net could only pick transactions that were likely to be fraudulent. That's why a human must get involved in making the final determination.

Luckily if you remembered your mother's maiden name, the transaction would have been approved and you would have gone home with your purchase.

Neural networks are among the most complicated of the classification and regression algorithms. Although training a neural network can be time-consuming, a trained neural network can speedily make predictions for new cases. For example, a trained neural network can detect fraudulent transactions in real time. They can also be used for other data mining applications, such as clustering. Neural nets are used in other applications as well, such as handwriting recognition or robot control.

Despite their broad application, we will restrict our discussion here to neural nets used for classification and regression. The output from a neural network is purely predictive. Because there is no descriptive component to a neural network model, a neural net's choices are difficult to understand. This often discourages its use. In fact, this technique is often referred to as a 'black box' technology.

A key difference between neural networks and other techniques that we have examined is that neural nets only operate directly on numbers. As a result, any non-numeric data in either the independent or dependent (output) columns must be converted to numbers before the data can be used with a neural net.

Neural networks are based on an early model of human brain function. Although they are described as 'networks', a neural net is nothing more than a mathematical function that computes an output based on a set of input values. The network paradigm makes it easy to decompose the larger function to a set of related sub-functions, and it enables a variety of learning algorithms that can estimate the parameters of the sub-functions.

1.5.3 Conceptual Clustering and Classification

Most clustering and classification approaches depend on numerically calculating a similarity, or distance measure. Because of this they are often called similarity based methods. The knowledge used for classification assignment is often an algorithm which is opaque and essentially a black box. Conceptual clustering and classification, on the other hand, develops a qualitative language for describing the knowledge used for clustering. It is basically in the form of production rules or decision trees which are explicit and transparent. The inductive system C5.0 (previously C4.5) is a typical approach. It is able to automatically generate decision trees and production rules from databases. Decision trees and rules have a simple representative form, making the inferred model relatively easy to comprehend by the user. However, the restraint to a particular tree or rule representation can significantly restrict the representation's power. In addition, available approaches have been developed, mainly for problem domains where variables only take categorical values, such as color being green and red. They are not effective in dealing with variables that take numerical values. The use of discretization of numerical variables to categorical descriptions is a useful approach. However more power discretization techniques are required.

1.5.4 Dependency Modeling

Dependency modeling describes dependencies among variables. Dependency models exist at two levels: structural and quantitative. The structural level of the model specifies (often in graphical form) which variables are locally dependent. The quantitative level specifies the strengths of the dependencies, using some numerical scale. Examples of tools for dependency modeling include probabilistic (or Bayesian) graphs and fuzzy digraph graphs.

Take probabilistic networks as an example. Table 1.2 shows a collection of 10 data patterns. Each is described by three attributes. The task of dependency modeling, by using probabilistic networks, is to learn both the network structure and a conditional probabilistic table. For the data collection of Table 1.3, it is not possible to know, all at once the most probable dependencies. Theoretically, for a given database there is a unique structure which has the highest joint probability and can be found by certain algorithms such as those developed by Cooper and Herskovits [Cooper-Herskovits 1991]. When a structure is identified, the next step is to find a probabilistic table such as that shown in Table 1.3.

Probabilistic graphical models are very powerful representation schemes which allow for fairly efficient inference and for probabilistic reasoning. However, few methods are available for inferring the structure from data, and they are limited to very small databases. Therefore, normally there is the need to find the structure by interviewing domain experts. For a given data structure there are several successful reports on learning conditional probabilities from data.

Other dependency modeling approaches include statistical analysis (e.g., correlation coefficients, principal component and factor analysis) and sensitivity analysis using neural networks.

1.5.5 Summarization

Summarization provides a compact description for a subset of data. Simple examples would be the mean and standard deviations. More sophisticated functions involve summary rules, multi-variate visualization techniques, and functional relationships between variables.

A notable technique for summarization is that of mining association rules. Given a database, the association rule mining techniques finds all associations of the form:

IF {set of values} THEN {set of values}

Table 1.2. A database example

case	Variable values		
	x_1	x_2	x_3
1	1	0	0
2	1	1	1
3	0	0	1
4	1	1	1
5	0	0	0
6	0	1	1
7	1	1	1
8	0	0	0
9	1	1	1
10	0	0	0

Table 1.3. The probabilistic table associated with the probabilistic structure

$p(x_1 = 1) = 0.5$	$p(x_1 = 0) = 0.5$
$p(x_2 = 1\|x_1 = 1) = 0.8$	$p(x_2 = 0\|x_1 = 1) = 0.2$
$p(x_2 = 1\|x_1 = 0) = 0.2$	$p(x_2 = 0\|x_1 = 0) = 0.8$
$p(x_3 = 1\|x_2 = 1) = 1$	$p(x_3 = 0\|x_2 = 1) = 0$
$p(x_3 = 1\|x_2 = 0) = 0.2$	$p(x_3 = 0\|x_2 = 0) = 0.8$

A rule is valid given two parameters *minsupport* and *minconfidence*, such that the rule holds with certainty $>$ *minconfidence* and the rule is supported by at least *minsupport* cases. Some commercial systems have been developed using this approach.

1.5.6 Regression

Linear (or non-linear) regression is one of the most common approaches used for correlating data. Statistical regression methods often require the user to specify the function over which the data is to be fitted. In order to specify the function, it is necessary to know the forms of the equations governing the correlation for the data. The advantage of such methods is that it is possible to gain from the equation, some qualitative knowledge about input-output relationships. However, if prior knowledge is not available, it is necessary to find out the most probable function by trial-and-error. This may require a great deal of time-consuming effort. Feed-forward neural networks (FFNNs) do not need functions to be fixed in order to learn. They have shown quite remarkable results in representing non-linear functions. However the resulting function using a FFNN is not easy to understand and is virtually a black box with no explanations.

1.5.7 Case-Based Learning

Case-based learning is based on acquiring knowledge represented by cases. It employs reasoning by analogy. Case-based learning focuses on the indexing and retrieval of relevant precedents. Typically, the solution sequence is a parameterized frame, or schema, where the structure is more or less fixed, rather than expressed in terms of an arbitrary sequence of problem-solving operators. Case-based reasoning is particularly useful for utilizing data which has complex internal structures. Differing from other data mining techniques, it does not require a large number of historical data patterns. Only a few reports have been produced on the application of case-based reasoning in process industries. These include case-based learning for historical equipment failure databases and equipment design.

1.5.8 Mining Time-Series Data

Many industries and businesses deal with time-series or dynamic data. It is apparent that all statistical and real-time control data used in process monitoring and control is essentially time-series. Most KDD techniques cannot account for time series of data. Time series data can be dealt with by carrying out preprocessing of the data in order to use minimum data points to capture the features and remove noise. These techniques include filters, e.g., Kalman filters, Fourier and wavelet transforms, statistical approaches and neural networks, as well as various qualitative signal interpretation methods.

1.6 Data Mining and Marketing

The standard success stories of KDD [Piatetsky-Matheus 1992] come primarily from marketing. Suppose you own a mail-order firm. You have a database in which, for fifteen years, you have kept data on which clients reacted to what mailings, and what products they bought. Naturally, such a database contains a great deal of potentially interesting data. A number of queries become possible: first you will want to know what groups of clients there are. Then you need to know whether to classify these according to region, age, product groups, or spending patterns.

It would probably be wisest to use a different classification for each marketing action. For example,: generally the response to mailing is 3 to 4% at most; and the rest of the letters might as well not have been sent. A neural network can analyze mailing from the past and in this way select only those addresses that give a fair chance of response. Thus one can sometimes save as much as 50% of mailing costs, while maintaining a steady response. A clustering of one's clients can be found in various ways—via statistical methods, genetic algorithms, attribute-value learners, or neural networks. The next question which can be asked concerns with the relationship between groups. It also concerns with trends. Clients buying baby clothes today may buy computer games in ten years, and fifteen years later a mopped.

It is obvious that knowing and applying these kinds of rules creates great commercial opportunities. However, it is not an easy task to choose the right pattern-recognition technique for your data. There are many different techniques, including Operations Research (OR) and genetic algorithms. If one technique finds a pattern, the others will often find one as well, provided the translation of the problem to the learning technique (the so-called representational engineering) has been done by a specialist. In the case of neural networks, the problem must be translated into values that can be fed to the input nodes of a network. In the case of genetic algorithms, the problem has to be considered in terms of strings of characters (chromosomes). A translation to points in a multi-dimensional space has to be made with OR-techniques, such as k-nearest neighbor.

Data mining has become widely recognized as a critical field by companies of all types. The use of valuable information 'mined' from data is recognized as necessary to maintain competitiveness in today's business environments. With the advent of data warehousing making the storage of vast amounts of data common place and the continued breakthroughs in increased computing power, businesses are now looking for technology and tools to extract usable information from detailed data.

Data mining has received the most publicity and success in the fields of database marketing and credit-card fraud detection. For example, in database marketing, great accomplishments have been achieved in the following areas.

- *Response modeling*, predicts which prospects are likely to buy, based on previous purchase history, demographics, geographics, and life-style data.
- *Cross-selling* maximizes sales of products and services to a company's existing customer base by studying the purchase patterns of products frequently purchased together.
- *Customer valuation* predicts the value or profitability of a customer over a specified period of time based on previous purchase history, demographics, geographics, and life-style data.
- *Segmentation and profiling* improves understanding of a customer segment through data analysis and profiling of prototypical customers.

As to credit-card fraud detection, data mining techniques have been applied in situations such as break-in and misuse detection and user identity verification.

1.7 Solving Real-World Problems by Data Mining

Several years ago, data mining was a new concept for many people. Data mining products were new and marred by unpolished interfaces. Only the most innovative or daring early adopters were attempting to apply these emerging tools. Today's products have matured and they are accessible to a much wider audience [Fayyad-Simoudis 1997]. We briefly recall some well-known data mining products below.

One of the most popular and successful applications of database systems is in the area of marketing where a great deal of information about customer behavior is collected. Marketers are interested in finding customer preferences so as to target them in their future campaigns [Berry, 1994, Fayyad-Simoudis 1997].

Development of a knowledge-discovery system is complex. It not only involves a plethora of data mining tools, it usually depends on the application domain which is determined by the extent of end-user involvement.

The following brief description of several existing knowledge-discovery systems exemplifies the nature of the problems being tackled and helps to visualize the main design issues arising therein.

(1) The SKICAT (Sky Image Cataloging and Analysis Tool) [Fayyad-Piatetsky 1996] system concerns an automation of reduction and analysis of the large astronomical dataset known as the Palomar Observatory Digital Sky Survey (POSS-II). The database is huge: three terabytes of images containing in the order of two billion sky objects. This research was initiated by George Djorgovski from the California Institute of Technology who realized that new techniques were required in order to analyze such huge amounts of data. He teamed up with Jet Propulsion Laboratory's Usama Fayyad and others. The result was SKICAT.

The SKICAT system integrates techniques for image processing, data classification, and database management. The goal of SKICAT is to classify sky objects which have been too faint to be recognized by astronomers. In order to do this the following scheme was developed: First, faint objects were selected from "normal" sky images. Then, using data from a more powerful telescope, the faint objects were classified. Next, the rules were generated from the already classified set of faint objects directly from "normal" sky images. These rules were then used for classifying faint objects directly from "normal" sky images. The learning was carried out in a supervised mode. In the first step the digitized sky images were divided into classes. The initial feature extraction is done by association with SKICAT image processing software. Additional features, invariant within and across sky images, were then derived to assure that designed classifiers would make accurate predictions on new sky images.

These additional, derived, features are important for the successful operation of the system. Without them the performance of the system drops significantly. To achieve this, the sky image data is randomly divided into training and testing data sets. For each training data set a decision tree is generated and rules are derived and checked on the corresponding testing data. From all the rules generated, a greedy set-covering algorithm selects a minimal subset of 'best' rules.

(2) Health-KEFIR (Key Findings Reporter) is a knowledge discovery system used in health-care as an early warning system [Fayyad-Piatetsky 1996]. The system concentrates on ranking deviations according to measures of how

interesting these events are to the user. It focuses on discovering and explaining key findings in large and dynamic databases. The system performs an automatic drill-down through data along multiple dimensions to determine the most interesting deviations of specific quantitative measures relative to their previous and expected values. The deviation technique is a powerful tool used in KEFIR to identify interesting patterns from the data. The deviations are then ranked using some measure of 'interestingness', such as looking at the actions which can be taken in response to the relevant deviations, and may even generate recommendations for corresponding actions. KEFIR uses Netscape to present its findings in a hypertext report, using natural language and business graphics.

(3) TASA (Telecommunication Network Alarm Sequence Analyzer) was developed for predicting faults in a communication network [Fayyad-Piatetsky 1996]. A typical network generates hundreds of alarms per day. TASA system generates rules like 'if a certain combination of alarms occur within (...) time then an alarm of another type will occur within (...) time'. The time periods for the 'if' part of the rules are selected by the user, who can rank or group the rules once they are generated by TASA.

(4) R-MINI system uses both deviation detection and classification techniques to extract useful information from noisy domains [Fayyad-Piatetsky 1996]. It uses logic to generate a minimal size rule set that is both complete and consistent.

First it generates one rule for each example. Then it reduces the number of rules by two subsequent steps. Step 1: it generalizes the rule so it covers more positive examples without allowing it to cover any negative examples. Step 2: weaker redundant rules are deleted.

Second, it replaces each rule with a rule that is simpler and will not leave any examples uncovered. This system was tested on Standard and Poor 500 data over a period of 78 months. It was concerned with 774 securities described by 40 variables each. The decision, discretized, variable was the difference between the S&P 500 average return and the return of a given portfolio. The discretization is from 'strongly performing' (6% above market), through "neutral" (plus or minus 2%) to "strongly underperforming" (6% below). The generated rules can then be used for prediction of a portfolio return. Obviously the rules have to be regenerated periodically as new data becomes available.

It is noted that the above knowledge discovery systems rely quite heavily on the application domain constraint implicit relationships observed in the problem, etc. The role of the user interface is also essential. Below are examples of domain-independent systems.

(5) Knowledge Discovery Workbench (KDW) by Piatetsky-Shapiro and Matheus (1992). This is a collection of methods used for interactive analysis of large business databases. It includes many different methods for clustering, classification, deviation detection, summarization, dependency analysis, etc.

It is the user, however, who needs to guide the system in searches. Thus, if the user is knowledgeable in both the domain and the tools used, the KDW system can be domain-independent and versatile.

(6) Clementine is a commercial software package for data mining (Integrated Solutions, Ltd.) [Fayyad-Piatetsky 1996]. Basically it is a classifier system based on neural networks and inductive machine learning. It has been applied for the prediction of viewing audiences for the BBC, selection of retail outlets, anticipating toxic health hazards, modeling skin corrosivity, and so on.

1.8 Summary

In this chapter, we have briefly introduced some background knowledge of association rule mining with reference to its parent topic: data mining. By way of a summary, we firstly discuss the trends of data mining. An outline of this book is then presented.

1.8.1 Trends of Data Mining

It is expected that data mining products will evolve into tools that support more than just the data mining step in knowledge discovery and that they will help encourage a better overall methodology [Wu 2000]. Data mining tools operate on data, so we can expect to see algorithms move closer to the data, perhaps into the DBMS itself.

The major advantage that data mining tools have over traditional analysis tools is that they use computer cycles to replace human cycles [Fayyad-Piatetsky 1996]. The market will continue to build on that advantage with products that search larger and larger spaces to find the best model. This will occur in products that incorporate different modeling techniques in the search. It will also contribute to ways of automatically creating new variables, such as ratios or rollups. A new type of decision tree, known as an oblique tree, will soon be available. This tree generates splits based on compound relationships between independent variables, rather than the one-variable-at-a-time approach used today.

Many data mining tools [Fayyad-Simoudis 1997] still require a significant level of expertise from users. Tool vendors must design better user interfaces if they hope to gain wider acceptance of their products, particularly for use in mid-size and smaller companies. User friendly interfaces will allow end user analysts with limited technical skills to achieve good results. At the same time experts will be able to tweak models in any number of ways, and rush users, at any level of expertise, quickly through their learning curves.

Recently, many meetings and conferences have offered forums to explore the progress and future possible work concerning data mining. For example, a group of researchers met in Chicago in July 1997, in La Jolla in March 1997, and February, 1998 to discuss the current state of the art of data mining, data intensive computing, and the opportunities and challenges for the future. The focus of the discussions was on mining large, massive, and distributed data sets.

As we have seen, there have been many data mining systems developed in recent years. This trend of research and development is expected to continue to flourish because of the huge amount of data which have been collected in databases, and the necessity to understand research and make good use of, such data in decision making. This serves as the driving force in data mining [Fayyad-Stolorz 1997, Han 1999].

The diversity of data, data mining tasks, and data mining approaches pose many challenging research issues. Important tasks presenting themselves for data mining researchers and data mining system and application developers are listed below:

- establishing a powerful representation for patterns in data;
- designing data mining languages;
- developing efficient and effective data mining methods and systems;
- exploring efficient techniques for mining multi-databases, small databases, and other special databases;
- constructing of interactive and integrated data mining environments; and
- applying data mining techniques to solve large application problems.

Moreover, with increasing computerization, the social impact of data mining should not be under-estimated. When a large amount of inter-related data is effectively analyzed from different perspectives, it can pose threats to the goal of protecting data security and guarding against the invasion of privacy. It is a challenging task to develop effective techniques for preventing the disclosure of sensitive information in data mining. This is especially true as the use of data mining systems is rapidly increasing in domains ranging from business analysis and customer analysis to medicine and government.

1.8.2 Outline

The rest of this book focuses on techniques for mining association rules in databases. Chapter 2 presents the preliminaries for identifying association rules, including the required concepts, previous efforts, and techniques necessary for constructing mining models upon existing mathematical techniques so that the required models are more appropriate to the applications.

Chapters 3, 4, and 5 demonstrate techniques for discovering hidden patterns, including negative association rules and causal rules. Chapter 3 proposes techniques for identifying negative association rules that have *low-frequency* and *strong-correlation*. Existing mining techniques do not work well on low-frequency (infrequent) itemsets because traditional association rule mining has, in the past, been focused only on frequent itemsets.

Chapter 4 explores techniques for mining another kind of hidden pattern causal rules between pairs of multi-value variables X and Y by partitioning, for which the causal rule is represented in the form $X \rightarrow Y$ with conditional probability matrix $M_{Y|X}$. This representation is apparently more powerful than item-based association rules and quantitative-item-based association rules. However, the causal relations are represented in a non-linear form a matrix for which it is rather difficult to make decisions by the rules. So, in Chapter 5, we also advocate a causal rule analysis.

Chapter 6 presents techniques for mining very large databases based on 'instance selection'. It includes four models as: (1) identifying approximate association rules by sampling; (2) searching real association rules according to approximate association rules (3) incremental mining; and (4) anytime algorithm.

In Chapter 7 we develop a new technique for mining association rules in databases that utilizes external data. It includes collecting external data, selecting believable external data, and synthesizing external data to improve the mined association rules in a database. This technique is particularly useful to companies such as nuclear power plants and earthquake bureaus, which might have very small databases.

Finally, we summarize this book in Chapter 8. In particular, we suggest four important open problems in this chapter.

2. Association Rule

This chapter recalls some of the essential concepts related to association rule mining, which will be utilized throughout the book. Some existing research into the improvement of association rule mining techniques is also introduced to clarify the process.

The chapter is organized as follows. In Section 2.1, we begin by outlining certain necessary basic concepts. Some measurements of association rules are discussed in Section 2.2. In Section 2.3, we introduce the Apriori algorithm. This algorithm searches large (or frequent) itemsets in databases. Section 2.4 introduces some research into mining association rules. Finally, we summarize this chapter in Section 2.5.

2.1 Basic Concepts

Association rule mining can be defined formally as follows:

$I = \{i_1, i_2, \cdots, i_m\}$ is a set of literals, or *items*. For example, goods such as milk, sugar and bread for purchase in a store are items; and $A_i = v$ is an item, where v is a domain value of the attribute A_i, in a relation $R(A_1, \cdots, A_n)$.

X is an *itemset* if it is a subset of I. For example, a set of items for purchase from a store is an itemset; and a set of $A_i = v$ is an itemset for the relation $R(PID, A_1, A_2, \cdots, A_n)$, where PID is a key.

$D = \{t_i, t_{i+1}, \cdots, t_n\}$ is a set of transactions, called a *transaction database*, where each transaction t has a tid and a t-itemset $t = (tid, t\text{-itemset})$. For example, a customer's shopping trolley going through a checkout is a transaction; and a tuple $(v_1, \cdots, v_n)$ of the relation $R(A_1, \cdots, A_n)$ is a transaction.

A transaction t contains an itemset X iff, for all items, where $i \in X$, i is a t-itemset. For example, a shopping trolley contains all items in X when going through the checkout; and for each $A_i = v_i$ in X, v_i occurs at position i in the tuple $(v_1, \cdots, v_n)$.

There is a natural *lattice structure* on the itemsets 2^I, namely the subset/superset structure. Certain nodes in this lattice are natural grouping categories of interest (some with names). For example, items from a particular department such as clothing, hardware, furniture, etc; and, from within say clothing, children's, women's and men's clothing, toddler's clothing, etc.

An itemset X in a transaction database D has a *support*, denoted as $supp(X)$. (For descriptive convenience in this book, we sometimes use $p(X)$ to stand for $supp(X)$.) This is the ratio of transactions in D containing X. Or

$$supp(X) = |X(t)|/|D|$$

where $X(t) = \{t$ in $D|t$ contains $X\}$.

An itemset X in a transaction database D is called as a large, or frequent, itemset if its support is equal to, or greater than, the threshold minimal support (*minsupp*) given by users or experts.

The *negation* of an itemset X is $\neg X$. The support of $\neg X$ is $supp(\neg X) = 1 - supp(X)$.

An *association rule* is the implication $X \rightarrow Y$, where itemsets X and Y do not intersect.

Each association rule has two quality measurements, *support* and *confidence*, defined as

- the support of a rule $X \rightarrow Y$ is the support of $X \cup Y$; and
- the confidence of a rule $X \rightarrow Y$ is $conf(X \rightarrow Y)$ as the ratio $|(X \cup Y)(t)|/|X(t)|$, or $supp(X \cup Y)/supp(X)$.

That is, support = frequencies of occurring patterns; confidence = strength of implication.

Support-confidence framework ([Agrawal-Imielinski-Swami 1993]): Let I be a set of items in a database D, $X, Y \subseteq I$ be itemsets, $X \cap Y = \emptyset$, $p(X) \neq 0$ and $p(Y) \neq 0$. Minimal support (*minsupp*) and minimal confidence (*minconf*) are given by users or experts. Then $X \rightarrow Y$ is a valid rule if

(1) $supp(X \cup Y) \geq minsupp$,
(2) $conf(X \rightarrow Y) = \frac{supp(X \cup Y)}{supp(X)} \geq minconf$,

where '$conf(X \rightarrow Y)$' stands for the confidence of the rule $X \rightarrow Y$.

Mining association rules can be broken down into the following two subproblems.

(1) Generating all itemsets that have support greater than, or equal to, user specified minimum support. That is, generating all frequent itemsets.
(2) Generating all rules that have minimum confidence in the following simple way: For every frequent itemset X, and any $B \subset X$, let $A = X - B$. If the confidence of a rule $A \rightarrow B$ is greater than, or equal to, the minimum confidence (or $supp(X)/supp(A) \geq minconf$), then it can be extracted as a valid rule.

To demonstrate the use of the support-confidence framework, we outline an example of the process of mining association rules below.

Table 2.1. A transaction database

TID	Items			
100	A		C	D	
200		B	C		E
300	A	B	C		E
400		B			E

Let item universe be $I = \{A, B, C, D, E\}$ and transaction universe be $TID = \{100, 200, 300, 400\}$.

In Table 2.1, 100, 200, 300, and 400 are the unique identifiers of the four transactions: A = sugar, B = bread, C = coffee, D = milk, and E = cake.

Each row in the table can be taken as a transaction. We can identify association rules from these transactions using the support-confidence framework. Let

$minsupp = 50\%$ (to be frequent, an itemset must occur in at least 2 transactions); and

$minconf = 60\%$ (to be a high-confidence, or valid, rule, at least 60% of the time you find the antecedent of the rule in the transactions, you must also find the consequence of the rule there).

By using the support-confidence framework, we present a two-step association rule mining as follows.

(1) The first step is to count the frequencies of k-itemsets. In Table 2.1, item $\{A\}$ occurs in the two transactions, $TID = 100$ and $TID = 300$. Its frequency is 2, and its support, $supp(A)$, is 50%, which is equal to $minsupp = 50\%$. Item $\{B\}$ occurs in the three transactions, $TID = 200$, $TID = 300$ and $TID = 400$. Its frequency is 3, and its support, $supp(B)$, is 75%, which is greater than $minsupp$. Item $\{C\}$ occurs in the three transactions, $TID = 100$, $TID = 200$ and $TID = 300$. Its frequency is 3, and its support, $supp(C)$, is 75%, which is greater than $minsupp$. Item $\{D\}$ occurs in the one transaction, $TID = 100$. Its frequency is 1, and its support, $supp(D)$, is 25%, which is less than $minsupp$. Item $\{E\}$ occurs in the three transactions, $TID = 200$, $TID = 300$ and $TID = 400$. Its frequency is 3, and its support, $supp(E)$, is 75%, which is greater than $minsupp$. This is summarized in Table 2.2.

Table 2.2. 1-itemsets in the database

Itemsets	Frequency	$> minsupp$
$\{A\}$	2	y
$\{B\}$	3	y
$\{C\}$	3	y
$\{D\}$	1	n
$\{E\}$	3	y

We now consider 2-itemsets. In Table 2.1, itemset $\{A, B\}$ occurs in the one transaction, $TID = 300$. Its frequency is 1, and its support, $supp(A \cup B)$, is 25%, which is less than $minsupp = 50\%$. In the formulas used in this book, $A \cup B$ stands for $\{A, B\}$. Itemset $\{A, C\}$ occurs in the two transactions, $TID = 100$ and $TID = 300$, its frequency is 2, and its support, $supp(A \cup C)$, is 50%, which is equal to $minsupp = 50\%$. Itemset $\{A, D\}$ occurs in the one transaction, $TID = 100$. Its frequency is 1, and its support, $supp(A \cup D)$, is 25%, which is less than $minsupp = 50\%$. Itemset $\{A, E\}$ occurs in the one transaction, $TID = 300$. Its frequency is 1, and its support, $supp(A \cup E)$, is 25%, which is less than $minsupp = 50\%$. Itemset $\{B, C\}$ occurs in the two transactions, $TID = 200$ and $TID = 300$. Its frequency is 2, and its support, $supp(B \cup C)$, is 50%, which is equal to $minsupp$. This is summarized in Table 2.3.

Table 2.3. 2-itemsets in the database

Itemsets	Frequency	$> minsupp$
$\{A, B\}$	1	n
$\{A, C\}$	2	y
$\{A, D\}$	1	n
$\{A, E\}$	1	n
$\{B, C\}$	2	y
$\{B, E\}$	3	y
$\{C, D\}$	1	n
$\{C, E\}$	2	y

In the same way, 3-itemsets and 4-itemsets can be obtained. This is listed in Tables 2.4 and 2.5.

Table 2.4. 3-itemsets in the database

Itemsets	Frequency	$> minsupp$
$\{A, B, C\}$	1	n
$\{A, B, E\}$	1	n
$\{A, C, D\}$	1	n
$\{A, C, E\}$	1	n
$\{B, C, E\}$	2	y

Table 2.5. 4-itemsets in the database

Itemsets	Frequency	$> minsupp$
$\{A, B, C, E\}$	1	n

However, the 5-itemset in the database is null. According to the above definitions, $\{A\}$, $\{B\}$, $\{C\}$, $\{E\}$, $\{A, C\}$, $\{B, C\}$, $\{B, E\}$, $\{C, E\}$ and $\{B, C, E\}$ in Table 2.1 are frequent itemsets.

(2) The second step is to generate all the association rules from the frequent itemsets. Because there is no frequent itemset in Table 2.5, the 4-itemsets contribute no valid association rules. In Table 2.4, there is one frequent itemset, $\{B, C, E\}$, with $supp(B \cup C \cup E) = 50\% = minsupp$. For the frequent itemset $\{B, C, E\}$, because $supp(B \cup C \cup E)/supp(B \cup C) = 2/2 = 100\%$ greater than $minconf = 60\%$, $B \cup C \rightarrow E$ can be extracted as a valid rule. In the same way, because $supp(B \cup C \cup E)/supp(B \cup E) = 2/3 = 66.7\%$, which is greater than $minconf$, $B \cup E \rightarrow C$ can be extracted as a valid rule and, because $supp(B \cup C \cup E)/supp(C \cup E) = 2/2 = 100\%$ is greater than $minconf$, $C \cup E \rightarrow B$ can be extracted as a valid rule. Also, because $supp(B \cup C \cup E)/supp(B) = 2/3 = 66.7\%$ is greater than $minconf$, $B \rightarrow C \cup E$ can be extracted as a valid rule. The association rules generated from $\{B, C, E\}$ are listed in Tables 2.6 and 2.7.

Table 2.6. Association rules with 1-item consequences from 3-itemsets

RuleNo	Rule	Confidence	support	$> minconf$
Rule1	$B \cup C \rightarrow E$	100%	50%	y
Rule2	$B \cup E \rightarrow C$	66.7%	50%	y
Rule3	$C \cup E \rightarrow B$	100%	50%	y

Table 2.7. Association rules with 2-item consequences from 3-itemsets

RuleNo	Rule	Confidence	support	$> minconf$
Rule4	$B \rightarrow C \cup E$	66.7%	50%	y
Rule5	$C \rightarrow B \cup E$	66.7%	50%	y
Rule6	$E \rightarrow B \cup C$	66.7%	50%	y

Also, we can generate all association rules from frequent 2-itemsets in Table 2.3. This is illustrated in Tables 2.8, 2.9, 2.10 and 2.11.

Table 2.8. Association rules for $\{A, C\}$

RuleNo	Rule	Confidence	support	$> minconf$
Rule7	$A \rightarrow C$	100%	50%	y
Rule8	$C \rightarrow A$	66.7%	50%	y

According to the above definitions, the 14 association rules listed above can be extracted as valid rules for Table 2.1.

Table 2.9. Association rules for $\{B, C\}$

RuleNo	Rule	Confidence	support	$> minconf$
Rule9	$B \rightarrow C$	66.7%	50%	y
Rule10	$C \rightarrow B$	66.7%	50%	y

Table 2.10. Association rules for $\{B, E\}$

RuleNo	Rule	Confidence	support	$> minconf$
Rule11	$B \rightarrow E$	100%	75%	y
Rule12	$E \rightarrow B$	100%	75%	y

Table 2.11. Association rules for $\{C, E\}$

RuleNo	Rule	Confidence	support	$> minconf$
Rule13	$C \rightarrow E$	66.7%	50%	y
Rule14	$E \rightarrow C$	66.7%	50%	y

2.2 Measurement of Association Rules

Piatetsky-Shapiro ([Piatetsky 1991]) have proposed that rules from relational tables are of the form $C_1 \rightarrow C_2$, where C_1 and C_2 are conditions on tuples of the relational table. Such a rule may be *exact*, meaning that all tuples that satisfy C_1 also satisfy C_2. It may be *strong*, meaning that tuples satisfying C_1 almost always satisfy C_2. Or, it may be *approximate*, meaning that some of the tuples satisfying C_1 also satisfy C_2. One of the important results in [Piatetsky 1991] is that a rule $X \rightarrow Y$ is not interesting if $support(X \rightarrow Y) \approx support(X) \times support(Y)$. Now, this argument has been taken as an important critique of mining interesting association rules. In this section, we briefly recall several well-known measurements of association rules.

2.2.1 Support-Confidence Framework

Agrawal et al. have built a support-confidence framework (see Section 2.1) for mining association rules from databases ([Agrawal-Imielinski-Swami 1993]). This framework has since become a common model for mining association rules.

The support-confidence framework is generally used as a framework for capturing a certain type of dependence among items represented in a database. This model measures the uncertainty of an association rule with two factors: support and confidence. However, the measure is not adequate for modeling all uncertainties of association rules. For instance, the measurement does not provide a test for capturing the correlation of two itemsets. Also, the support is limited in informative feedback because it represents the number of transactions containing an itemset but not the number of items. In order to improve this framework, some measurements on the support and confidence of association rules, such as the chi-squared test model ([Brin-Motwani-Silverstein 1997]) and collective strength based measure ([Agrawal-Yu 1998]), have been recently proposed. These different measurements on support and confidence lead to different models for mining association rules. Hence, the measuring of uncertainty of association rules has recently become one of the crucial problems when mining association rules.

In fact, the measurement of the uncertainty of an event has been a popular topic for research over the years. Mathematical probability theory and statistics offer many well-developed techniques for measuring uncertainty. Thus, there are many measuring models that can be applied for the estimation of the uncertain factors ($supp$ and $conf$) of an association rule. We now recall three well-known measurements for association rules.

2.2.2 Three Established Measurements

1. Piatetsky-Shapiro has argued that a rule $X \to Y$ is not interesting if

$$support(X \to Y) \approx support(X) \times support(Y)$$

According to the probability interpretation in [Brin-Motwani-Silverstein 1997], $support(X \cup Y) = p(X \cup Y)$ and $confidence(X \to Y) = p(Y|X) = p(X \cup Y)/p(X)$. Then, Piatetsky-Shapiro's argument can be denoted as

$$p(X \cup Y) \approx p(X)p(Y)$$

This means that $X \to Y$ cannot be extracted as a rule if $p(X \cup Y) \approx p(X)p(Y)$. In fact, in probability theory, $p(X \cup Y) \approx p(X)p(Y)$ denotes that X is approximately independent of Y.

2. A statistical definition of dependence for the sets X and Y is

$$Interest(X, Y) = \frac{p(X \cup Y)}{p(X)p(Y)},$$

with the obvious extension to more than two sets ([Brin-Motwani-Silverstein 1997]). This formula, which we shall refer to as the *interest* of Y given X, is one of the main measurements of uncertainty of association rules. In this case, the further the value is from 1, the greater the dependence. Or, for $1 > mininterest > 0$, if

$$|\frac{p(X \cup Y)}{p(X)p(Y)} - 1| \geq mininterest$$

then $X \to Y$ is a rule of interest.

By Piatetsky-Shapiro's argument, we can divide $Interest(X, Y)$ into 3 cases as follows:

(1) if $p(X \cup Y)/(p(X)p(Y)) = 1$, then $p(X \cup Y) = p(X)p(Y)$, or Y and X are independent;

(2) if $p(X \cup Y)/(p(X)p(Y)) > 1$, or $p(X \cup Y) > p(X)p(Y)$, then Y is positively dependent on X; and

(3) if $p(X \cup Y)/(p(X)p(Y)) < 1$, or $p(X \cup Y) < p(X)p(Y)$, then Y is negatively dependent to X, or $\neg Y$ is positively dependent on X.

In this way, we can define another form of interpretation of rules of interest as follows. For $1 > mininterest > 0$,

(a) if

$$\frac{p(X \cup Y)}{p(X)p(Y)} - 1 \geq mininterest$$

then $X \Rightarrow Y$ is a rule of interest; and

(b) if

$$-(\frac{p(X \cup Y)}{p(X)p(Y)} - 1) \geq mininterest$$

then $X \rightarrow \neg Y$ is a rule of interest.

This leads to two new definitions of association rules of interest as follows.

Definition 2.1 (*the Piatetsky-Shapiro argument*) *Let I be a set of items in the database TD, $X, Y \subseteq I$ be itemsets, $X \cap Y = \emptyset$, $p(X) \neq 0$, and $p(Y) \neq 0$. Also, minsupp, minconf and mininterest > 0 are given by users or experts. Then, $X \rightarrow Y$ can be extracted as a valid rule of interest if*

(1) $p(X \cup Y) \geq minsupp$,

(2) $p(Y|X) \geq minconf$, and

(3) $|p(X \cup Y) - p(X)p(Y)| \geq mininterest$.

Definition 2.2 (*the Brin, Motwani and Silverstein argument*) *Let I be a set of items in the database D; X, Y ($\subseteq I$) be itemsets; $X \cap Y = \emptyset$; $p(X) \neq 0$; and $p(Y) \neq 0$. The thresholds: minimum support (minsupp), minimum confidence (minconf), and minimum interest (mininterest > 0) are given by users or experts. Then, $X \rightarrow Y$ can be extracted as a valid rule of interest if*

(1) $p(X \cup Y) \geq minsupp$,

(2) $p(Y|X) \geq minconf$, and

(3) $|\frac{p(X \cup Y)}{p(X)p(Y)} - 1| \geq mininterest$.

Here, condition (3) ensures that $X \rightarrow Y$ is a rule of interest.

3. According to the support-confidence framework, and the Brin, Motwani and Silverstein argument, we can take

(1) $X \cap Y = \emptyset$,

(2) $p(X \cup Y) \geq minsupp$,

(3) $p(Y|X) \geq minconf$ (e.g. $conf(X \rightarrow Y) \geq minconf$), and

(4) $|\frac{p(X \cup Y)}{p(X)p(Y)} - 1| \geq mininterest$,

as the *conditions* that association rule $X \rightarrow Y$ can be extracted to a valid rule of interest, where the thresholds, *minimum support* (*minsupp*), *minimum confidence* (*minconf*) and *minimum interest* (*mininterest* > 0), are given by users or experts.

Mathematical probability theory and statistics are certainly the oldest and most widely used techniques for measuring uncertainty in many applications. Therefore, we can also apply these rope techniques to estimate the uncertain factors (*supp* and *conf*) of an association rule.

2.3 Searching Frequent Itemsets

Identifying frequent itemsets is one of the most important issues faced by the knowledge discovery and data mining community. There have been a number of excellent algorithms developed for extracting frequent itemsets in very large databases. Apriori is a famous, and widely-used, algorithm for mining frequent itemsets (see [Agrawal-Imielinski-Swami 1993]). For efficiency, many variations of this approach, such as the hash-based algorithm (see [Park-Chen-Yu 1995]) and the OPUS-based algorithm (see [Webb 2000]), have been constructed. To match the algorithms already developed, we first present the Apriori algorithm, we then design an optimized algorithm by pruning all uninteresting frequent itemsets.

2.3.1 The Apriori Algorithm

As we have seen in Section 2.1, the first step of association rules mining is finding frequent itemsets in databases. The complexity of an association rules mining system is heavily dependent upon the complexity of the corresponding algorithm for identifying frequent itemsets.

The following algorithm *FrequentItemsets* is used to generate all frequent itemsets in a given database D. This is the Apriori algorithm. The parameter *dbsize* is the total number of tuples in the database.

Algorithm 2.1 *FrequentItemsets*
begin
    Input: D: data set; minsupp: minimum support;
    Output: L: frequent itemsets;
    let frequent itemset set $L \leftarrow \{\}$;
    let frontier set $F \leftarrow \{\{\}\}$;
    while $F \neq \{\}$ **do begin**

−make a pass over the database D
    let candidate set $C \leftarrow \{\}$;
   forall database tuples t **do**
   forall itemsets f in F **do**
    if t contains f **then begin**
     let $C_f \leftarrow$ candidate itemsets that are extensions
        of f and contained in t;
     forall itemsets c_f in C_f **do**
      if $c_f \in C$ **then**
       $c_f.count \leftarrow c_f.count + 1$;
      else
       $c_f.count \leftarrow 0$; $C \leftarrow C \cup \{c_f\}$;
    end

−consolidate
    let $F \leftarrow \{\}$;
   forall itemsets c in C **do begin**
    if $c.count/dbsize > minsupp$ **then**
     $L \leftarrow L \cup c$;
    if c should be used as a frontier in the next pass **then**
     $F \leftarrow F \cup c$;
   end
  end
end

The Apriori algorithm makes multiple passes over a given database. The *frontier set* for a pass consists of those itemsets that are extended during the pass. In each pass, the support for certain itemsets is measured. These itemsets, referred to *candidate itemsets*, are derived from the tuples in the database and the itemsets contained in the frontier set.

Associated with each itemset is a counter that stores the number of transactions in which the corresponding itemset has appeared. This counter is initialized to zero when an itemset is created.

Initially, the frontier set consists of only one element, which is an empty set. At the end of a pass, the support for a candidate itemset is compared to *minsupp* to determine whether it is a frequent itemset. At the same time, it is determined whether this itemset should be added to the frontier set for the next pass. The algorithm terminates when the frontier set becomes empty. The support count for the itemset is preserved when an itemset is added to the frequent/frontier set.

However, in a given large database, the Apriori algorithm *FrequentItemsets* used for identifying frequent itemsets, involves a search with little heuristic information in a space with an exponential amount of items and possible itemsets. This algorithm may suffer from large computational overheads when the number of frequent itemsets is very large ([Webb 2000]). For example, suppose there are 1000 items in a given large database, the average number of items in each transaction is 6. Then there are almost 10^{15} possible itemsets to be counted in the database. In the next subsection, we present an efficient algorithm for picking up itemsets of interest.

To illustrate the use of the Apriori algorithm, we use the data in Table 2.1 where $minsupp = 50\%$.

Firstly, the 1-itemsets $\{A\}$, $\{B\}$, $\{C\}$, $\{D\}$, and $\{E\}$ are generated as candidates at the first pass over the dataset, where $A.count = 2$, $B.count = 3$, $C.count = 3$, $D.count = 1$, and $E.count = 3$. Because $minsupp = 50\%$ and $dbsize = 4$, $\{A\}$, $\{B\}$, $\{C\}$, and $\{E\}$ are frequent itemsets. Three are listed in Table 2.12.

Table 2.12. Frequent 1-itemsets in the dataset in Table 2.1

Itemsets	Frequency	$> minsupp$
$\{A\}$	2	y
$\{B\}$	3	y
$\{C\}$	3	y
$\{E\}$	3	y

Secondly, the frequent 1-itemsets $\{A\}$, $\{B\}$, $\{C\}$, and $\{E\}$ are appended into the frontier set F, and the second pass begins over the dataset to search for 2-itemset candidates. Each such candidate is a subset of F. The 2-itemset candidates are $\{A, B\}$, $\{A, C\}$, $\{A, E\}$, $\{B, C\}$, $\{B, E\}$, and $\{C, E\}$, where $A \cup B.count = 1$, $A \cup C.count = 2$, $A \cup E.count = 1$, $B \cup C.count = 2$, $B \cup E.count = 3$, and $C \cup E.count = 2$. $A \cup C$, $B \cup C$, $B \cup E$ and $C \cup E$ are frequent itemsets. They are listed in Table 2.13.

Table 2.13. Frequent 2-itemsets in the dataset in Table 2.1

Itemsets	Frequency	$> minsupp$
$\{A, C\}$	2	y
$\{B, C\}$	2	y
$\{B, E\}$	3	y
$\{C, E\}$	2	y

Thirdly, the frequent 1-itemsets and 2-itemsets are appended into the frontier set F, and the third pass begins over the dataset to search for 3-itemset candidates. Frequent 3-itemsets are listed in Table 2.14.

Table 2.14. Frequent 3-itemsets in the dataset

Itemsets	Frequency	$> minsupp$
$\{B, C, E\}$	2	y

Fourthly, the frequent 1-itemsets, 2-itemset, and 3-itemsets are appended into the frontier set F, and the fourth pass begins over the dataset to search for 4-itemset candidates. There is no frequent 4-itemset, and the algorithm is ended.

2.3.2 Identifying Itemsets of Interest

Recalling Piatetsky-Shapiro's argument, if

$$p(X \cup Y) \approx p(X)p(Y)$$

then $X \to Y$ cannot be extracted as a rule. In fact, in probability theory, $p(X \cup Y) \approx p(X)p(Y)$ denotes X as approximately independent of Y. In other words, if $|p(X \cup Y) - p(X)p(Y)| \geq mininterest$, the rule $X \to Y$ is of interest, and $X \cup Y$ is called an *interested itemset*, where $mininterest$ is a minimum interest value specified by users. In the reverse case, if $|p(X \cup Y) - p(X)p(Y)| < mininterest$, the rule $X \to Y$ is not of interest, and $X \cup Y$ is called an *uninteresting itemset*. For this argument, we can establish a faster algorithm for picking out all itemsets of interest in a given database.

As we will see shortly, many of the frequent itemsets will relate to rules that are not of interest. If only frequent itemsets of interest are extracted, the search space can be greatly reduced. Therefore, we now construct an efficient algorithm for identifying frequent itemsets of interest, by pruning.

Normally, the Apriori algorithm is used to generate all frequent itemsets in a given database. We want only the interesting frequent itemsets in the database to be generated. Thus, the uninteresting frequent itemsets are pruned in the following algorithm.

Algorithm 2.2 *FrequentItemsetsbyPruning*
begin
Input: D: data set; minsupp: minimum support; mininterest: minimum interest;
Output: Frequentset: frequent itemsets;
(1) **let** frequent set $Frequentset \leftarrow \{\}$;
(2) **let** $L_1 \leftarrow$ {frequent 1-itemsets};
   let $Frequentset \leftarrow Frequentset \cup L_1$;
(3) **for** $(k = 2; L_{k-1} \neq \{\}; k++)$ **do**
      begin
   //Generate all possible k-itemsets of interest in D.
      let $C_k \leftarrow \{\{x_1, \ldots x_{k-2}, x_{k-1}, x_k\} \mid \{x_1, \ldots x_{k-2}, x_{k-1}\} \in L_{k-1} \wedge \{x_1, \ldots x_{k-2}, x_k\} \in L_{k-1}\}$;
      for any transaction t in D **do**
         begin
   //Check which k-itemsets are included in transaction t.
         let $C_t \leftarrow$ the k-itemsets in t that are contained by C_k;

      for any itemset A in C_t **do**
         let $A.count \leftarrow A.count + 1$;
      end
      let $L_k \leftarrow \{c | c \in C_k \wedge (p(c) = (c.count/|D|) >= minsupp)\}$;
    //Prune all uninteresting k-itemsets in L_k
      for any itemset i in L_k **do**
        if an itemset i is not of interest **then**;
          let $L_k \leftarrow L_k - \{i\}$;
      end
      let $Frequentset \leftarrow Frequentset \cup L_k$;
  (4) **output** the frequent itemsets $Frequentset$ in D;
end

The algorithm $FrequentItemsetsbyPruning$ is used to generate all frequent itemsets of interest in a database D. This algorithm is similar to the former algorithm, $FrequentItemsets$, so we simply elucidate the differences in Step (3). This step generates all sets L_k for $k \geq 2$ by way of a loop, where L_k is the set of all frequent k-itemsets in D generated in the kth pass of the algorithm, and the end-condition of the loop is $L_{k-1} = \{\}$. For $k \geq 2$, we need to prune all uninteresting k-itemsets from the set C_k. That is, for any itemset i in C_k, if $|p(X \cup Y) - p(X)p(Y)| < mininterest$ for any expressions $i = X \cup Y$ of i, then i is an uninteresting frequent itemset, and it must be pruned from C_k.

After all uninteresting frequent itemsets are pruned, the searched space for extracting frequent itemsets is obviously reduced, and all data can be maintained in the memory. To demonstrate the use of the above algorithm, we present the following example.

Example 2.1 *Let D be a given transaction database with 10 transactions from a grocery store (see Table 2.15). Let $A = bread$, $B = coffee$, $C = tea$, $D = sugar$, $E = beer$, and $F = butter$. Assume $minsupp = 0.3$ and $mininterest = 0.07$. The supports of frequent itemsets in both the set L by $FrequentItemsets$ and the set $Frequentset$ by $FrequentItemsetsbyPruning$ are shown below.*

In Table 2.15, there are six 1-itemsets: A, B, C, D, E and F, in RD. For $minsupp = 0.3$, all are frequent 1-itemsets in both of the sets L and $Frequentset$. This is listed in Table 2.16 below. And $L_1 = \{A, B, C, D, E, F\}$.

In Table 2.15, the set C_2 of the 2-itemsets is: AB [1], AC, AD, AE, AF, BC, BD, BE, BF, CD, CE, CF, DE, DF and EF. Each of the above 2-itemsets contains at least one subset of L_1. For $minsupp = 0.3$, $L_2 = \{AB, AC, AD, BC, BD, BF, CD, CF\}$ are all frequent 2-itemsets of L, as listed in Table 2.17, for the algorithm $FrequentItemsets$.

---

[1] For simplicity, we sometimes use AB for $\{A, B\}$.

Table 2.15. Transaction databases in RD

Transaction ID	Items
T_1	A, B, D
T_2	A, B, C, D
T_3	B, D
T_4	B, C, D, E
T_5	A, C, E
T_6	B, D, F
T_7	A, E, F
T_8	C, F
T_9	B, C, F
T_{10}	A, B, C, D, F

Table 2.16. 1-items in both of L and $Frequentset$

Item	Number of Transactions	Support $p(X)$
A	5	0.5
B	7	0.7
C	6	0.6
D	6	0.6
E	3	0.3
F	5	0.5

Table 2.17. 2-itemsets in L

Item	Number of Transactions	Support $p(X)$
A, B	3	0.3
A, C	3	0.3
A, D	3	0.3
B, C	4	0.4
B, D	6	0.6
B, F	3	0.3
C, D	3	0.3
C, F	3	0.3

However, for $minsupp = 0.3$ and $mininterest = 0.07$, $L_2 = \{BD\}$ are all frequent 2-itemsets in $Frequentset$ as listed in Table 2.18, for the algorithm $FrequentItemsetsbyPruning$. Certainly, because $|p(A \cup B) - p(A)p(B)| = |0.3 - 0.5 * 0.7| = 0.05 < mininterest = 0.07$, $|p(A \cup C) - p(A)p(C)| = 0 < mininterest$, $|p(A \cup D) - p(A)p(D)| = 0 < mininterest$, $|p(B \cup C) - p(B)p(C)| = 0.02 < mininterest$, $|p(B \cup F) - p(B)p(F)| = 0.05 < mininterest$, $|p(C \cup D) - p(C)p(D)| = 0.06 < mininterest$, and $|p(C \cup F) - p(C)p(F)| = 0 < mininterest$. Therefore, AB, AC, AD, BF, CD, and CF are not of interest. Hence, AB, AC, AD, BF, CD and CF are pruned from L_2 before it is appended into $Frequentset$.

Table 2.18. 2-itemsets in *Frequentset*

Item	Number of Transactions	Support $p(X)$
B, D	6	0.6

In Table 2.15, the set C_3 of the 3-itemsets is: *ABC*, *ABD*, *ACD*, *BCD*, *BCF*, *BDF*, and *CDF*. For *minsupp* = 0.3, $L_3 = \{ABD, BCD\}$ are all frequent itemsets in L, as listed in Table 2.19, for the algorithm *FrequentItemsets*.

Table 2.19. Supports of frequent itemsets in L

Itemset	Number of Transactions	Support $p(X)$
A, B, D	3	0.3
B, C, D	3	0.3

However, in the algorithm *FrequentItemsetsbyPruning*, for *minsupp* = 0.3 and *mininterest* = 0.07, $C_3 = \{\}$ and $L_3 = \{\}$, as all 3-itemsets are pruned from C_3 because of interest. Thus, Step 2 ends. The frequent itemsets in *Frequentset* are the output.

The algorithm *FrequentItemsets* still needs to identify the longer frequent itemsets in *RD*. In Table 2.15, the set C_4 of the 4-itemsets is: *ABCD*. For *minsupp* = 0.3, $L_4 = \{\}$. Thus, Step 2 ends, and the frequent itemsets in L are the output.

The above example show that, there are eight frequent 2-itemsets in L as a result of the algorithm *FrequentItemsets*, and only one frequent 2-itemset in *Frequentset* created by *FrequentItemsetsbyPruning*, after the uninteresting frequent itemsets are pruned. In total, there are sixteen frequent itemsets in L, and eight frequent itemsets of interest in *Frequentset*. Furthermore, we can also cut down the searched space by focusing on association rules of interest in the algorithm *FrequentItemsetsbyPruning*. This is the same technique as that used in the algorithm based on OPUS ([Webb 2000]).

2.4 Research into Mining Association Rules

Much of the research activity in the field of data mining has centered around association rules. There are many excellent publications which summarize this research, such as [Chen-Han-Yu 1996, Fayyad-Piatetsky 1996, Fayyad-Stolorz 1997]. The main task of mining association rules is to derive a set of strong association rules in the form of $I \rightarrow J$, where I and J are disjoint sets of items ([Agrawal-Imielinski-Swami 1993, Brin-Motwani-Silverstein 1997,

Han-Karypis-Kumar 1997, Miller-Yang 1997, Park-Chen-Yu 1997, Srikant-Agrawal 1997]). In order to implement this task, a wide range of problems have been investigated covering such diverse topics as efficient algorithms for mining association rules ([Agrawal-Srikant 1994, Brin-Motwani-Silverstein 1997, Park-Chen-Yu 1997]), measures of itemsets ([Brin-Motwani-Silverstein 1997, Aggarawal-Yu 1998]), parallel data mining for association rules ([Han-Karypis-Kumar 1997]), and so on. In this section, we simply recall three typical approaches of mining association rules established in current literature: the chi-squared test ([Brin-Motwani-Silverstein 1997]), the FP-tree based model ([Han-Pei-Yin 2000]), and the OPUS based algorithm ([Webb 2000]).

2.4.1 Chi-squared Test Method

The chi-squared test method was presented by Brin, Motwani and Silverstein ([Brin-Motwani-Silverstein 1997]). This method measures the significance of associations via the chi-squared test for correlation used in classical statistics. This leads to a measure that is upward closed in the itemset lattice, enabling reduction of the mining problem to a search for a border between correlated and uncorrelated itemsets in the lattice. This approach is useful because it not only captures correlation, but also detects negative implication. We now demonstrate this using an example.

Example 2.2 *Suppose we have the market basket data from a grocery store, consisting of n baskets. Let us focus on the purchase of tea and coffee. In the following table, rows t and ¬t correspond to baskets that do and do not, contain tea, and similarly columns c and ¬c correspond to coffee. The numbers represent the percentage of baskets.*

Table 2.20. Purchase of tea and coffee

	c	$\neg c$	$\sum_{row}$
t	20	5	25
$\neg t$	70	5	75
$\sum_{col}$	90	10	100

We can apply the support-confidence model to the potential association rule $t \rightarrow c$. The support for this rule is 20%, which is fairly high. The confidence is the conditional probability that a customer buys coffee, given that he/she buys tea, i.e., $P[t \wedge c]/P[t] = 20/25 = 0.8$, or 80%, which is also fairly high. At this point, we may conclude that the rule $t \rightarrow c$ is a valid rule.

Let us consider the fact that a *priori* probability that a customer buys coffee is 90%. In other words, a customer who is known to buy tea is less likely to buy coffee (by 10%) than a customer about whom we have no information.

This means that the correlation value would be taken as a parameter to determine whether a rule is valid or not. For this purpose, Brin, Motwani and Silverstein have offered a measure for discovering association rules using the chi-squared test as follows.

Let $p(A)$ be the probability that event A occurs, and $p(\neg A) = 1 - p(A)$ the probability that event A does not occur. Likewise, $p(A \wedge B)$ is the probability that both event A and event B occur together, and $p(\neg A \wedge B)$ is the probability that event B occurs but event A does not, and so on.

Definition 2.3 *The events A and B are independent if $p(A \wedge B) = p(A)p(B)$.*

Similarly, if $p(A \wedge B \wedge C) = p(A)p(B)p(C)$, then A, B, and C are *3-way independent*.

Definition 2.4 *If two events are not independent, they are dependent or correlated.*

If there is a series of n trials, the number of times event A occurs is denoted by $O_n(A)$, or just $O(A)$ when n is understood. $p(A)$ can be estimated by $O_n(A)/n$. In this way it can be estimated whether $p(A \wedge B) \neq p(A)p(B)$.

To put this in the context of mining association rules, $\{i_{a_1}, \cdots, i_{a_m}\} \subset I$ is a correlation rule if the occurrences of the items $i_{a_1}, \cdots, i_{a_m}$ are correlated. Let R be $\{i_1, \neg i_1\} \times \cdots \times \{i_k, \neg i_k\}$ and $r = r_1 \cdots r_k \in R$. Here R is the set of all possible basket values, and r is a single basket value. Each value of r denotes a *cell*. This terminology comes from viewing R as a k-dimensional table, known as a contingency table. Let $O(r)$ denote the number of baskets falling into cell r. To test whether a given cell is dependent, we must determine whether the actual count in cell r differs sufficiently from the expectation.

In the chi-squared test, expectation is calculated under the assumption of independence. Thus, $E[i_j] = O_n(i_j)$ for a single item, $E[\neg i_j] = n - O_n(i_j)$, and $E[r] = n \times E[r_1]/n \times \cdots \times E[r_k]/n$. Then the chi-squared statistic is defined as follows:

$$\chi^2 = \sum_{r \in R} (O(r) - E[r])^2 / E[r]$$

In short, this is a normalized deviation from expectation. The chi-squared statistic, as defined, will specify whether all k items are k-way independent. In order to determine whether some subsets of items are correlated, for instance A, B and C in Example 2.1, we merely restrict the range of r to $\{A, \neg A\} \times \{B, \neg B\} \times \{C, \neg C\}$. If all the variables were really independent, the chi-squared value would be 0 (allowing for fluctuations if $n < \infty$). If it is higher than a cutoff value (3.84 at the 95% significance level) we reject the independence assumption. Note that the cutoff value for any given significance level can be obtained from widely available tables for the chi-squared distribution. We now demonstrate the use of the test with the data from Example 2.1.

Example 2.3 *Let the contingency table for itemsets C and D in Example 2.1 be as follows:*

Table 2.21. The contingency table of C and D

	D	$\neg D$	$\sum_{row}$
C	3	3	6
$\neg C$	3	1	4
$\sum_{col}$	6	4	10

Now $E[C] = O(C) = 6$, while $E[D] = O(D) = 6$. Note that $E[C]$ is the sum of row 1, while $E[D]$ is the sum of column 1. The chi-squared value is

$$(3 - 6 \times 6/10)^2/(6 \times 6/10) + (3 - 6 \times (10 - 6)/10)^2/(6 \times (10 - 6)/10)$$
$$+ (3 - (10 - 6) \times 6/10)^2/((10 - 6) \times 6/10)$$
$$+ (1 - (10 - 6) \times (10 - 6)/10)^2/((10 - 6) \times (10 - 6)/10)$$
$$+ 0.1 + 0.15 + 0.15 + 0.225 = 0.625$$

Since 0.625 is less than 3.84, we do not reject the independence assumption at the 95% confidence interval.

Example 2.4 *Consider itemsets B and D in Example 2.1. The contingency table is as follows:*

Table 2.22. The contingency of B and D

	D	$\neg D$	$\sum_{row}$
B	6	1	7
$\neg B$	0	3	3
$\sum_{col}$	6	4	10

Now $E[B] = O(B) = 7$, while $E[D] = O(D) = 6$. The chi-squared value is

$$(6 - 6 \times 6/10)^2/(6 \times 6/10) + (1 - 6 \times (10 - 6)/10)^2/(6 \times (10 - 6)/10)$$
$$+ (0 - (10 - 7) \times 6/10)^2/((10 - 7) \times 6/10)$$
$$+ (3 - (10 - 7) \times (10 - 6)/10)^2/((10 - 7) \times (10 - 6)/10)$$
$$= 1.6 + 0.8167 + 1.8 + 2.7 = 6.9167$$

This chi-squared value of 6.9167 is significant at the 95% significance level. Furthermore, the largest contribution to the χ^2 value comes from the bottom-right cell, indicating that the dominant dependence is a veteran, being over 40. This matches our intuition.

2.4.2 The FP-tree Based Model

Traditional frequent patterns mining adopt an Apriori-like candidate set generation-and-test approach. However, a candidate set generation is still costly, especially when there exist prolific patterns and/or long patterns. To overcome this difficulty, Han, Pei and Yin have proposed a novel frequent pattern mining model based on the frequent pattern tree (FP-tree) ([Han 2000]). The FP-tree structure is defined as follows.

Definition 2.5 *(FP-tree): A frequent pattern tree is a tree structure defined below.*

- *It consists of one root labelled 'null', a set of item prefix subtrees which are the children of the root, and a frequent-item header table.*
- *Each node in the item prefix subtree consists of three fields: item-name, count and node-link, where item-name registers which item the particular node represents, count registers the number of transactions represented by the portion of the path reaching the node, and node-link links to the next node in the FP-tree which carries the same item-name; or it is null if there are none.*
- *Each entry in the frequent-item header table consists of two fields, (1) item-name and (2) head of node-link, which points to the first node in the FP-tree carrying the item-name.*

The process of the FP-tree based model is as follows.

First, an FP-tree is constructed, which is an extended prefix-tree structure storing crucial, quantitative information about frequent patterns. Only frequent length-1 items will have nodes in the tree, and the tree nodes are arranged in such a way that more frequently occurring nodes will have a better chance of sharing nodes than less frequently occurring ones.

Second, an FP-tree-based pattern fragment growth mining method is developed, which starts from a frequent length-1 pattern (as an initial suffix pattern), and examines only its conditional pattern base (a 'sub-database' which consists of the set of frequent items co-occurring with the suffix pattern). It then constructs its (conditional) FP-tree, and performs mining recursively with such a tree. The pattern growth is achieved via concatenation of the suffix pattern with the new patterns generated from a conditional FP-tree. Since a frequent itemset in any transaction is always encoded in the corresponding path of the frequent pattern trees, pattern growth ensures the completeness of the result. In this context, the method is not an Apriori-like restricted generation-and-test but a restricted test only. The major operations of mining are count accumulation and prefix path count adjustment, which are usually much less costly than the candidate generation and pattern matching operations performed in most Apriori-like algorithms.

Third, the search technique employed in mining is a partitioning-based, divide-and-conquer method rather than the Apriori-like bottom-up generation of frequent itemsets combinations. This dramatically reduces the size of the conditional pattern base generated at the subsequent level of search, as well as the size of its corresponding conditional FP-tree. Moreover, it transforms the problem of finding long frequent patterns into looking for shorter ones and then concatenating the suffix. It employs the least frequent items as the suffix, which offers good selectivity. All these techniques contribute to a substantial reduction in search costs.

2.4.3 OPUS Based Algorithm

Identifying frequent itemsets is a procedure for searching an exponential space that consists of all possible combinations of items and itemsets in a given database. This is necessary because the items are randomly combined in the transactions of a database, and the considered itemsets in the database are apparently of an exponential amount. For example, suppose we have market basket data from a grocery store with 1000 items. There are then 2^{1000} possible itemsets occurring in the database. Conventional mining approaches are Apriori-like. Each is a two-stage process consisting of: (1) generating frequent itemsets, and (2) generating association rules. (for details, please see 'support-confidence framework' in Sections 2.1 and 2.2.) However, this can impose large computational overheads when the number of frequent itemsets is very large ([Webb 2000]). This will often be the case when association rule analysis is performed on domains other than basket analysis, or when it is performed for basket analysis with basket information augmented by other customer information.

Webb has presented an alternative approach to direct search for association rules for some applications ([Webb 2000]). This method applies the OPUS search to prune the search space on the basis of inter-relationships between itemsets.

Therefore, we can see that mining association rules can be tackled as a search process that starts with general rules (rules with one condition on the left hand side (LHS)) and searches through successive specializations (rules formed by adding additional conditions to the LHS). Such a search is unordered. That is, the order in which successive specializations are added to an LHS is significant, and $A \wedge B \wedge C \rightarrow X$ is the same as $C \wedge B \wedge A \rightarrow X$. An important component of an efficient search in this context is minimizing the number of association rules that need to be considered. A key technique used to eliminate potential association rules from consideration is 'optimistic pruning'. Optimistic pruning operates by forming an optimistic evaluation of the highest rule value that might occur in a region of the search space. An optimistic evaluation is one that cannot be lower than the actual maximum value. If the optimistic value for the region is lower than the lowest value that is of interest, then that region can be pruned. If a search seeks the top m association rules, then it can maintain a list of the top m rules encountered at that point during the search. If an optimistic evaluation is lower than the lowest value of a rule in the top m, then the corresponding region of the search space may be pruned. Other pruning rules could perhaps identify regions that can be pruned because they contain only rules that fail to meet prespecified constrains such as:

– minimum support (the frequency in the data of the right hand side (RHS) or of the RHS and LHS in combination);
– minimum *lift*; or
– being one of the top m association rules on some specified criteria.

Here, 'lift' is a frequently utilized measure of association rule utility. The lift of an association rule $= \frac{|LHS \wedge RHS|}{|LHS|} / \frac{|RHS|}{n}$, where $|X|$ is the number of cases with conditions X, and n is the total number of cases in the data set.

The term *credible rule* is used to denote association rules for which, at some given point in a search, it is possible that the rule will be of interest, using whatever criteria of interest applies for the given search.

If we restrict association rules to having a single condition on the RHS, two search strategies are plausible:

(1) for each potential RHS, the condition explores the space of possible LHS conditions; or
(2) for each potential LHS combination of conditions, the space of possible RHS conditions is explored.

The former strategy leads to the most straight-forward implementation as it involves a simple iteration through a straight-forward search for each potential RHS condition. However, this implies accessing the count of the number of cases covered by the LHS many times, once for each RHS condition for which an LHS is considered. At the very least, this entails computational overheads for caching information. At worst, it requires a pass through the data each time the value is to be utilized. While a pass through the data has lower overheads when the data is stored in memory rather than on disk, it is still a time-consuming operation that must be avoided if computation is to be efficient.

The algorithm, which applies the OPUS search algorithm to obtain an efficient search for association rules, is designed as a recursive procedure with three arguments:

(1) **CurrentLHS**: the set of conditions in the LHS of the rule currently being considered;
(2) **AvailableLHS**: the set of conditions that may be added to the LHS of rules to be explored below this point;
(3) **AvailableRHS**: the set of conditions that may appear on the RHS of a rule in the search space at this point and below.

This algorithm is computationally efficient for association rule analysis during which the number of rules to be found can be constrained and all data can be maintained in memory.

2.5 Summary

Knowledge discovery in databases has been an active and attractive research challenge both in the areas of Artificial Intelligence and Databases ([Wu 1995, Zhang 1989]). A prevailing topic in this area is mining association rules from databases. Agrawal, Imielinski and Swami have proposed a support-confidence framework for discovering association rules ([Agrawal-Imielinski-Swami 1993]). This framework is now widely accepted as a measure of uncertainty in association rules. However, because different measures on uncertainty lead to different models for mining association rules, measuring of uncertainty of association rules has become one of the crucial problems concerning mining association rules. For this reason, we have systematically studied possible means of measuring association rules in this chapter. The key points of this chapter are:

- presented some needed concepts for dealing with association rules;
- recalled previous efforts concerning association rule mining;
- designed an efficient algorithm for identifying association rules of interest; and
- introduced three efforts on mining association rules: the chi-squared test model ([Brin-Motwani-Silverstein 1997]), the FP-tree based model ([Han-Pei-Yin 2000]) and the OPUS based algorithm ([Webb 2000]).

3. Negative Association Rule

During decision making, we are often confronted by a huge amount of factors. These factors may be either an advantage or a disadvantage to a decision objective. For the purpose of low-risk (high-profit), we must scrutinize the possible behavior of these factors. It is particularly useful to grasp which of the disadvantage factors will rarely occur when the expected advantage factors occur, by using past data. Also, we take into account that there are essential differences between positive and negative association rule mining. Using a pruning algorithm we can reduce the search space, however, some pruned itemsets may be useful in the extraction of negative rules.

In this chapter, we present new techniques for identifying negative association rules of interest in databases. The chapter is organized as follows. We begin by introducing our motivation for the research in Section 3.1. We argue why our algorithm is focused on discovering positive and negative itemsets of interest in databases. This argument is illustrated in Section 3.2. In Section 3.3, we illustrate the effectiveness of focusing on negative association rules of interest. In Section 3.4, we first define the conditions of negative itemsets of interest, and then propose an algorithm for generating all possible positive and negative itemsets of interest for a given database. In Section 3.5, we build a new model for extracting and measuring positive and negative association rules of interest using the argument of Piatetsky-Shapiro, and probability theory. In Section 3.6, we compare our model with some existing mining techniques and, finally, we summarize the contents of the chapter in Section 3.7.

3.1 Introduction

Traditional association rule mining has been mainly focused on identifying the relationships strongly associated among itemsets that have *frequent* and *high-correlation*. Association rules enable us to detect the items that commonly occur together in an application. Association rules from the support-confidence framework are *positive rules* (see Chapter 2). They indicate that the presence of some itemsets will imply the presence of other itemsets within the same transactions.

In applications, an association rule $A \rightarrow B$ is used to predict that 'if A occurs, then B generally also occurs'. For efficiency, we can apply this association rule to place 'B near to A' for applications such as store layout, product placement and supermarket management. For a store, associations analyzing suggests:

(1) higher-rank items, or itemsets, should be placed near to a seller;
(2) B should be placed near to A if there is a rule $A \rightarrow B$ for itemsets A and B.

The first strategy leads to highly efficient marketing due to the fact that goods frequently purchased every day in the store can easily be reached by the seller. The second strategy saves time for the seller because a group of goods often purchased together in the store are selectively laid out. Below we look at two examples with different types of association rules.

Example 3.1 *Consider six itemsets, A, B, C, D, E and F, two association rules, saying ,$A \rightarrow B$ and $E \rightarrow F$ (from the support-confidence model), and two aisles in a supermarket to place these six itemsets. We know that A and B should be put in the same aisle, as should E and F. How about C and D?*

From the two positive association rules, C and D are not positively associated with any of the other itemsets. What if we have a rule such as $A \rightarrow \neg C$, which says that the presence of A in a transaction implies that C is highly unlikely to be present in the same transaction? We call rules of the form $A \rightarrow \neg C$ *negative rules*. (In the following sections, we will also have negative rules in the forms $\neg A \rightarrow C$ and $\neg A \rightarrow \neg C$.) Negative rules indicate that the presence of some itemsets will imply the absence of other itemsets in the same transactions. In our current example, if we have a negative association between A and C (and no other negative associations with C), we would put C in the same aisle as E and F.

Example 3.2 *Investors in an estate will encounter problems of environmental quality, natural resource use, and problems also of an economic and political nature. Analysis of circumstances that give rise to environmental problems, resource use conflicts, and possible policy solutions to these problems and conflicts, must depend, not only on positive, but also on negative association rules from past data.*

This example shows that negative association rules become very important if a decision maker wants, for application purposes, to know which disadvantage factors rarely occur when certain advantage factors occur. Because negative association rules are hidden in infrequent itemsets, existing mining techniques do not work well when identifying these rules.

There are two issues that have motivated our research into mining, not only positive association rules, but also negative association rules. First, decision making in many applications, such as product placement and investment analysis, often involves a number of factors, including advantage factors and disadvantage factors. To minimize negative impacts, and maximize possible benefits, we must scrutinize which of the side-effect factors will rarely (if ever) occur when the expected advantage factors occur. Negative association rules such as $A \rightarrow \neg C$ are very important in decision making because $A \rightarrow \neg C$ can tell us that C (which may be a disadvantage factor) rarely occurs when A (which may be an advantage factor) occurs. Therefore, the above two examples demonstrate that associations among different factors, both positive and negative, are useful.

Second, experience in the areas of science and engineering have shown that negative relationships (such as negative numbers in mathematics, and negative assertions in logic) play the same important role as positive relationships do. Association rules like $A \rightarrow \neg C$ describe another type of relationship among itemsets: *negation*. Therefore, negative association rules can be as important as positive rules in association analysis, although negative rules are hidden and differ.

For the above reasons, we advocate a way to discover negative association rules when identifying (positive) association rules in databases. Mining negative association rules brings us two direct benefits.

- Logically, the first benefit is to further complete associated relationships among items as a system in science and technology, in the same way as we require negative (real) numbers in applications after systems of natural numbers and positive real numbers are formed.
- The second benefit is to offer more information which might be of use in supporting decisions for applications.

To illustrate how negative association rules hidden in databases can be identified, we use the example below.

Example 3.3 *Suppose we have market basket data from a grocery store, consisting of n baskets. Let us focus on the purchase of tea (t) and coffee (c). And let supp(t) = 0.25 and supp(t ∪ c) = 0.2.*

We now apply the support-confidence framework (see [Agrawal-Imielinski-Swami 1993]) to the potential association rule t → c. The support for this rule is 0.2, which is fairly high. The confidence is the conditional probability that a customer buys coffee, given that he/she buys tea, i.e.,

$$supp(t \cup c)/supp(t) = 0.2/0.25 = 0.8$$

which is also pretty high. At this point, we may conclude that the rule t → c is a valid rule.

Now, let $supp(c) = 0.6$, $supp(t) = 0.4$, $supp(t \cup c) = 0.05$, and $minconf = 0.52$. Then the conditional probability is

$$supp(t \cup c)/supp(t) = 0.05/0.4 = 0.125 < minconf = 0.52,$$

and $supp(t \cup c) = 0.05$ are low. This means that $t \cup c$ is an infrequent itemset, and $t \to c$ cannot be extracted as a rule in the support-confidence framework. But

$$supp(t \cup \neg c) = supp(t) - supp(t \cup c) = 0.4 - 0.05 = 0.35$$

is very high, and

$$supp(t \cup \neg c)/supp(t) = 0.35/0.4 = 0.875 > minconf$$

Therefore, $t \to \neg c$ should be extracted from the database.

The rule $t \to \neg c$ is a negative rule. From Example 3.3, we need to examine infrequent itemsets (such as $t \cup c$) to identify negative association rules. Existing algorithms for association analysis have concentrated on identifying only frequent itemsets in a given database. This indicates that existing algorithms for discovering frequent itemsets are inadequate for mining negative association rules.

In fact, for many applications, such as catalog design, store layout, product placement, supermarket management and planning, mining positive association rules enables us to determine which itemsets occur associated with an itemset A. And it is also important to apply negative association rules to determine which itemsets rarely occur associated with A.

However, from the above examples, identifying negative association rules requires *infrequent itemsets* in databases. And, as we know, previous algorithms have generally been involved with identifying only *frequent itemsets* in a given database. This means that existing algorithms for discovering frequent itemsets are inadequate for extracting negative association rules.

On the other hand, the identification of infrequent itemsets of interest will involve confronting search spaces of an exponential size. To solve these problems, we construct a novel and efficient algorithm for picking out, not only all *positive itemsets of interest*, but also *negative itemsets of interest* in databases. The main advantage of this algorithm is to reduce the size of the searched space which consists of all possible items and itemsets in a database.

The approach in this chapter differs from existing work in association analysis in two aspects. First, infrequent itemsets in databases are of interest to us for mining negative association rules. Second, to design an efficient model for mining both positive and negative association rules in databases, we estimate the confidence of association rules, using an increasing degree of the rule's conditional probability relative to its priori probability.

3.2 Focusing on Itemsets of Interest

Although data mining is commonly defined as a non-trivial process of identifying valid, novel, potentially useful, and ultimately understandable patterns in data (see [Fayyad-Piatetsky 1996]), positive association rules mining has, to date, solved the only useful aspect of data mining. As we advance into a more mature stage, researchers are exploring alternatives for finding hidden patterns. One of hidden patterns is negative association rule among itemsets that have *infrequent* and *high-correlation*. Negative patterns are important in applications, which tell us which of items rarely occur together. Unfortunately, up until now, mining negative association rules has received little attention. The aim of this chapter is to develop techniques for identifying negative association rules of interest in databases.

As we will see, mining negative association rules is very different from that of mining positive association rules in databases. In particular, identifying negative association rules presents new problems. These include:

(1) identification of infrequent itemsets of interest;
(2) the exponential increase of the amount of involved (infrequent and frequent) itemsets in databases;
(3) how to efficiently identify both frequent and infrequent itemsets of interest in databases; and
(4) the construction of an alternative model for measuring negative association rules in databases.

So, specified models for extracting negative association rules must be developed. Before constructing an efficient mining model, we now elucidate why our algorithm is focused on discovering association rules of interest in databases.

As we have seen, mining both positive and negative association rules requires, not only frequent itemsets, but also some infrequent itemsets. However, identifying frequent itemsets is itself a procedure for searching an exponential space which consists of all possible items and itemsets in a given database. This is because the items are randomly combined in the transactions of the database. And the number of itemsets to be considered in the database can be of an exponential size. For example, suppose we have market basket data from a grocery store, consisting of n baskets with 1000 items. Then there are 2^{1000} possible itemsets which might occur in the database. Although the Apriori algorithm (see [Agrawal-Srikant 1994]), which is a famous procedure in knowledge discovery and data mining, only deals with frequent itemsets in databases, it can impose large computational overheads when the number of frequent itemsets is very large (see [Han-Pei-Yin 2000, Webb 2000]). To overcome this difficulty, Han, Pei and Yin proposed a novel frequent pattern mining model based on an FP-tree (see [Han-Pei-Yin 2000]). Meanwhile, Webb presented an alternative approach to the association rule discovery ([Webb 2000]). This was a one-step mining approach, which applies an OPUS-search to prune the search space on the basis of inter-relationships between itemsets. According to their experiments, both of the above algorithms are more efficient than the Apriori algorithm and its derivatives.

Now, we have to consider some of the infrequent itemsets which are used to discover negative association rules in databases. The amount of handled itemsets is obviously very large. We note that some itemsets pruned in the OPUS based algorithm might be useful for extracting negative association rules in a database. In other words, perhaps a frequent itemset should not be pruned in spite of the fact that it is not contained in any association rules. Some such frequent itemsets in databases might still be helpful to negative association rules. So, the existing pruning techniques are not appropriate for the discovery of negative association rules.

On the other hand, as we will see shortly, the number of possible infrequent itemsets for negative association rules is often far greater than the number of frequent itemsets in a database. This means that the amount of itemsets involved in a database (including possible positive and negative) grows to almost double. Hence, an efficient algorithm for mining negative associations must be developed.

For efficiency, when we mine, we focus our attention on only positive and negative itemsets of interest. In this way, we clarify what negative itemsets are, and which are interesting negative itemsets for applications. To do so, we use the argument of Piatetsky-Shapiro on association rules of interest ([Piatetsky 1991]).

Even if we do so, there might still be the problem of exponential searching spaces for some applications. Indeed, the data sets faced by miners can be very large. Complete computation for mining this kind of database might not be feasible, or indeed warranted, when the sources are bounded. To facilitate mining large scale databases, we advocate a two-phase approach. In the first phase, we locate all approximate positive and negative itemsets of interest within a selected instance set of a given large scale database by using a pruning technique. The second phase adds up the accurate values for all approximate positive and negative itemsets of interest in the database. The key problem is how to construct an instance set. It must fit two requirements:

(1) the set must be infrequent enough to be tackled in the memory; and
(2) the frequency of itemsets in the instance set must be approximate to that in the original database.

Sampling is naturally the fastest and best way to obtain approximate itemsets of interest from databases.

To select instances in a given large database, we first apply the *central limit theorem* to determine, by precision, the size of the instance set. We then choose at random the instances in the database by using a pseudo-random number generator. Experience with statistics tells us that the selected instance set can approximately hold to the distribution of itemsets in a given database if the data in the database follows a Bernoulli distribution or a binomial distribution.

Actually, a transaction randomly appended into a database has two possible outcomes for an itemset A. They are 1 or 0. Suppose the probability of A occurring in the database is p, and the probability of A not occurring is $q = 1 - p$, then the itemset A in this database has a Bernoulli distribution according to the definition in [Durrett 1996]. Note that an itemset with a Bernoulli distribution can also be taken with a binomial distribution. Since operations (not including the 'sort' operation) on a database are random, an operated database can also be taken as a Bernoulli trial (or a binomial distribution) for an itemset, if the database has not been sorted. Hence, the above method is generally sound enough to deal with large scale databases.

Note that the above approximating discovery can be useful in many applications, including marketing and stock investment, where time might be limited and only approximate association rules are required. Indeed, for a short-term stock investor, time is money. Thus, if an investor can obtain approximate frequent itemsets from data in the stock databases quickly, these itemsets might be sufficient to enable profitable decisions on investments to be made. On the other hand, if a stock investor tried to extract all accurate supports of frequent itemsets from the databases, too much time might be spent to make decisions and the most opportune time for investment might pass.

However, looking into reducing search space is not the main aim of this chapter. For further details of some techniques which lessen the amount of handled positive and negative itemsets in searched spaces, please see Chapter 6. Meanwhile, this chapter focuses on identifying itemsets of interest in applications. To demonstrate the utility, we cut down the number of attributes of each transaction in a given database to an appropriate integer so as to avoid exponential research space. In doing so, we implement an algorithm specially designed for mining negative associations.

3.3 Effectiveness of Focusing on Infrequent Itemsets of Interest

As we have seen, negative association rule mining presents more challenges than positive association rule mining due to the fact that negative association rules can be hidden in huge amounts of infrequent itemsets. Unfortunately, existing algorithms are inadequate for identifying negative association rules. Focusing on identifying negative association rules from interesting infrequent itemsets can reduce search space. We will demonstrate the effectiveness of our approach by an example, but first, let us examine, by example, existing techniques to ascertain whether any can serve the purpose of identifying negative association rules. We assume that $minsupp = 0.4$ and $minconf = 0.6$.

Example 3.4 *Consider a database* $TD = \{(A,B, D); (B, C, D); (B, D); (B, C, D, E); (A, B, D, F)\}$, *which has 5 transactions, separated by semicolons. Each transaction contains several items, separated by commas.*

1. The first solution (a traditional association rule mining technique) is used to identify positive association rules $A \to B$ ($supp = 0.6$ and $conf = 1$), $A \to D$ ($supp = 0.6$ and $conf = 1$), $A \to BD$ ($supp = 0.6$ and $conf = 1$), $AB \to D$ ($supp = 0.6$ and $conf = 1$), $AD \to B$ ($supp = 0.6$ and $conf = 1$), $C \to B$ ($supp = 0.4$ and $conf = 1$), $C \to D$ ($supp = 0.4$ and $conf = 1$), and so on, from **7 frequent itemsets**: $AB, AD, BC, BD, CD, ABD,$ and BCD, in TD. This method cannot be used to identify negative association rules.

2. The second solution is to directly extend a traditional mining algorithm to identify negative association rules when positive rules are searched for in TD. The negative association rules are $A \to \neg C, A \to \neg E, A \to \neg F, B \to \neg E, B \to \neg F, C \to \neg A, C \to \neg E, C \to \neg F, D \to \neg E, D \to \neg F,$ and so on, from **49 infrequent itemsets**:

   $AC, AE, AF, BE, BF, CE, CF, DE, DF, EF, ABC, ABE,$
   $ABF, ACD, ACE, ACF, ADE, ADF, AEF, BCE, BCF, BDE, BDF,$
   $BEF, CDE, CDF, CEF, DEF, ABCD, ABCE, ABCF, ABDE, ABDF,$
   $ABEF, ACDE, ACDF, ACEF, ADEF, BCDE, BCDF, BDEF, CDEF,$
   $ABCDE, ABCDF, ABCEF, ABDEF, ACDEF, BCDEF, ABCDEF.$

   There are at least **818** possible negative association rules generated from the 49 infrequent itemsets by using this solution. For example, there are at least **110 possible negative rules** generated from the infrequent itemset $ABCDEF$ alone.

   People may argue that existing techniques, such as the OPUS based algorithm [Webb 2000], can be used to reduce search space. However, some itemsets that are pruned in the OPUS based algorithm may be useful for extracting negative association rules from a database. This is the essential difference between positive and negative association rule mining. In this chapter, we develop new techniques which reduce search space. We demonstrate the effectiveness of our approach in the continuation of Example 3.4 as follows.

3. The third solution (Our approach) is to search those itemsets that are of interest. The simplest method is to consider expressions consisting of frequent itemsets. That is, if X is an infrequent itemset of interest, there is at least one expression $X = AB$ where both A and B are frequent itemsets. In this way, we can reduce the search space to 4 interesting infrequent itemsets: $AC, ABC, ACD,$ and $ABCD$.

From the first observation, traditional approaches cannot directly help identify negative rules. Using the second solution, it needs to search huge amounts of negative association rules (at least 818) for a rather small database. It would be difficult for a user to browse negative rules when the database is even slightly large. In particular, it is a challenge to identify which of the rules are really useful to applications. Also, existing techniques are inefficient in reducing search space. So, at present, we must search huge spaces to identify negative rules. This strongly encourages us to develop new techniques for identifying negative rules. In fact, our solution (3) explores efficient techniques which overcome various difficulties in negative rule mining. This chapter goes on to exploit efficient techniques which confront the size and complications of negative association rules in data.

Based on the above analysis, the problem can be formulated as follows.

Research is focused on identifying negative association rules of the form: $A \rightarrow \neg B$ (or $\neg A \rightarrow B$ or $\neg A \rightarrow \neg B$), of interest in applications, where A and B are itemsets, and $\neg X$ stands for the negation of an itemset X.

3.4 Itemsets of Interest

As we have seen, there can be almost exponential infrequent itemsets in a database, and only some are useful for mining negative association rules of interest. So we must make clear which of the negative association rules are significant for applications. In this section, we first determine the conditions for identifying negative itemsets of interest in databases. Then, we construct a procedure for identifying positive and negative itemsets of interest.

3.4.1 Positive Itemsets of Interest

Previous work on the amount of 'usefulness' or 'interest' of a rule has focused on how much the actual support of a rule exceeded the expected support, based on the support of the antecedent and consequent ([Srikant-Agrawal 1997]). Piatetsky-Shapiro argued that a rule $X \rightarrow Y$ is not interesting if

$$support(X \rightarrow Y) \approx support(X) \times support(Y)$$

(see [Piatetsky 1991]). This argument reaches a significant probabilistic level, so we take it as one of the conditions for judging which are the itemsets of interest.

Because $confidence(X \rightarrow Y)$ and $support(X \cup Y)$ can be interpreted according to probability theory as:

$$support(X \cup Y) = p(X \cup Y)$$

$$confidence(X \rightarrow Y) = p(Y|X) = \frac{p(X \cup Y)}{p(X)}$$

([Brin-Motwani-Silverstein 1997, Srikant-Agrawal 1996]) then the Piatetsky-Shapiro argument can be represented as

$$p(X \cup Y) \approx p(X)p(Y)$$

This formula is referred to as the *interest* of Y given X, and is one of the main measurements of uncertainty in association rules. Certainly, the further the value is from 1, the more the dependence. Using Piatetsky-Shapiro's argument, we present a new concept for mining association rules from large databases with the following theorem.

Theorem 3.1 (*Piatetsky-Shapiro's argument*) *Let I be a set of items in the database TD, $X, Y \subseteq I$ be itemsets, $X \cap Y = \emptyset$, $supp(X) \neq 0$, and $supp(Y) \neq 0$, where $minsupp, minconf$ and $mininterest > 0$ are given by users or experts. Then $X \rightarrow Y$ can be extracted as a rule of interest if*

(1) $supp(X \cup Y) \geq minsupp$,
(2) $supp(Y|X) \geq minconf$, and
(3) $|supp(X \cup Y) - supp(X)supp(Y)| \geq mininterest$.

Proof: We need only prove that

$$|\frac{supp(X \cup Y)}{supp(X)supp(Y)} - 1| \geq mininterest$$

For (3),

$$\frac{|supp(X \cup Y) - supp(X)supp(Y)|}{supp(X)supp(Y)} \geq \frac{mininterest}{supp(X)supp(Y)},$$

or

$$|\frac{supp(X \cup Y)}{supp(X)supp(Y)} - 1| \geq \frac{mininterest}{supp(X)supp(Y)}$$

Because $supp(X)supp(Y) \leq 1$, so

$$\frac{mininterest}{supp(X)supp(Y)} \geq \frac{mininterest}{1} = mininterest.$$

Hence,

$$|\frac{supp(X \cup Y)}{supp(X)supp(Y)} - 1| \geq mininterest$$

According to the definition of interest, $X \rightarrow Y$ can be extracted as a rule of interest.

∇

As we can see, there are three thresholds: *minimum support* (*minsupp*), *minimum confidence* (*minconf*) and *minimum interest* (*mininterest*) required for rules of interest. According to Piatetsky-Shapiro's argument in Theorem 3.1, if $X \rightarrow Y$ is a rule of interest, the condition $|supp(X \cup Y) - supp(X)supp(Y)| \geq mininterest$ must be satisfied. However, different applications may require different values of minimum interest (*mininterest*). For example, *mininterest* = 0.08 is a valid choice in Example 3.3, but it is a poor choice when all supports of the itemsets are less than 0.08. Hence, we must determine an appropriate minimum interest (*mininterest*) for an application.

By the condition of interest rules, if $supp(X \cup Y) = minsupp$ for itemset $X \cup Y$, $X \rightarrow Y$ would be possibly extracted as a rule of interest. In particular, if $supp(X \cup Y) = supp(X) = supp(Y) = minsupp$, $X \rightarrow Y$ might also be extracted as a rule of interest. This means that all the necessary conditions of interest rules would be satisfied. And for minimum interest (*mininterest*), the condition

$$|supp(X \cup Y) - supp(X)supp(Y)| = minsupp - minsupp^2 \geq mininterest$$

must hold. Therefore, we can take $minsupp - minsupp^2$ as an *upper bound* of *mininterest*. For example, for $minsupp = 0.2$,

$$mininterest \leq minsupp - minsupp^2 = 0.2 - 0.2^2 = 0.16$$

and if $minsupp = 0.001$,

$$mininterest \leq minsupp - minsupp^2 = 0.001 - 0.001^2 = 0.00099$$

Theorem 3.1 indicates that $X \rightarrow Y$ cannot be extracted as a rule of interest if $supp(X \cup Y) \approx supp(X)supp(Y)$. Actually, $supp(X \cup Y) \approx supp(X)supp(Y)$ denotes X is very nearly independent of Y in probability theory terms. Generally, if $supp(X \cup Y) - supp(X)supp(Y) \geq mininterest$, the rule $X \rightarrow Y$ is of interest. Strictly speaking, if

(1) $X \cap Y = \emptyset$,
(2) $supp(X \cup Y) \geq minsupp$,
(3) $supp(X \cup Y) - supp(X)supp(Y) \geq mininterest$, and
(4) $supp(X \cup Y)/supp(X) \geq minconf$

and then $X \rightarrow Y$ is a valid association rule of interest, where *mininterest* is a minimum interest value specified by users. And $X \cup Y$ is called a *positive itemset of interest*. Otherwise, if $|supp(X \cup Y) - supp(X)supp(Y)| < mininterest$ or $supp(X \cup Y)/supp(X) \leq minconf$, the rule $X \rightarrow Y$ is not of interest, and $X \cup Y$ is called an *uninteresting itemset*.

In the reverse case, if i is a positive itemset of interest, there is at least an expression $i = X \cup Y$ such that X and Y satisfy the above four conditions for positive association rules of interest.

3.4.2 Negative Itemsets of Interest

To mine negative association rules, all itemsets for such rules in a given database must be generated. For example, if $A \rightarrow \neg B$ (or $\neg A \rightarrow B$, or $\neg A \rightarrow \neg B$) can be found, then $supp(A \cup \neg B) \geq minsupp$ (or $supp(\neg A \cup B) \geq minsupp$, or $supp(\neg A \cup \neg B) \geq minsupp$) must hold. This means that $supp(A \cup B) < minsupp$ may hold. And the itemset $A \cup B$ may not be generated as a frequent itemset when using conventional algorithms. In other words, $A \cup B$ may be an infrequent itemset. However, numbers of infrequent itemsets are usually too large in databases to be easily handled. Therefore, we have to pick out only the infrequent itemsets useful to applications. Which infrequent itemsets are of interest? To answer this question, we must define some conditions for recognizing all infrequent itemsets of interest.

Generally, in a large scale database, if A is a frequent itemset and B is an infrequent itemset with frequency 1, then $A \rightarrow \neg B$ is a valid negative rule. In fact, $supp(A) \geq minsupp$ and $supp(B) \approx 0$. So

$$supp(A \cup \neg B) \approx supp(A) \geq minsupp$$

and

$$conf(A \rightarrow \neg B) = supp(A \cup \neg B)/supp(A) \approx 1 \geq minconf$$

This means that rule $A \rightarrow \neg B$ is valid. There can be a number of itemsets of this kind in databases. For example, some rarely purchased goods in a store fit into this category. However, it is frequent itemsets that usually attract attention to in applications. Hence, any patterns mined in databases would commonly relate to frequent itemsets. This means that if $A \rightarrow \neg B$ (or $\neg A \rightarrow B$, or $\neg A \rightarrow \neg B$) is a negative rule of interest, A and B would involve only frequent itemsets. This is one of the main reasons for identifying interesting negative association rules.

For applications and probability significance, the itemsets for negative association rules of the form $A \rightarrow \neg B$ (or $\neg A \rightarrow B$, or $\neg A \rightarrow \neg B$) would satisfy the following conditions:

(1) $A \cap B = \emptyset$;
(2) $supp(A) \geq minsupp$ and $supp(B) \geq minsupp$; and
(3) $supp(A \cup \neg B) \geq minsupp$ (or $supp(\neg A \cup B) \geq minsupp$, or $supp(\neg A \cup \neg B) \geq minsupp$).

Here condition (2) can guarantee the probability significance of negative association rules. The others assure the rules to be valid. Generally, an infrequent itemset i is called a *negative itemset* if there is at least one expression of $i = A \cup B$ such that A and B match the above three conditions.

For the Piatetsky-Shapiro argument, if $supp(A \cup \neg B) - supp(A) supp(\neg B) \geq mininterest$, the rule $A \rightarrow \neg B$ is of interest. Therefore if

(1) $A \cap B = \emptyset$,

(2) $supp(A) \geq minsupp$, $supp(B) \geq minsupp$, and $supp(A \cup \neg B) \geq minsupp$,

(3) $supp(A \cup \neg B) - supp(A)supp(\neg B) \geq mininterest$, and

(4) $supp(A \cup \neg B)/supp(A) \geq minconf$,

then $A \rightarrow \neg B$ is a valid negative association rule of interest, where *mininterest* is a minimum interesting value specified by users. And $A \cup B$ is a *negative itemset of interest*. Otherwise, the rule $A \rightarrow \neg B$ is not of interest, and $A \cup B$ is an *uninteresting itemset*. Thus, uninteresting itemsets are any itemsets in a database which exclude both positive and negative itemsets of interest. These itemsets need to be pruned to reduce the space searched when we mine.

On the other hand, if i is a negative itemset of interest, there is at least one expression $i = A \cup B$ such that one of the rules: $A \rightarrow \neg B$, or $\neg A \rightarrow B$, or $\neg A \rightarrow \neg B$, is a valid negative association rule of interest.

As we will see shortly, there are many frequent itemsets related to association rules that are not of interest. If the extracted itemsets deal only with positive and negative itemsets of interest, the search space can be extremely reduced. Therefore, the algorithm in the next subsection focuses on only searching for frequent itemsets of interest from a given database.

3.5 Searching Interesting Itemsets

As mentioned, the Apriori algorithm identifies only frequent itemsets, and does not include any infrequent ones. On the other hand, it takes only a little heuristic information to search an exponential space consisting of items and possible itemsets in a given database. However, this algorithm may suffer from large computational overheads when the number of frequent itemsets is very large ([Han-Pei-Yin 2000, Webb 2000]). For this reason, we now construct an efficient focussed algorithm for picking up all positive and negative itemsets of interest in a given database.

3.5.1 Procedure

Procedure 3.1 *InterestItemsetsbyPruning*
begin

    Input: D: data set; minsupp: minimum support; mininterest: minimum interest;

    Output: PL: set of positive itemsets of interest; NL: set of negative itemsets of interest;

(1) **let** the set of positive itemsets of interest $PL \leftarrow \emptyset$;

    let the set of negative itemsets of interest $NL \leftarrow \emptyset$;

(2) **let** $Frequent_1 \leftarrow \{\text{frequent 1-itemsets}\}$;

    let $PL \leftarrow PL \cup Frequent_1$;

(3) **for** $(k = 2; (L_{k-1} \neq \emptyset \text{ and } S_{k-1} \neq \emptyset); k++)$ **do**
begin
//Generate all possible positive and negative k-itemsets of interest in D.
  (3.1) **let** $Tem_k \leftarrow$ the k-itemsets constructed from $Frequent_i$ ($1 \leq i \leq k - 1$);
  (3.2) **for** any transaction t in D **do**
    begin
    //Check which k-itemsets are included in transaction t.
        let $Tem_t \leftarrow$ the k-itemsets in t and are also contained by Tem_k;
        for any itemset A in Tem_t **do**
          let $A.count \leftarrow A.count + 1$;
    end
  (3.3) **let** $C_k \leftarrow$ the k-itemsets in Tem_k that each k-itemset contains at least a subset in L_{k-1};
    let $Frequent_k \leftarrow \{c | c \in C_K \wedge (supp(c) = (c.count/|D|) >= minsupp)\}$;
    let $L_k \leftarrow Frequent_k$;
    let $N_k \leftarrow Tem_k - Frequent_k$;
    //Prune all uninteresting k-itemsets in L_k
  (3.4) **for** any itemset i in L_k **do begin**
      if an itemset i is uninteresting **then**
        let $L_k \leftarrow L_k - \{i\}$;
        let $PL \leftarrow PL \cup L_k$;
  (3.5) **let** $S_k \leftarrow \{i | i \in N_k \text{ and } i \text{ is a negative itemset}\}$;
    //Prune all uninteresting k-itemsets in S_k
    for any itemset i in S_k **do begin**
      if an itemset i is uninteresting **then**
        let $S_k \leftarrow S_k - \{i\}$;
      let $NL \leftarrow NL \cup S_k$;
  end
(4) **output** the positive and negative itemsets of interest as PL and NL;
end

The algorithm $InterestItemsetsbyPruning$ is used to generate all positive and negative itemsets of interest in a given database D, where PL is the set of all positive (or frequent) itemsets of interest in D, and NL is the set of all negative (or infrequent) itemsets of interest in D. However, though PL and NL contain only positive and negative itemsets of interest respectively, all frequent itemsets in $Frequent_i$ ($i > 0$) must be saved for generating future negative itemsets of interest. So, there are three kinds of sets: PL, NL, and $Frequent_i$ ($i > 0$) to be retained during the running of the above algorithm. In this chapter, the pruning is limited to reduce PL and NL.

The initialization is done in Step (1). Step (2) generates the set $Frequent_1$ of all frequent 1-itemsets in the database D as the first pass of the algorithm in the database D. And $Frequent_1$ is also appended into PL.

Step (3) generates all sets L_k and S_k for $k \geq 2$ by a loop, where L_k is the set of all positive k-itemsets of interest in the database D generated in the kth pass of the algorithm, S_k is the set of all negative k-itemsets of interest in the database D generated in the kth pass of the algorithm, and the end-condition of the loop is of both $L_{k-1} = \emptyset$ and $S_{k-1} \neq \emptyset$. Each subsequent pass in Step (3), for example pass k, consists of five phases as follows.

The first phase (3.1) is to generate the set Tem_k of all k-itemsets in the database D, where each itemset in Tem_k is the union of two certain frequent itemsets in $Frequent_i$ for $1 \leq i \leq k-1$. That is, for itemsets A in $Frequent_{i_0}$ and B in $Frequent_{i_1}$ $(1 \leq i_0, i_1 \leq k-1)$, if $A \cup B$ is a k-itemset, $A \cup B$ is appended into Tem_k. Meanwhile, each itemset in Tem_k is counted in the database D by a loop in phase (3.2). And C_k, $frequent_k$, L_k, and N_k are generated in the second phase (3.3). C_k is the set of all possible frequent k-itemsets in Tem_k, for which each of this kind of k-itemset must contain at least a subset that is an element of L_{k-1}. Both $frequent_k$ and L_k are the set of all frequent k-itemsets in C_k where their supports are greater than, or equal to, $minsupp$, and where $|D|$ is the number of transactions in the database D. That is, L_k is the set of all positive k-itemsets in C_k. N_k is the set of all infrequent k-itemsets in Tem_k, where their supports are less than $minsupp$. Or, $N_k = Tem_k - frequent_k$, and N_k is the set of all possible negative k-itemsets in Tem_k.

Selection of all positive and negative k-itemsets of interest is carried out in phases (3.4) and (3.5). In phase (3.4), if an itemset i in L_k satisfies $|supp(X \cup Y) - supp(X)supp(Y)| < mininterest$ for any expressions $i = X \cup Y$ of i, then i is an uninteresting frequent itemset and it must be pruned from L_k. After all uninteresting frequent itemsets are pruned from L_k, the set L_k is appended into PL. In phase (3.5), all negative itemsets in N_k are first assigned to S_k. Then all negative itemsets of interest in S_k are selected. That is, if an itemset i in S_k satisfies $|supp(X \cup Y) - supp(X)supp(Y)| < mininterest$ for any expression $i = X \cup Y$ of i, then i is an uninteresting frequent itemset and it must be pruned from S_k. After all uninteresting frequent itemsets are pruned from S_k, the set S_k is appended into NL.

Step (4) outputs the positive and negative itemsets of interest as PL and NL in the database D, where each itemset i in PL must be, together with its support $supp(i)$, greater than, or equal to, the minimum support $minsupp$, and each itemset i in PL must satisfy the conditions that determine which itemset is a negative itemset of interest. The algorithm is ended in Step (5).

We have noticed that, although the sets PL and NL of the positive and negative itemsets of interest in the database D are minimized in the algorithm, the searched space for negative itemsets of interest is still huge. We will approach this problem in a later chapter.

3.5.2 An Example

After all uninteresting frequent itemsets are pruned, the searched space for extracting positive and negative itemsets of interest is obviously reduced. This is more efficient than using the Apriori algorithm and its derivatives. To demonstrate the use of the above algorithm, we present the following example. (The data has been already dealt with in Example 2.1 of Chapter 2.)

Example 3.5 *In Table 3.1, a transaction database TD with 10 transactions is obtained from a grocery store. Let $A = bread$, $B = coffee$, $C = tea$, $D = sugar$, $E = beer$, $F = butter$. Assume $minsupp = 0.3$ and $mininterest = 0.07$.*

Table 3.1. Transaction database TD

Transaction ID	Items
T_1	A, B, D
T_2	A, B, C, D
T_3	B, D
T_4	B, C, D, E
T_5	A, C, E
T_6	B, D, F
T_7	A, E, F
T_8	C, F
T_9	B, C, F
T_{10}	A, B, C, D, F

For comparison, we first list all positive and negative itemsets. The supports of the single positive frequent items in database TD are shown in Table 3.2 and other positive itemsets in TD are listed in Table 3.3. The possible negative itemsets in TD are given in Table 3.4.

Table 3.2. Frequent items in TD

Item	Number of Transactions	Support $supp(X)$
A	5	0.5
B	7	0.7
C	6	0.6
D	6	0.6
E	3	0.3
F	5	0.5

We now mine this database using the efficient algorithm above. In Table 3.1, there are six 1-itemsets: A, B, C, D, E, and F in the database TD.

Table 3.3. Frequent itemsets in TD

Itemset	Support $supp(X)$	Itemset	Support $supp(X)$
A, B	0.3	A, C	0.3
A, D	0.3	B, C	0.4
B, D	0.6	B, F	0.3
C, D	0.3	C, F	0.3
A, B, D	0.3	B, C, D	0.3

Table 3.4. All negative itemsets in TD

Itemset	Support $supp(X)$	Itemset	Support $supp(X)$
A, E	0.2	A, F	0.2
B, E	0.1	C, E	0.2
D, E	0.1	D, F	0.2
E, F	0.1	A, B, C	0.2
A, B, F	0.1	A, C, D	0.2
A, C, F	0.1	A, B, E	0.2
A, D, E	0	A, D, F	0.1
B, C, E	0.1	B, C, F	0.2
B, D, E	0.1	B, D, F	0.2
B, E, F	0	C, E, F	0
D, C, F	0.1	A, B, C, D	0.2
A, B, D, F	0.1	A, B, D, E	0
A, B, C, F	0.1	B, C, D, E	0.1
B, C, D, F	0.1		

For $minsupp = 0.3$, all are frequent 1-itemsets in PL. These are the same as those listed in Table 3.2. Also, $Frequent_1 = \{A, B, C, D, E, F\}$.

For Table 3.1, the set Tem_2 of the 2-itemsets is: AB, AC, AD, AE, AF, BC, BD, BE, BF, CD, CE, CF, DE, DF, and EF, constructed by $Frequent_1$. For $minsupp = 0.3$, $Frequent_2 = L_2 = \{AB, AC, AD, BC, BD, BF, CD, CF\}$ all are frequent 2-itemsets. So $N_2 = \{AE, AF, BE, CE, DE, DF, EF\}$, and $S_2 = N_2$.

However, the pruning technique[1] is applied in our algorithm so as to reduce the searched space. That is, we prune all uninteresting itemsets from L_k and S_k in each loop. For $mininterest = 0.07$, $L_2 = \{BC, BD\}$ is the set of all positive 2-itemsets of interest in PL as listed in Table 3.5 below, for the algorithm $InterestItemsetsbyPruning$. Certainly, because $|supp(A \cup B) - supp(A)supp(B)| = 0.05 < mininterest$, $|supp(A \cup C) - supp(A)supp(C)| = 0 < mininterest$, $|supp(A \cup D) - supp(A)supp(D)| = 0 < mininterest$, $|supp(B \cup F) - supp(B)supp(F)| = 0.05 < mininterest$, $|supp(C \cup D) - supp(C)supp(D)| = 0.06 < mininterest$, and $|supp(C \cup F) -$

---

[1] Note that the following results in this example are generated according to only the first three conditions of positive or negative itemsets of interest. The fourth condition for confidence will be considered in the next section. The searched space is further reduced if the fourth condition is involved when we identify all positive and negative itemsets of interest in a database.

$supp(C)supp(F)| = 0 < mininterest$, so AB, AC, AD, BC BF, CD and CF are not of interest. Hence, AB, AC, AD, BC, BF, CD and CF are pruned from L_2 before it is appended into PL. Also, $S_2 = \{BE\}$ is the set of all negative 2-itemsets of interest in NL listed in Table 3.6 below, for the algorithm $InterestItemsetsbyPruning$.

Table 3.5. Positive 2-itemsets of interest in PL

Item	Number of Transactions	Support $supp(X)$
B, D	6	0.6

Table 3.6. Negative 2-Iitemsets of interest in NL

Item	Number of Transactions	Support $supp(X)$
B, E	1	0.1

For Table 3.1, the set Tem_3 of the 3-itemsets is: ABC, ABD, ABE, ABF, ACD, ACE, ACF, ADE, ADF, AEF, BCD, BCE, BCF, BDE, BDF, BEF, CDE, CDF, CEF, and DEF constructed by $Frequent_1$ and $Frequent_2$. For $minsupp = 0.3$, $Frequent_3 = L_3 = \{ABD, BCD\}$ are all frequent 3-itemsets. So $N_3 = \{ABC, ABF, ACD, ACF, ABE, ADE, ADF, BCE, BCF, BDE, BDF, BEF, CEF\}$, and $S_3 = N_3$. However, for $mininterest = 0.07$ $L_3 = \{ABD, BCD\}$ the set of all positive 3-itemsets of interest in PL is listed in Table 3.7 below, after all uninteresting itemsets have been pruned from L_3. Thus, $S_3 = \{ABE, ADE, BDE, BEF, CDF, CEF\}$ is the set of all negative 3-itemsets of interest in NL listed in Table 3.8 as follows, after all uninteresting itemsets have been pruned from S_3.

Table 3.7. Positive 3-itemsets of interest in PL

Itemset	Number of Transactions	Support $supp(X)$
A, B, D	3	0.3
B, C, D	3	0.3

For Table 3.1, the set Tem_4 of the 4-itemsets is: $ABCD$, $ABCF$, $ABDE$, $ABDF$, $BCDE$, and $BCDF$. For $minsupp = 0.3$, $Frequent_4 = L_4 = \emptyset$. Thus, $S_4 = N_4 = Tem_4$. Meanwhile, $S_4 = \{ABCD, ABDF, BCDF\}$ is the set of all negative 4-itemsets of interest in NL listed in Table 3.9 below, after all uninteresting itemsets have been pruned from S_3.

Algorithm $InterestItemsetsbyPruning$ still needs to identify longer frequent itemsets in D for NL. In Table 3.1, the set Tem_5 of the 5-itemsets is:

Table 3.8. Negative 3-itemsets of interest in NL

Itemset	Number of Transactions	Support $supp(X)$
A, B, E	2	0.2
A, D, E	0	0.0
B, D, E	1	0.1
B, E, F	0	0.0
C, D, F	1	0.1
C, E, F	0	0.0

Table 3.9. Negative 4-itemsets of interest in NL

Itemset	Number of Transactions	Support $supp(X)$
A, B, C, D	2	0.2
A, B, D, F	1	0.1
B, C, D, F	1	0.1

$ABCDF$. For $minsupp = 0.3$, $Frequent_5 = L_5 = \emptyset$. So $S_5 = N_5 = Tem_5$, and $S_4 = \emptyset$ after all uninteresting itemsets are pruned from S_3. Step (3) is now ended. Then the results listed in the above tables are output in Step (4).

Certainly, there are 16 frequent itemsets, and only 10 positive itemsets of interest, in PL. There are 27 negative itemsets, and only 10 negative itemsets of interest in NL. Note that we do not consider that the confidence of a rule has to be greater than, or equal to, the minimum confidence $minconf$ in this example, when identifying positive and negative itemsets of interest. This is because, in the next section, the above data will be used to test our measure model for confidences in association rules. If we seriously consider this factor, there are only 8 positive itemsets of interest in PL, where 6 positive itemsets of interest in PL are 1-itemsets. And there are 9 negative itemsets of interest in NL.

3.5.3 A Twice-Pruning Approach

As we have seen, the search space for NL is still very large. The algorithm based on OPUS will be modified for mining negative association rules. (For details of OPUS, see [Webb 2000].) Webb's OPUS based model argues that, for some applications, we can directly search for association rules. This means that some frequent itemsets can be pruned if these itemsets do not occur in any association rules. However, the technique cannot be applied directly to identify infrequent itemsets of interest. The reason is that some itemsets pruned by the OPUS based algorithm may be useful in extracting negative association rules of interest in applications. So we now present an alternative, efficient and effective approach for mining itemsets of interest by pruning.

For the procedure $InterestItemsetsbyPruning$, pruning is used in Step (3.4) and (3.5) for positive and negative itemsets, respectively. The conditions of pruning are the first three conditions for itemsets of interest both positive and negative. To direct search positive and negative association rules, we must consider the fourth condition of each of the positive and negative itemsets of interest defined in Section 3.4.1 and Section 3.4.2. We now describe the OPUS based method for identifying negative association rules.

To identify infrequent itemsets of interest efficiently, we propose building a *twice-pruning approach* by using OPUS. It is outlined as follows. If a frequent itemset is pruned straight away when frequent itemsets of interest are searched, it cannot occur any longer in the frequent itemsets. But it can occur in infrequent itemsets of interest. If the itemset is then pruned when infrequent itemsets of interest are searched, it is removed from the rest of the searched space. If an infrequent itemset is pruned when infrequent itemsets of interest are searched, it does not then impact on searching for frequent itemsets of interest.

3.6 Negative Association Rules of Interest

Mathematical probability theory and statistics are the oldest and most widely used techniques for measuring uncertainty in many applications. These techniques can be applied to estimate the uncertainty factors (*support* and *confidence*) of an association rule. In this section we present a model based on the Piatetsky-Shapiro argument, and on probability theory, for mining association rules of interest in databases.

3.6.1 Measurement

Recall the relationship between $p(Y|X)$ and $p(Y)$ for a possible rule $X \rightarrow Y$ in Subsection 3.4.1. Here, Piatetsky-Shapiro's argument also stands for the statistical definition of dependence of the sets X and Y below (see [Brin-Motwani-Silverstein 1997])

$$Interest(X,Y) = \frac{p(X \cup Y)}{p(X)p(Y)} = \frac{p(Y|X)}{p(Y)}$$

This formula is referred to as the *interest* of Y, given X. Certainly, the further the value is from 1, the greater the dependence. When $Interest(X,Y) = 1$, then $p(Y|X) = p(Y)$ means that Y and X are independent. When $Interest(X,Y) > 1$, $p(Y|X) > p(Y)$ means that Y is positively dependent on X, or the probability that the occurrence of Y is increased when X occurs. Also, when $Interest(X,Y) < 1$, then $p(Y|X) < p(Y)$ means that Y is negatively dependent on X, or the probability that the occurrence of Y is decreased when X occurs.

Considering the relationship between the conditional probability $p(Y|X)$ and the probability $p(Y)$, we can divide $Interest(X,Y)$ into three cases as follows.

(1) If $Interest(X,Y) = 1$ or $p(Y|X) = p(Y)$, then Y and X are independent.
(2) If $Interest(X,Y) > 1$ or $p(Y|X) > p(Y)$, then Y is positively dependent on X, and $p(Y|X) - p(Y)$ satisfies:

$$0 < p(Y|X) - p(Y) \leq 1 - p(Y)$$

In particular, we have

$$0 < \frac{p(Y|X) - p(Y)}{1 - p(Y)} \leq 1$$

Certainly, the bigger the ratio $(p(Y|X) - p(Y))/(1 - p(Y))$ is, the heavier the positive dependence.

(3) If $Interest(X,Y) < 1$ or $p(Y|X) < p(Y)$, then Y is negatively dependent on X (or $\neg Y$ is positively dependent on X). And $p(Y|X) - p(Y)$ satisfies:

$$0 > p(Y|X) - p(Y) \geq -p(Y)$$

In particular, we have

$$0 < \frac{p(Y|X) - p(Y)}{-p(Y)} \leq 1$$

Certainly, the bigger the ratio $(p(Y|X) - p(Y))/(-p(Y))$ is, the heavier the negative dependence will be.

For the first case, the rule $X \rightarrow Y$ and the negative rules between X and Y are not of interest because X and Y are independent. In particular, an infrequent neighbor of 1 is not of interest. That is, if $|p(Y|X) - p(Y)| < mininterest$, $X \rightarrow Y$, and the negative rules between X and Y are not of interest as yet.

The second case has been widely explored in previous data mining models, where the rule $X \rightarrow Y$ may be an association rule of interest. The last case has received little attention. In this case, because Y is negatively dependent on X, then $X \rightarrow \neg Y$ may be a negative association rule of interest. To offer more information to applications, this category of negative association rules of interest would also be mined.

Accordingly, we can obtain the following theorem.

Theorem 3.2 *Let I be the set of items in a database TD; $X, Y \subseteq I$ be itemsets; $X \cap Y = \emptyset$; $p(X) \neq 0$; and $p(Y) \neq 0$. Also, $minsupp, minconf$ and $mininterest > 0$ are given by users or experts. Then $X \rightarrow Y$ can be extracted as a rule if*

(1) $p(X \cup Y) \geq minsupp$,
(2) $p(Y|X) \geq minconf$, and
(3) $|p(Y|X) - p(Y)| \geq mininterest$.

Proof: We need only prove $|\frac{p(X \cup Y)}{p(X)p(Y)} - 1| \geq mininterest$. For (3) of the above theorem, we have

$$\frac{|p(Y|X) - p(Y)|}{p(Y)} \geq \frac{mininterest}{p(Y)},$$

or

$$|\frac{p(X \cup Y)}{p(X)p(Y)} - 1| \geq \frac{mininterest}{p(Y)}$$

Because $0 < p(Y) \leq 1$, thus

$$\frac{mininterest}{p(Y)} \geq mininterest$$

Hence,

$$|\frac{p(X \cup Y)}{p(X)p(Y)} - 1| \geq mininterest$$

Hence, $X \rightarrow Y$ can be extracted as a rule of interest.

$$\triangledown$$

The certainty factor model is an excellent model to reflect the above relationships between $p(Y|X)$ and $p(Y)$ (see [Shortliffe 1976]). This is denoted as PR (*probability ratio*) in this chapter, and is the ratio of the conditional probability and the priori probability describing the increased degree of $p(Y|X)$ relative to $p(Y)$ as follows.

$$PR(Y|X) = \begin{cases} if & \frac{p(Y|X)-p(Y)}{1-p(Y)} \quad p(Y|X) \geq p(Y), p(Y) \neq 1 \\ \frac{p(Y|X)-p(Y)}{p(Y)}, if & p(Y) > p(Y|X), p(Y) \neq 0 \end{cases}$$

According to $p(Y|X) = p(X \cup Y)/p(X)$, we have

$$PR(Y|X) = \begin{cases} \frac{p(X \cup Y)-p(X)p(Y)}{p(X)(1-P(Y))} \\ if \quad p(X \cup Y) \geq p(X)p(Y) \\ \quad p(X)(1-p(Y)) \neq 0 \\ \\ \frac{p(X \cup Y)-p(X)p(Y)}{p(X)p(Y)} \\ if \quad p(X \cup Y) < p(X)p(Y) \\ \quad p(X)p(Y) \neq 0 \end{cases}$$

Or,

$$PR(Y|X) = \begin{cases} \frac{supp(X\cup Y)-supp(X)supp(Y)}{supp(X)(1-SUPP(Y))} \\ if \quad supp(X\cup Y) \geq supp(X)supp(Y) \\ \quad supp(X)(1-supp(Y)) \neq 0 \\ \\ \frac{supp(X\cup Y)-supp(X)supp(Y)}{supp(X)supp(Y)} \\ if \quad supp(X\cup Y) < supp(X)supp(Y) \\ \quad supp(X)supp(Y) \neq 0 \end{cases}$$

where $supp(Y|X)$ in the certainty factor model is replaced by $supp(X \cup Y)/supp(X)$ for the convenience of mining association rules in databases. We note that, PR has properties as follows.

Property 3.1 *Assuming $\Omega_Y = \{Y, \neg Y\}$ is the hypothesis frame of discernment, and $X \subseteq \Omega_Y$ is the available evidence based on observations, the increased ratio PR of conditional probability relative to priori probability satisfies:*

$$PR(Y|X) + PR(\neg Y|X) = 0$$

Proof: (a) Let $p(Y|X) \geq p(Y)$. Then, because

$$p(Y|X) + p(\neg Y|X) = 1,$$
$$p(\neg Y|X) = 1 - p(Y|X) \leq 1 - p(Y)$$
$$= p(\neg Y)$$

Therefore,

$$PR(Y|X) = \frac{p(Y|X) - p(Y)}{1 - p(Y)}$$
$$PR(\neg Y|X) = \frac{p(\neg Y|X) - p(\neg Y)}{p(\neg Y)}$$

Hence,

$$PR(Y|X) + PR(\neg Y|X)$$
$$= \frac{p(Y|X) - p(Y)}{1 - p(Y)} + \frac{p(\neg Y|X) - p(\neg Y)}{p(\neg Y)}$$
$$= \frac{p(Y|X) - p(Y)}{1 - p(Y)} + \frac{(1 - p(Y|X)) - (1 - p(Y))}{1 - p(Y)}$$
$$= 0$$

(b) If $p(Y|X) < p(Y)$ then, because

$$p(Y|X) + p(\neg Y|X) = 1$$
$$p(\neg Y|X) = 1 - p(Y|X) > 1 - p(Y)$$
$$= p(\neg Y)$$

Therefore,

$$PR(Y|X) = \frac{p(Y|X) - p(Y)}{p(Y)}$$

$$PR(\neg Y|X) = \frac{p(\neg Y|X) - p(\neg Y)}{1 - p(\neg Y)}$$

Hence,

$$PR(Y|X) + PR(\neg Y|X)$$
$$= \frac{p(Y|X) - p(Y)}{p(Y)} + \frac{p(\neg Y|X) - p(\neg Y)}{1 - p(\neg Y)}$$
$$= \frac{p(Y|X) - p(Y)}{1 - p(Y)} + \frac{(1 - p(Y|X)) - (1 - p(Y))}{1 - (1 - p(Y))}$$
$$= 0$$

So, we have $PR(Y|X) + PR(\neg Y|X) = 0$.

$$\nabla$$

To discover and measure both positive and negative association rules, we take $PR(Y|X)$ as the confidence level of the association rule for given itemsets X and Y. We can see that $confidence(X \to Y)$ matches certain special cases, as follows.

- Using probability theory, if $p(Y|X) = p(Y)$, Y and X are independent. The confidence of the association rule $X \to Y$ would be assigned as

$$confidence(X \to Y) = PR(Y|X) = 0$$

- If $p(Y|X) - p(Y) > 0$, Y is positively dependent on X. When $p(Y|X) = 1$ is the strongest condition, Y is positively dependent on X, and the confidence of the association rule $X \to Y$ would be assigned as

$$confidence(X \to Y) = PR(Y|X) = 1$$

- Again, if $p(Y|X) - p(Y) < 0$, Y is negatively dependent on X. When $p(Y|X) = p(Y)$ is the weakest condition, Y is negatively dependent on X, and the confidence of the association rule $X \to \neg Y$ would be assigned as

$$confidence(X \to \neg Y) = PR(Y|X) = 0$$

- When $p(Y|X) = 0$ is the strongest condition, Y is negatively dependent on X, and the confidence of the association rule $X \to \neg Y$ would be assigned as

$$confidence(X \to \neg Y) = PR(Y|X) = 1$$

By way of description, we take half of the above formula, $PR(Y|X) = (p(Y|X) - p(Y))/(1 - p(Y))$, or

$$PR(Y|X) = \frac{supp(X \cup Y) - supp(X)supp(Y)}{supp(X)(1 - supp(Y))}$$

if $supp(X \cup Y) \geq supp(X)supp(Y)$
$supp(X)(1 - supp(Y)) \neq 0,$

as a metric for the confidence of rule $X \rightarrow Y$ in the following discussion. We now present the definition of association rules of interest using this metric as follows.

Definition 3.1 *Let I be a set of items in a database TD, $i = A \cup B \subseteq I$ be an itemset, $A \cap B = \emptyset$, $supp(A) \neq 0$, and $supp(B) \neq 0$. Also, $minsupp, minconf$ and $mininterest > 0$ are given by users or experts. Then,*

(1) if $supp(A \cup B) \geq minsupp$, $supp(A \cup B) - supp(A)supp(B) \geq mininterest$, and $PR(B|A) \geq minconf$, then $A \rightarrow B$ can be extracted as a rule of interest;

(2) if $supp(A \cup \neg B) \geq minsupp$, $supp(A) \geq minsupp$, $supp(B) \geq minsupp$, $supp(A \cup \neg B) - supp(A)supp(\neg B) \geq mininterest$, and $PR(\neg B|A) \geq minconf$, then $A \rightarrow \neg B$ can be extracted as a rule of interest;

(3) if $supp(\neg A \cup B) \geq minsupp$, $supp(A) \geq minsupp$, $supp(B) \geq minsupp$, $supp(\neg A \cup B) - supp(\neg A)supp(B) \geq mininterest$, and $PR(B|\neg A) \geq minconf$, then $\neg A \rightarrow B$ can be extracted as a rule of interest; and

(4) if $supp(\neg A \cup \neg B) \geq minsupp$, $supp(A) \geq minsupp$, $supp(B) \geq minsupp$, $supp(\neg A \cup \neg B) - supp(\neg A)supp(\neg B) \geq mininterest$, and $PR(\neg B|\neg A) \geq minconf$, then $\neg A \rightarrow \neg B$ can be extracted as a rule of interest.

This definition shows four kinds of valid association rules of interest. Case 1 defines the positive association rules of interest. Case 2, Case 3 and Case 4 deal with negation. In the definition, $supp(*) \geq minsupp$ guarantees that association rules describe the relationships between two frequent itemsets; $supp(X \cup Y) - supp(X)supp(Y) \geq mininterest$ leads to the association rules that are of interest; and $PR(*) \geq minconf$ is the condition that association rules are valid and believable.

3.6.2 Examples

We now demonstrate how to apply this model to identify association rules. We use the data in Example 3.5, letting $minsupp = 0.2$, $minconf = 0.4$ and $mininterest = 0.08$.

Example 3.6 *For itemset $B \cup D$ in PL, $supp(B) = 0.7$, $supp(D) = 0.6$ and $supp(B \cup D) = 0.6$, we have $supp(B \cup D) - supp(B)supp(D) = 0.18 >$*

mininterest $= 0.08$. *This means that the belief increases, or $B \to D$, can be extracted as an association rule. Furthermore,*

$$PR(D|B) = \frac{supp(D \cup B) - supp(B)supp(D)}{supp(B)(1 - supp(D))} = \frac{0.6 - 0.7 * 0.6}{0.7 * (1 - 0.6)} = 0.642857$$

Therefore,

$$supp(B \cup D) = 0.6, PR(D|B) = 0.642857$$

is the support and the confidence of $B \to D$. According to our model, $B \to D$ can be extracted as a valid rule of interest.

Example 3.7 *For itemset $B \cup E$ in NL, $supp(B) = 0.7$, $supp(\neg E) = 0.7$, and $supp(B \cup \neg E) = 0.6$, we have $supp(B \cup \neg E) - supp(B)supp(\neg E) = 0.11 > mininterest = 0.08$. This means that the belief increases, or that $B \to \neg E$ can be extracted as an association rule. Furthermore,*

$$PR(\neg E|B) = \frac{supp(B \cup \neg E - supp(B)supp(\neg E)}{supp(B)(1 - supp(\neg E))} = \frac{0.6 - 0.7 * 0.7}{0.7 * (1 - 0.7)} = 0.5238,$$

and so,

$$supp(B \cup \neg E) = 0.6, PR(\neg E|B) = 0.5238$$

is the support and the confidence of $B \to \neg E$. According to our model, $B \to \neg E$ can be extracted as a valid rule of interest due to the fact that $PR(\neg E|B) > minconf$, $supp(B \cup \neg E) > minsupp$, $supp(B) > minsupp$, and $supp(E) = minsupp$.

By the PR model, $B \to D$ and $A \cup B \to D$ can be extracted as rules of interest. And $\{B, D\}$ and $\{A, B, D\}$ are all the positive itemsets of interest in Example 3.5.

Similarly, for itemsets in NL, we can use the PR model to extract all negative association rules. Using the PR model, $B \to \neg E$, $A \cup B \to \neg E$, $A \cup D \to \neg E$, $B \cup D \to \neg E$, $B \cup F \to \neg E$, $C \cup F \to \neg E$, $D \to \neg C \cup F$, $A \cup B \cup D \to \neg E$ and $B \cup D \to \neg C \cup F$ can be extracted as rules of interest. And $\{B, E\}$, $\{A, B, E\}$, $\{A, D, E\}$, $\{B, D, E\}$, $\{B, F, E\}$, $\{C, F, E\}$, $\{D, C, F\}$, $\{A, B, D, E\}$ and $\{B, D, C, F\}$ are all negative itemsets of interest in Example 3.5.

As we have seen, if all conditions of positive and negative itemsets of interest are considered when we mine, the searched space can further be reduced.

For $minsupp = 0.2$, $minconf = 0.4$ and TD in Example 3.5, all association rules in the support-confidence framework are as follows:

$$A \to B, supp(A \cup B) = 0.3, conf(A \to B) = 0.6$$
$$A \to C, supp(A \cup C) = 0.3, conf(A \to C) = 0.6$$
$$A \to D, supp(A \cup D) = 0.3, conf(A \to D) = 0.6$$

$B \to C, supp(B \cup C) = 0.4, conf(B \to B) = 0.571$

$B \to D, supp(B \cup D) = 0.6, conf(B \to D) = 0.857$

$B \to F, supp(B \cup F) = 0.3, conf(B \to F) = 0.43$

$C \to D, supp(C \cup D) = 0.3, conf(C \to D) = 0.5$

$C \to F, supp(C \cup F) = 0.3, conf(C \to F) = 0.5$

$A \to B \cup D, supp(A \cup B \cup D) = 0.3, conf(A \to B \cup D) = 0.6$

$A \cup B \to D, supp(A \cup B \cup D) = 0.3, conf(A \cup B \to D) = 1$

$A \cup D \to B, supp(A \cup B \cup D) = 0.3, conf(A \cup D \to D) = 1$

$B \to C \cup D, supp(B \cup C \cup D) = 0.3, conf(B \to C \cup D) = 0.43$

$B \cup C \to D, supp(B \cup C \cup D) = 0.3, conf(B \cup C \to D) = 0.75$

$B \cup D \to C, supp(B \cup C \cup D) = 0.3, conf(B \cup D \to C) = 0.5$

As we have seen, the itemsets of some rules (such as $A \to C$, $A \to D$, $C \to F$, and $A \to B \cup D$) are independent, but are extracted as valid association rules in the support-confidence framework. On the other hand, mining negative association rules enables us to determine which itemsets do not occur collectively. This means that negative association rules are also important in applications.

3.7 Algorithms Design

The task of mining association rules in our PR model is to discover all positive and negative association rules of interest. In fact, this can be broken down into the following two issues.

(1) Generating the set PL of all positive frequent itemsets, and the set NL of all negative frequent itemsets;
(2) Generating all the rules of the form $A \to B$ or $B \to A$ in PL, and all the rules of the form $\neg A \to B$, or $B \to \neg A$, or $\neg A \to \neg B$, or $\neg B \to \neg A$ in NL.

Let D be a database, and *minsupp, minconf* and *mininterest* be given by users. The algorithm for searching for association rules in our probability ratio model is constructed as follows.

Algorithm 3.1 *PRModel*
begin
    Input*: D: database; minsupp, minconf, mininterest: threshold values;*

Output: $X \rightarrow Y$: *association rule;*

(1) **call** routine *InterestItemsetsbyPruning;*
   // Generating all positive association rules in PL.
(2) **for** any frequent itemset A in PL **do**
   for any itemset $X \cup Y = A$ and $X \cap Y = \emptyset$ **do begin**
      if $supp(X \cup Y) - supp(X)supp(Y) \geq mininterest$ **then**
      if $PR(Y|X) \geq minconf$ **then**
         output the rule $X \rightarrow Y$
            with confidence $PR(Y|X)$ and support $supp(A)$;
      if $PR(X|Y) \geq minconf$ **then**
         output the rule $Y \rightarrow X$
            with confidence $PR(X|Y)$ and support $supp(A)$;
   end;
   // Generating all negative association rules in NL.
(3) **for** any itemset A in NL **do**
   for any itemsets $X \cup Y = A$ and $X \cap Y = \emptyset$ **do begin**
   // Generating negative association rules of the form: $\neg X \rightarrow Y$ or
   $Y \rightarrow \neg X$.
   (3.1) $supp(X) \geq minsupp$ and $supp(Y) \geq minsupp$ and $supp(\neg X \cup Y) \geq minsupp$ **then**
      if $supp(\neg X \cup Y) - supp(\neg X)supp(Y) \geq mininterest$ **then begin**
         if $PR(Y|\neg X)| \geq minconf$ **then**
            output the rule $\neg X \rightarrow Y$
               with confidence $PR(Y|\neg X)$ and support $supp(\neg X|Y)$;
         if $PR(\neg X|Y)| \geq minconf$ **then**
            output the rule $Y \rightarrow \neg X$
               with confidence $PR(\neg X|Y)$ and support $supp(Y \cup \neg X)$;
   end;
   // Generating negative association rules of the form: $\neg X \rightarrow \neg Y$
   or $\neg Y \rightarrow \neg X$.
   (3.2) **if** $supp(X) \geq minsupp$ and $supp(Y) \geq minsupp$ and
   $supp(\neg X \cup \neg Y) \geq minsupp$ **then**
      if $supp(\neg X \cup \neg Y) - supp(\neg X)supp(\neg Y) \geq mininterest$ **then**
      begin
         if $PR(\neg Y|\neg X)| \geq minconf$ **then**
         output the rule $\neg X \rightarrow \neg Y$
            with confidence $PR(\neg Y|\neg X)$ and support $supp(\neg X|\neg Y)$;
         if $PR(\neg X|\neg Y)| \geq minconf$ **then**
            output the rule $\neg Y \rightarrow \neg X$
               with confidence $PR(\neg X|\neg Y)$ and support $supp(\neg Y \cup \neg X)$;
   end;
      end;
   end.

The algorithm $PRModel$ generates, not only all positive association rules in PL, but also all negative association rules in NL. The initialization is done in Step (1), where the procedure $InterestItemsetsbyPruning$ is called in for handling the sets PL and NL of all positive and negative itemsets of interest respectively, in the database D.

Step (2) generates all positive association rules of interest of the form $X \rightarrow Y$, in the set PL, where $supp(X \cup Y) - supp(X)supp(Y) \geq mininterest$. If $PR(Y|X) \geq minconf$, $X \rightarrow Y$ is extracted as a valid rule of interest, with confidence $PR(Y|X)$ and support $supp(X \cup Y)$. And if $PR(X|Y) \geq minconf$, $Y \rightarrow X$ is extracted as a valid rule of interest, with confidence $PR(X|Y)$ and support $supp(X \cup Y)$.

Step (3) generates all negative association rules of interest of the form $\neg X \rightarrow Y$, or $Y \rightarrow \neg X$, or $\neg X \rightarrow \neg Y$, or $\neg Y \rightarrow \neg X$, in the set NL. This is completed in Step (3.1) and Step (3.2). In Step (3.1), for $supp(X) \geq minsupp$ and $supp(Y) \geq minsupp$, $supp(\neg X \cup Y) \geq minsupp$, and $supp(\neg X \cup Y) - supp(\neg X)supp(Y) \geq mininterest$. If $PR(Y|\neg X) \geq minconf$, $\neg X \rightarrow Y$ is extracted as a valid rule of interest, with confidence $PR(Y|\neg X)$ and support $supp(\neg X \cup Y)$. And, for $PR(\neg X|Y) \geq minconf$, $Y \rightarrow \neg X$ is extracted as a valid rule of interest, with confidence $PR(\neg X|Y)$ and support $supp(\neg X \cup Y)$.

In Step (3.2), for $supp(X) \geq minsupp$ and $supp(Y) \geq minsupp$, $supp(\neg X \cup \neg Y) \geq minsupp$, and $supp(\neg X \cup \neg Y) - supp(\neg X)supp(\neg Y) \geq mininterest$. If $PR(\neg Y|\neg X) \geq minconf$, $\neg X \rightarrow \neg Y$ is extracted as a valid rule of interest, with confidence $PR(\neg Y|\neg X)$ and support $supp(\neg X \cup \neg Y)$. And, for $PR(\neg X|\neg Y) \geq minconf$, $\neg Y \rightarrow \neg X$ is extracted as a valid rule of interest, with confidence $PR(\neg X|\neg Y)$ and support $supp(\neg X \cup \neg Y)$.

3.8 Identifying Reliable Exceptions

Mining exceptions in databases have been studied recently in [Liu et al. 1999] and [Liu et al. 2000]. For comparison, this section simply recalls the techniques.

Patterns hidden in databases can fall into three categories as follows.

- *strong patterns*: regularities for numerous objects;
- *weak patterns*: reliable exceptions representing a relatively small number of objects; and
- *random patterns*: random and unreliable exceptions.

Liu et al. present techniques for mining the weak 'patterns-reliable' exceptions, which are infrequent and high-confidence.

3.8.1 Confidence Based Interestingness

When no other information is given, an event with lower occurring probability gives more information than an event with higher probability. From information theory, we know that the number of bits required to describe the occurrence is defined as

$$I = -\log_2 P$$

where $P =$ the probability that the event will occur.

Similarly, for a given rule $AB \rightarrow X$, with confidence $Pr(X|AB)$, we will require $-\log_2(Pr(X|AB))$ and $-\log_2(Pr(\neg X|AB))$ number of bits to describe the events X and $\neg X$, given AB. Thus, the total number of bits required to describe the rule $AB \rightarrow X$ is

$$I_C^{AB_0} = (-Pr(X|AB)\log_2 Pr(X|AB)) + (-Pr(\neg X|AB)\log_2 Pr(\neg X|AB))$$

where, $I_C^{AB_0} =$ number of bits required to describe $AB \rightarrow X$ when no other knowledge has been applied.

However, the difference in the number of bits in describing the rule $AB \rightarrow X$ in terms of $A \rightarrow X$ and $B \rightarrow X$ can bring surprises. The bigger the difference in describing the rule $AB \rightarrow X$, the more interesting it is. Therefore, to estimate the relative interestingness in terms of $A \rightarrow X$ and $B \rightarrow X$, we need to know the number of bits required to describe the event X when the probability of that event occurring given A and B, is $Pr(X|A)$ and $Pr(X|B)$, respectively.

Since the rule $AB \rightarrow X$ describes the event X in terms of A and B, therefore, to describe a similar event X, in terms of A and B using the rule $A \rightarrow X$ and $B \rightarrow X$ we need $-\log_2 Pr(X|A)$ and $-\log_2 Pr(X|B)$ number of bits. Now, in rule $AB \rightarrow X$, the probability of the event X occurring is $Pr(X|AB)$. Therefore, the expected number of bits required to describe all the X events in rule $AB \rightarrow X$, in terms of A and B using the two rules is $-Pr(X|AB)(\log_2 Pr(X|A) + \log_2 Pr(X|B))$. Similarly, for the event $\neg X$ in rule $AB \rightarrow X$, $-Pr(\neg X|AB)(\log_2 Pr(\neg X|A) + \log_2 Pr(\neg X|B))$ number of bits will be required. Thus the total number of bits required to describe the event X and $\neg X$ in the rule $AB \rightarrow X$ by the rules $A \rightarrow X$ and $B \rightarrow X$ is

$$I_C^{AB_1} = (-Pr(X|AB)[\log_2 Pr(X|A)) + \log_2 Pr(X|B))] \\ - Pr(\neg X|AB)[\log_2 Pr(\neg X|A) + \log_2 Pr(\neg X|B)]$$

where $I_C^{AB_1} =$ number of bits required when $AB \rightarrow X$ is described by $A \rightarrow X$ and $B \rightarrow X$.

Thus, the relative surprise, or relative interestingness, that comes from the difference between two descriptions for the given rule $AB \rightarrow X$ is

$$RI_C^{AB} = I_C^{AB_1} - I_C^{AB_0} \\ = -Pr(X|AB)[\log_2 \frac{Pr(X|A)Pr(X|B)}{Pr(X|AB)}$$

$$- Pr(\neg X|AB)[\log_2 \frac{Pr(\neg X|A)Pr(\neg X|B)}{Pr(\neg X|AB)}$$

$$= Pr(X|AB)[\log_2 \frac{Pr(X|AB)}{Pr(X|A)Pr(X|B)}$$

$$+ Pr(\neg X|AB)[\log_2 \frac{Pr(\neg X|AB)}{Pr(\neg X|A)Pr(\neg X|B)}$$

where RI_C^{AB} = the relative surprise or interestingness of the rule, considering the confidence and knowledge about other rules.

The interestingness of a rule that we have formulated in terms of confidence gives the exact impression of relative entropy. Here the entropy of a rule is calculated relative to the other rules. It is a measure of distance between two distributions. In statistics, this arises as an expected logarithm of the likelihood ratio. The relative entropy $D(p(x)||q(x))$ is a measure of the inefficiency of assuming that the distribution is $q(x)$, when the true distribution is $p(x)$. The relative entropy, or *Kullback Leibler distance*, between two probability functions is defined as,

$$D(p(x)||q(x)) = \sum_{x \in X} p(x) log \frac{p(x)}{q(x)}$$

In estimating the interestingness of the rule $AB \rightarrow X$ with true confidence $Pr(X|AB)$ we approximated its confidence from the rules $A \rightarrow X$ and $B \rightarrow X$.

3.8.2 Support Based Interestingness

By stating that the support of a rule $AB \rightarrow X$, we mean thet the frequency of the rule's consequent evaluation is A by AB, relative to the whole dataset. When we know the support of the two common sense rules $A \rightarrow X$ and $B \rightarrow X$, we know the relative frequency of the consequent X and $\neg X$ evaluated by A and B respectively. A similar relative entropy measure can be applied to estimate the surprise from the support. Now, for the newly discovered rule $AB \rightarrow X$, the true distributions of the consequent X and $\neg X$ evaluated by A and B are $Pr(ABX)$ and $Pr(AB\neg X)$ respectively. From the knowledge of one of our common sense rules, $A \rightarrow X$, for which the relative frequencies of X and $\neg X$ are $Pr(AX)$ and $Pr(A\neg X)$ respectively, thiscan be used to find the distance between two distributions of consequence using relative entropy. The relative entropy of $AB \rightarrow X$, relative to the rule $A \rightarrow X$ in terms of their support, is thus

$$D(AB \rightarrow X || A \rightarrow X) = Pr(ABX)\log\frac{Pr(ABX)}{Pr(AX)} + Pr(AB\neg X)\log\frac{Pr(AB\neg X)}{Pr(A\neg X)}$$

Similarly, for rule $B \to X$, the relative entropy is

$$D(AB \to X||B \to X) = Pr(ABX)\log\frac{Pr(ABX)}{Pr(BX)} + Pr(AB\neg X)\log\frac{Pr(AB\neg X)}{Pr(B\neg X)}$$

Thus the total relative interestingness due to the rule's support that comes from the relative entropy of $AB \to X$ for the two common-sense rules is,

$$RI_s^{AB} = D(AB \to X||A \to X) + D(AB \to X||B \to X)$$
$$= Pr(ABX)\log\frac{Pr(ABX)}{Pr(AX)Pr(BX)}$$
$$+ Pr(AB\neg X)\log\frac{Pr(AB\neg X)}{Pr(A\neg X)Pr(B\neg X)}$$

Hence, the total interestingness of a rule $AB \to X$ relative to $A \to X$ and $B \to X$ is

$$RI = RI_c^{AB} + RT_s^{AB}$$

This includes support, confidence and consideration of other rules in the estimation of the relative surpriseness.

3.8.3 Searching Reliable Exceptions

To search for weak patterns (i.e., reliable exceptions) from databases, a simple and efficient approach was proposed in [Liu et al. 2000], which uses deviation analysis to identify interesting exceptions and explore reliable ones. The approach is based on the following observations.

(1) An exception might occur when a low support is found in the data, or it might be a strong pattern.
(2) A reasonable induction algorithm can summarize data and learn rules.
(3) Attributes in the rules are salient features.

Observation (1) suggests that exceptions cannot be extracted from the data by applying standard machine learning techniques. Observations (2) and (3) allow us to focus on important features so that an efficient method for finding reliable exceptions can be found. The approach consists of the four phases below.

Rule Induction and Focusing Obtaining strong patterns: normally, a user can stop here in his preliminary data mining probing. If the number of rules is too large, the user can choose to focus on the strongest rules. Let us assume that several rules have caught our attention and we are curious to know any reliable exceptions with respect to these strong patterns. This is a filtering step that helps us focus on a few attributes quickly. If we are confident about what we want to investigate, i.e., we know the relevant attributes, then this step can be replaced by user specification of relevant attributes.

Contingency Table and Deviation Now we focus on a particular attribute in a rule. We can use these attributes and the class attribute to build a two-way contingency table that allows us to calculate deviations.

Table 3.10. Contingency table

Class	Attribute				R-Total
	V_1	V_2	$\cdots$	V_c	
C_1	$(n_{11})x_{11}$	$(n_{12})x_{12}$	$\cdots$	$(n_{1c})x_{1c}$	$n_{1.}$
C_2	$(n_{21})x_{21}$	$(n_{22})x_{22}$	$\cdots$	$(n_{2c})x_{2c}$	$n_{2.}$
$\cdots$	$\cdots$	$\cdots$	$\cdots$	$\cdots$	$\cdots$
C_r	$(n_{r1})x_{r1}$	$(n_{r2})x_{r2}$	$\cdots$	$(n_{rc})x_{rc}$	$n_{r.}$
C-Total	$n_{.1}$	$n_{.2}$	$\cdots$	$n_{.c}$	n

In the table, x_{ij} are the frequencies of occurrence found in the data, and $n_{ij} = n_{i.}n_{.j}/n$ is the expected frequency of occurrence. Also, $n = \sum_{i=1}^{r}\sum_{j=1}^{c} x_{ij}$ —total, $n_{.j} = \sum j = 1^r x_{ij}$, a column total (C-Total), and $n_{i.} = \sum j = 1^c x_{ij}$ is a row total (R-Total). Using the expected frequency as the norm, we can define the deviation as

$$\delta_{ij} = \frac{x_{ij} - n_{ij}}{n_{ij}}$$

Positive, Negative, and Outstanding Deviations Using the above definition to calculate deviations, we can expect to have three types: positive, zero, or negative. If the deviation is positive, it suggests that what is concerned is consistent with strong patterns; if it is zero, it is the norm; and if it is negative, what's concerned is inconsistent with strong patterns. The value of *delta* displays the magnitude of deviation. A large value means the deviation could be caused by chance. Since we are concerned about reliable exceptions, and reliability is subject to user need, we specify that a threshold δ_t is positively outstanding; for $\delta_t < 0$, any deviation $\delta < \delta_t$ is negatively outstanding. Deviations are powerful, and useful in this case, as they provide a simple way of identifying interesting patterns in the data.

Reliable Exceptions After we have identified the outstanding, negative deviations of attribute-values with respect to the class label, we can get all the instances that contain these attribute-value and class pairs, and perform further mining on the focused dataset—a window, using any data mining techniques is preferable. For example, we can continue searching for frequent itemsets to investigate the above exceptional combinations. As the number of instances is much smaller now than originally, the mining performance should improve greatly. Reliable exceptions could be those longest frequent itemsets with high support in the window.

A strong association rule found in the window might itself be a strong rule that can be found in the whole data set. We need to make sure that what we find are indeed weak patterns—low support but high confidence. In other words, any sub-itemsets found in a reliable exception should be excluded if they hold high support in the whole data. A simple method is as follows. Assuming that X is a sub-itemset that does not include any negatively deviated attributes in a strong association rule found in the window, we can compare the support sup_{win} of X in the window, and its counterpart sup_{who} in the whole data. Note that what we really want to check is $P(X, c)$ for the window, and $P(X)$ for the whole data, with respect to $X \to c$. If we consider their ratio, they are actually the confidence values. Therefore, if the difference $sup_{win} - conf_{who}$ is sufficiently large (as $conf_{win}$ is always 1, the large difference means a low $conf_{who}$), we should be satisfied that X's high confidence is unique to the window, otherwise, X does not have sufficient evidence to be included in the final reliable exception.

3.9 Comparisons

For simplicity, we compare our proposed approach with the support-confidence framework outlined in Chapter 2, the interest model in Chapter 2, the exception mining model, and the strong negative association model described in this section.

3.9.1 Comparison with Support-Confidence Framework

We now compare the proposed PR model with the support-confidence framework (denoted by SCF) from the functions. The SCF model usually generates association rules in databases, some of which are not of interest, and it only deals with frequent itemsets. However, the PR model discovers both positive and negative association rules in databases, all of which are of interest. And it deals too with, not only frequent itemset of interest, but also infrequent itemsets of interest. Therefore, our probability ratio model offers more necessary information for applications than the SCF model does.

3.9.2 Comparison with Interest Models

Piatetsky-Shapiro has argued that a rule $X \to Y$ is not interesting if $support(X \to Y) \approx support(X) \times support(Y)$ ([Piatetsky 1991]). In order to fit this argument, Brin, Motwani and Silverstein have suggested measuring significance of association rules via the chi-squared test for correlation from classical statistics ([Brin-Motwani-Silverstein 1997]). Again, Srikant and Agrawal have applied the chi-square values to check whether association rules are statistically significant so as to implement Piatetsky-Shapiro's argument ([Srikant-Agrawal 1997]). For simplicity, we focus on the Chi-Squared test model here (denoted by CST).

Models based on the chi-square test depend upon eight probabilities — $supp(X)$, $supp(Y)$, $supp(\neg X)$, $supp(\neg Y)$, $supp(X \cup Y)$, $supp(X \cup \neg Y)$, $supp(\neg X \cup Y)$, and $supp(\neg X \cup \neg Y)$ — to construct a *contingency table* for the itemset $X \cup Y$ and to determine whether itemset $X \cup Y$ is the minimal dependent itemset using the chi-squared test.

Unfortunately, while Brin, Motwani and Silverstein mention that there are negative relationships among itemsets, their work does not build basic techniques, such as how to identify which negative associations are of interest or how to search for those associations. Because mining negative associations requires certain infrequent itemsets, it is very different from mining positive association rules. Therefore, an alternative mining model must be explored.

The PR model requires five probabilities — $supp(X)$, $supp(Y)$, $supp(X \cup Y)$, $supp(\neg X)$, and $supp(\neg X \cup Y)$ — to determine whether $X \rightarrow Y$ or $X \rightarrow \neg Y$ can be extracted as rules. In particular, this model has developed techniques for identifying negative association rules in databases.

On the other hand, the CST model usually generates association rules in databases, all of which are of interest, but it only deals with frequent itemsets. This method does not build basic techniques, such as how to identify which negative association rules are of interest, or how to search for those association rules. In particular, the model requires three procedures: the chi-square test, the $Interest(X, Y)$ test, and the computing confidence to discover association rules of interest. However, the PR model finds both positive and negative association rules in databases, all of which are of interest. It deals with, not only frequent itemset of interest, but also infrequent itemsets of interest. Also, a model for mining negative association rules of interest is advocated in the PR model. In particular, this model only requires the procedure *probability ratio* to discover association rules of interest.

From the above observations, it is clear that the PR model is a better measure of uncertainty for mining association rules.

3.9.3 Comparison with Exception Mining Model

Patterns in a database can be divided into strong, weak and random. Strong patterns can be helpful for applications. As we have argued, weak patterns can also be very useful to applications. However, most current data mining techniques cannot effectively support weak pattern mining or 'exception' mining as it is known ([Liu et al. 1999, Liu et al. 2000]).

Huan Liu and his group advocated an algorithm for finding weak patterns, known as reliable exceptions, from databases, and written as the EMM model. Negative association rules are an important kind of weak pattern.

In the EMM model, the interestingness of an exceptional rule $AB \rightarrow X$ is measured by dependence on the composition of knowledge concerning the rules $A \rightarrow X$ and $B \rightarrow X$.

Searching interesting exceptional rules by the EMM model is based on the chi-square test, and requires eight probabilities — $supp(X)$, $supp(Y)$,

$supp(\neg X)$, $supp(\neg Y)$, $supp(X \cup Y)$, $supp(X \cup \neg Y)$, $supp(\neg X \cup Y)$, and $supp(\neg X \cup \neg Y)$ — to construct the *contingency table* for the itemset $X \cup Y$ and to determine whether itemset $X \cup Y$ is the minimal dependent itemset using the chi-squared test.

For the PR model, we focus only on mining negative association rules of interest. The interestingness of a negative rule between itemsets X and Y is measured by four conditions as defined in Section 3.4. This requires only five probabilities — $supp(X)$, $supp(Y)$, $supp(X \cup Y)$, $supp(\neg X)$ and $supp(\neg X \cup Y)$ — to determine whether $X \to Y$ or $X \to \neg Y$ can be extracted as rules.

Note that the EMM model also generates negative association rules in databases, all of which are of interest. This often requires three steps: (1) testing confidence-based interestingness, (2) testing support-based interestingness, and (3) searching exceptional rules. However, if we wish to discover negative association rules by using the EMM model, it is not clear how we can identify which of $X \to \neg Y$, $\neg X \to Y$, $Y \to \neg X$, $\neg Y \to X$ can be extracted, using the same facts as in the CST model. Therefore, it is clear that the PR model is better than the EMM model for finding negative association rules of interest.

3.9.4 Comparison with Strong Negative Association Model

Savasere, Omiecinski and Navathe have developed a new approach for finding negative associations which leads to a very large number of rules with low interest measures ([Savasere-Omiecinski-Navathe 1998]). By combining previously discovered positive associations with domain knowledge to constrain the search space fewer, but more interesting negative rules can be mined.

In [Savasere-Omiecinski-Navathe 1998], a *negative association rule* is defined as an implication of the form $X \nrightarrow Y$, where $X \cap Y = \emptyset$, where X is called the antecedent, and where Y is the consequence of the rule. Every rule also has a rule interest measure. The interest measure RI of a negative association rule $X \nrightarrow Y$ is defined as follows:

$$RI = \frac{\varepsilon[support(X \cup Y)] - support(X \cup Y)}{support(X)}$$

where $\varepsilon[support(X)]$ is the *expected support* of an itemset X. The rule interest RI is negatively related to the actual support of the itemset $X \cup Y$. It is the highest if the actual support is zero, and zero if the actual support is the same as the expected support.

The problem of finding negative rules can now be stated as follows. Given a database of customer transactions, D, and a taxonomy T on the set of items, find all rules $X \nrightarrow Y$ such that (a) $support(X)$, and $support(Y)$ are greater than the minimum support $minsupp$; and (b) the rule interest measure is greater than $minRI$, where $minsupp$ and $minRI$ are specified by the user. Condition (a) is necessary to ensure that the generated rule is statistically significant. For example, even if the rule perfectly predicts 10 out of 10 million cases, it is not particularly useful because it is not general enough.

On the other hand, although the approach in [Savasere-Omiecinski-Navathe 1998] is able to discover negative relationships, it cannot identify concrete expressions of negative rules. In particular, the technique is knowledge-dependent. Knowledge is often poor and costly. This means that the approach is far from being useful in real-world applications.

Our PR model can identify negative association rules of the form $A \rightarrow \neg B$ (or $\neg A \rightarrow B$ or $\neg A \rightarrow \neg B$), which are of interest in applications. This distinguishes our model from the strong negative association model above.

3.10 Summary

As we know, many business decisions, such as sales and investments, involve a number of factors which include both advantage and disadvantage factors. To minimize disadvantage impacts and maximize possible benefits, we must consider the probability that factors occur, the probability that side-effect factors occur, and negative associations among the factors must be faced. Therefore, identifying negative association rules is useful to applications.

As we have seen, in order to identify negative association rules, we must face factors such as: infrequent itemsets, exponential search space, and measurement. Specific and efficient mining models must be developed for discovering negative association rules in databases.

Unfortunately, while Brin, Motwani and Silverstein mentioned that there are negative relationships among itemsets, their work did not build basic techniques, such as how to identify which negative associations are of interest. Nor did they demonstrate how to search for those associations.

However, exception mining has dealt with negative association rules mining ([Liu et al. 1999, Liu et al. 2000]). The work has focused on exceptional rules of the form $AB \rightarrow X$ whose interestingness is measured by dependence on the composition of knowledge concerning the rules $A \rightarrow X$ and $B \rightarrow X$. In real-world applications, negative associations often occur. They cannot always be classified into exceptional patterns. On the other hand, the approach for searching negative association rules requires many prior probabilities of conjunctions among A, B, and X.

In this chapter, we have constructed a new method for mining negative association rules in databases. Our approach is a novel one because

(a) infrequent itemsets are considered of interest in the PR method;
(b) we have used an increasing degree of conditional probability relative to prior probability to estimate confidences of positive and negative association rules; and

(c) the PR model can identify negative association rules of the form $A \to \neg B$ (or $\neg A \to B$ or $\neg A \to \neg B$), which are of interest in applications. This, in particular, also distinguishes the PR model from existing models.

The key points of this chapter are thus as follows.

(1) Created the conditions of negative itemsets of interest.
(2) Constructed an efficient algorithm to identify all possible positive and negative itemsets of interest in a given database.
(3) Proposed a new model to measure and extract both positive and negative association rules in databases.
(4) Evaluated the effectiveness of the proposed model by comparing.

4. Causality in Databases

A causal rule between two variables, $X \rightarrow Y$, captures the relationship that the presence of X causes the appearance of Y. Because of its usefulness (in comparison with association rules), the techniques for mining causal rules are beginning to be developed. However, the effectiveness of existing methods, such as LCD and CU-path algorithms, is limited for mining causal rules among invariable items. These techniques are not adequate for the discovery and representation of causal rules among multi-value variables. In this chapter, we propose techniques for mining causality between the variables X and Y by partitioning, where causality is represented in the form $X \rightarrow Y$, with the conditional probability matrix $M_{Y|X}$. These techniques are also applied to find causal rules in probabilistic databases.

This chapter begins by stating the problems faced in Section 4.1. Some necessary basic concepts are defined in Section 4.2. In Section 4.3 we first define a 'good partition' for generating item variables from items, and we then present a method of mining causality of interest from large databases. In Section 4.4 we advocate an approach for finding dependencies among variables. In Section 4.5 we apply the proposed causality mining techniques to mining probabilistic databases. And finally, we conclude in Section 4.6.

4.1 Introduction

Conventional association-rules mining techniques are mainly focused on three representative patterns in large databases as follows.

(1) **Item-based association rule.** Work on mining item-based association rules has been reported in such publications as [Agrawal-Imielinski-Swami 1993], [Agrawal-Srikant 1994], [Brin-Motwani-Silverstein 1997], [Piatetsky 1991], [Shintani-Kitsuregawa 1998] and [Srikant-Agrawal 1997]. For example, the rule $tea \rightarrow sugar$ with $supp = 20\%$ and $conf = 80\%$ is an item-based association rule. It implies that '80% of all customers who buy tea also buy sugar'.

(2) **Quantitative association rule.** Work on mining quantitative association rules has been reported in such publications as [Han-Cai-Cercone 1993], [Miller-Yang 1997] and [Srikant-Agrawal 1996]. For example, from [Srikant-Agrawal 1996] we have the following:

$$\langle Age : 30..39 \rangle \wedge \langle Married : Yes \rangle \rightarrow \langle NumCars : 2 \rangle$$

with $supp = 10\%$ and $conf = 100\%$ as a Quantitative association rule, where 'Age' and 'NumCars' are quantitive attributes and 'Married' is a categorical attribute. This means that '10% of married people between 30 and 39 have at least 2 cars'.

(3) **Causality.** Work on mining causality among variables in large databases has also been begun by [Cooper 1997], [Heckerman-Geiger-Chickering 1995] and [Silverstein-Brin-Motwani-Ullman 1998] because of its usefulness to practical applications such as decision-making and planning. An example from [Silverstein-Brin-Motwani-Ullman 1998] states that:

$$states \rightarrow united$$

is a causal rule. This means that 'the presence of *states* causes the appearance of *united* in the *clari.world* news.

Research into the first two patterns has resulted in a well-considered valuable framework. There have also been some research into mining causality, such as the LCD algorithm ([Cooper 1997]) and the CU-path algorithm ([Silverstein-Brin-Motwani-Ullman 1998]), which utilize constraint-based causal discovery for mining causal relationships in market basket data. In fact, the CU-path algorithm is an improved model of the LCD algorithm, which applies the chi-squared formula to test the dependence, independence, and conditional independence between variables, so as to find possible causal relationships between these variables.

However, previous techniques in causality mining can only identify causal rules among simple variables, such as the causal rule quoted above (*states* → *united*), used for words in the *clari.world* news hierarchy. These techniques are inadequate for discovering causal rules among multi-value variables from large databases and for representing them.

Mining causality among multi-value variables in many applications, such as decision-making, diagnosis and planning, can be useful for solving problems in applications. Accordingly, in this chapter, we propose a model based on partitioning, presented by [Zhang-Zhang 2001], for mining causality among multi-value variables in large databases. Here the causality is represented by the form $X \rightarrow Y$, with conditional probability matrix $M_{Y|X}$ (see [Pearl 1988]). The tasks of mining causality can be regarded simply as

(1) partitioning item variables, and
(2) estimating conditional probability matrices for rules of interest.

The second task will be implemented using the Piatetsky-Shapiro argument. However, the first task is more difficult, while problems in the second task include implementing an equi-depth partitioning model and finding a method of calculating the number of partitions required as posed by [Srikant-Agrawal 1996], unfortunately, because previous partitions on data are generally blind (relative to a given database), the quantitative items and item variables generated are sometimes bad, or at least not good. One of our main contributions in this chapter is to advocate a new partitioning model for determining all item variables for a given database, which decomposes the 'bad quantitative items' and 'bad item variables', and composes the 'not-good quantitative items' and the 'not-good item variables'.

Though causal rules among item variables can be both useful and expressive, mining item-based association rules and quantitative association rules is still necessary for many practical applications. For example, when the item variable X impacts on item variable Y at only a few point-values, this knowledge is represented in the item-based association rule and quantitative association rule more efficiently than in causality.

4.2 Basic Definitions

Assume I is a set of items in a database D, and a subset of the same type of items in I is referred to as a *quantitative item*. For convenience, we use the term 'quantitative item' as a set and its name interchangeably. Certainly, an item $A \in I$ can be taken as a special quantitative item. An *item variable* denotes a variable which represents a quantitative item in a set of quantitative items of the same domain.

An *item-based association rule* (formally defined in Chapter 2) is a relationship of the form

$$A \to B,$$

where A and B are itemsets and $A \cap B = \emptyset$. This has both support and confidence greater than, or equal to, the minimum support (*minsupp*) and the minimum confidence (*minconf*) thresholds, respectively.

A *quantitative association rule* is a relationship of the form

$$\langle attribute1, value1 \rangle \to \langle attribute2, value2 \rangle,$$

where *attribute1* and *attribute2* are attributes, *value1* and *value2* are subsets of the domains of *attribute1* and *attribute2* respectively, and $\langle attribute1, value1 \rangle$ and $\langle attribute2, value2 \rangle$ are quantitative items. We now illustrate the mining of quantitative association rules using an example.

Example 4.1 *Consider a personnel database at a university. The interest data is a set of records with 'educational level', and 'salary' of a first job. We* *extract* 30000 *such records from the database. The statistical results are listed in Table 4.1.*

Table 4.1. Statistical results of interest data

Education	Salary	Number
Doctor	$[3500, +\infty)$	8500
	$[2100, 3500)$	1400
	$[0, 2100)$	100
Master	$[3500, +\infty)$	1900
	$[2100, 3500)$	7100
	$[0, 2100)$	1000
UnderMaster	$[3500, +\infty)$	200
	$[2100, 3500)$	3000
	$[0, 2100)$	6800

In Table 4.1, the domain of *Education* can be partitioned into *Doctor*, *Master*, and *UnderMaster*; or *Doctor*, *Master*, and *UnderMaster* are quantitative items. The domain of *Salary* can be partitioned into three quantitative items $[3500, +\infty)$, $[2100, 3500)$ and $[0, 2100)$. And '*Number*' represents the statistical results, such as the number of transactions that contain the quantitative items *Master*, and $[2100, 3500)$ is 7100. In the light of the models in [Han 1993, Srikant 1996], we can extract quantitative association rules as follows.

Rule1 *Education* = *Doctor* $\Rightarrow$ *Salary* ≥ 3500
    with confidence 0.85
Rule2 *Education* = *Master* $\Rightarrow$ *Salary* $\in [2100, 3500)$
    with confidence 0.71
Rule3 *Education* = *UnderMaster* $\Rightarrow$ Salary < 2100
    with confidence 0.68

where Rule1, Rule2 and Rule3 are three quantitative association rules. This means that finding such quantitative rules is beneficial when mining databases with categorical attributes.

A *causal rule* is a relationship between X and Y of the form

$$X \Rightarrow Y,$$

where X and Y are variables with values in the *ranges* of $R(X)$ and $R(Y)$, respectively. Here, $x \in R(X)$ is called a *point-value* of X, where x is a quantitative item in data mining.

In order to mine these causal rules, we propose a new model for finding causality in large databases based on 'good partition'. Causality is represented by the form $X \rightarrow Y$, with a conditional probability matrix $M_{Y|X}$ according to Bayesian rules, where $M_{Y|X}$ is as

$$M_{Y|X} \triangleq P(y|x) \triangleq P(Y = y | X = x)$$

$$= \begin{bmatrix} p(y_1|x_1) & p(y_2|x_1) & \cdots & p(y_n|x_1) \\ p(y_1|x_2) & p(y_2|x_2) & \cdots & p(y_n|x_2) \\ & \cdots & & \\ p(y_1|x_m) & p(y_2|x_m) & \cdots & p(y_n|x_m) \end{bmatrix}$$

where $p(y_j|x_i) = p(Y = y_j | X = x_i)$ are the conditional probabilities, $i = 1, 2, \cdots, m$, and $j = 1, 2, \cdots, n$.

For example, if X and Y are two item variables with ranges {*Doctor*, *Master*, *UnderMaster*} and {$[3500, +\infty)$, $[2100, 3500)$, $[0, 2100)$} respectively, as in Example 4.1, we can obtain the causal rule $X \Rightarrow Y$ with a conditional probability matrix as follows.

$$M_{Y|X} = \begin{bmatrix} 0.85 & 0.14 & 0.01 \\ 0.19 & 0.71 & 0.1 \\ 0.02 & 0.3 & 0.68 \end{bmatrix}$$

where,

$$p(Y = [3500, +\infty) | X = Doctor) = 0.85,$$
$$p(Y = [2100, 3500) | X = Doctor) = 0.14,$$
$$p(Y = [0, 2100) | X = Doctor) = 0.01,$$
$$p(Y = [3500, +\infty) | X = Master) = 0.19,$$
$$p(Y = [2100, 3500) | X = Master) = 0.71,$$
$$p(Y = [0, 2100) | X = Master) = 0.1,$$
$$p(Y = [3500, +\infty) | X = UnderMaster) = 0.02,$$
$$p(Y = [2100, 3500) | X = UnderMaster) = 0.3, and$$
$$p(Y = [0, 2100) | X = UnderMaster) = 0.68.$$

This nice result is due to a better partition. However, because partitions on data are generally blind relative to a given database, it is difficult to construct a reasonable partition for applications. For example, if {*Doctor, UnderDoctor*} is a partition on R(*Education*) as in Example 4.1, then Rule2 and Rule3 can be neither generalized in the causal rule $X \rightarrow Y$ nor discovered as a valid rule. This means *UnderDoctor* is a **bad quantitative item** under the partition. Furthermore, if two quantitative items can compose a new quantitative item under a partition, and the new quantitative item is not a bad quantitative item, then the two quantitative items are referred to as **not-bad quantitative items**. If a quantitative item cannot be composed with any other quantitative item into a not-bad quantitative item under the partition, it is called a **good quantitative item**.

Also, if an item variable causes a quantitative rule not to be generalized in a certain causal rule, it is called a **bad item variable**. If two item variables can compose a new item variable under a partition, and the new item variable is not a bad item variable, then the two item variables are referred to as **not-bad item variables**. If an item variable cannot be composed with any other item variable into a not-bad item variable under the partition, it is called a **good item variable**.

A partition, which can cause bad quantitative items or bad item variables, is called a **bad partition**. A partition which can cause not-good item variables or not-good item variables, is called a **not-good partition**. If all quantitative items and item variables are good under a partition, this partition is called a **bad partition**.

For any two itemsets i_1 and i_2, i_1 and i_2 are *property tolerant* if, and only if, i_1 and i_2 have the same property, attribute or constraint. Thus, i_1 and i_2 are *associated tolerant* if, and only if, for any itemset i_3, $p(i_3|i_1) \approx p(i_3|i_2)$. Again, two quantitative items, q_1 and q_2, are *property tolerant* if, and only if, q_1 and q_2 have the same property, attribute or constraint. In addition, q_1 and q_2 are *associated tolerant* if, and only if, for any quantitative item q_3, $p(q_3|q_1) \approx p(q_3|q_2)$. And the two item variables X_1 and X_2 are *property tolerant* if, and only if, X_1 and X_2 have the same property, attribute or constraint. While, X_1 and X_2 are *associated tolerant* if, and only if, for any item variable Y, $p(Y|X_1) \approx p(Y|X_2)$.

4.3 Data Partitioning

Causality among variables is often hidden in data. Thus we must preprocess the faced data by partitioning. In this section, we propose techniques for partitioning data in a given database.

4.3.1 Partitioning Domains of Attributes

Although there are a great many existing data partitioning models, a major issue in mining causality research is still partitioning techniques on data and domains of attributes for specific applications. In data mining, there are two partitioning data models: the knowledge based partitioning model ([Han-Cai-Cercone 1993]) and the equi-depth partitioning model ([Srikant-Agrawal 1996]). Han, Cai and Cercone have put forward a knowledge based partitioning model, which requires background knowledge, such as concept hierarchies, data relevance, and expected rule forms ([Han-Cai-Cercone 1993]). This partitioning is efficient in discovering a certain kind of quantitative association rule from relational databases by using an attribute-oriented induction method. The other model, known as an equi-depth partitioning model, has been proposed by Srikant and Agrawal. This is an alternative method for the measurement of partial completeness ([Srikant-Agrawal 1996]). This partitioning model is useful for mining quantitative association rules in databases. Here, the number of partitions required can be calculated as

$$Number\ of\ Intervals = \frac{2n}{m(K-1)}$$

where n is the number of quantitative attributes, m is the minimum support, and K is the partial completeness level.

Generally, a quantitative item does not occur in the transactions of a database. When searching for quantitative association rules in databases, we say that a quantitative item i is contained by a transaction t of a database D if there exists at least one element of i occurring in t. (Note that each quantitative item consists of multiple simpler items.) The support of the quantitative item i is defined as $100 * s\%$ of transactions in D that contain at least one element of i. Or

$$s = |i(t)|/|D|$$

where $i(t) = \{t$ in $D|t$ contains at least one element of $i\}$.

In this way, we can map the quantitative association rules problem into a Boolean association rules problem. And some item-based mining techniques and algorithms can also be used to identify quantitative association rules.

However, such a partition on data is blind relative to a given database. It is possible that some quantitative items are bad, and some are not-good, because of the blindness of the partition to a given database. In fact, the number of partitions does not concern the 'associated tolerant'. We will use a so-called 'good partition' to generate quantitative items, and item variables, for a given database. This decomposes the 'bad item variables' and composes the 'good item variables'.

Let D be a given database and I the set of all items in D. Our partitioning model is described as follows.

(1) Generating relative properties, attributes, and constraint conditions for D.

(2) Generating the set QI of all quantitative items by way of those relative constraint conditions, where all quantitative items form a partition of I.

(3) Optimizing all the quantitative items, utilizing the decomposition and composition for quantitative items.

(4) Generating the set IV of all item variables by those relative properties and attributes, where all item variables form a partition of QI, and each item variable takes certain quantitative items as its point-values. This means, in a way, that each item variable can be viewed as a set of quantitative items with the same property (or attribute).

(5) Optimizing all the item variables, using the decomposition and composition for item variables.

As we have seen, when generating quantitative items and item variables by partitioning, we need to consider all data in a given database so as to obtain a 'good partition' on the data. However, databases in real applications are often very large, which makes partitioning a time-consuming procedure. For efficiency, we can essentially partition the faced data on a training set of given data sets.

4.3.2 Quantitative Items

Generally, there are different partitions for the domain of an attribute in different applications. Thus, we must consider user requirements and the reasonableness of a problem when determining a partition.

In previous sections, we partitioned the domains of *Education* and *Salary* as

$$\{Doctor, Master, UnderMaster\}$$

and

$$\{[3500, +\infty), [2100, 3500), [0, 2100)\}$$

respectively, where X and Y stood for *Education* and *Salary*. In this example, the constraint condition on the quantitative item *Doctor* is *Education* = *Doctor*, the constraint condition on the quantitative item *UnderMaster* is that *Education* is lower than *Master*, the constraint condition on the quantitative item $[3500, +\infty)$ is $3500 \leq Salary < +\infty$, and the constraint condition on the quantitative item $[2100, 3500)$ is $2100 \leq Salary < 3500$. For $R(Education)$,

$$q_1 = [x]_{Education=Doctor},$$
$$q_2 = [x]_{Education=Master}, and$$
$$q_3 = [x]_{Education=UnderMaster}$$

are three subsets of $R(Education)$. For $R(Salary)$,

$$q_4 = [x]_{3500 \leq Salary < +\infty},$$
$$q_5 = [x]_{2100 \leq Salary < 3500}, and$$
$$q_6 = [x]_{0 \leq Salary < 2100}$$

are three subsets of $R(Salary)$, where each subset is a set of discrete real numbers. For simplicity, q_4, q_5 and q_6 will be denoted as the three intervals: $[3500, +\infty), [2100, 3500)$ and $[0, 2100)$.

According to this, we can formally define quantitative items and the partition as follows.

Definition 4.1 *Assume I is a set of items. A quantitative item over I is a set of all items satisfying the constraint condition CR. A consequence of quantitative items, $q_1, q_2, \cdots, q_k$, is a partition of I if it satisfies:*

(1) $I = q_1 \cup q_2 \cup \cdots \cup q_k$;

(2) $q_i = \{A | A \in I \wedge [A]_{CR_i}\}$, where CR_i is a constraint relation, and $[A]_{CR_i}$ means that item A satisfies the constraint CR_i; and

(3) $q_i \cap q_j = \emptyset$ for $i \neq j, 1 \leq i, j \leq k$.

In fact, a quantitative item is the generalization of some items with the same constraint condition. For the above example, the consequence of the quantitative items $q_1, q_2, \cdots, q_6$ is a partition of I. And q_1 is a generalization of *Doctor* with education *Doctor*, q_3 is a generalization of *Bachelor*, *UnderBachelor* with education lower than Master, q_4 is a generalization of items with salary over 3500, and q_6 is a generalization of items with a salary less than 2100.

According to the different requirements of applications, we can divide them into different sets of quantitative items. For example, we can partition $R(Education)$ and $R(Salary)$ as

$$\{Doctor, UnderDoctor\},$$
$$\{Doctor, Master, Bachelor, UnderBacheor\},$$
$$\{Doctor, Master, UnderMaster\}$$

and

$$\{[7200, +\infty), [3500, 7200), [2100, 3500), [0, 2100)\},$$
$$\{[3500, +\infty), [2100, 3500), [0, 2100)\},$$
$$\{[3500, +\infty), [0, 3500)\},$$

respectively. However, a reasonable partition on data for data mining also needs to consider the identity on support of items and the associated degree of an item with other items. And so, we apply decomposition and composition for quantitative items to generate a good partition.

4.3.3 Decomposition and Composition of Quantitative Items

In order to find a 'good partition' for a given database, the quantitative items partitioned in properties must be optimized. We now define a method to decompose and compose quantitative items.

Lemma 4.1 *Let I be the set of all items of a given database, and QI be the set of all quantitative items under a partition.*

(i) For $q \in QI$, q is a bad quantitative item if, and only if, there are at least two items, i_1 and i_2, in I such that $i_1 \rightarrow i_3$ and $i_2 \rightarrow i_4$ can all be extracted as valid rules, and $i_3 \cap i_4 = \emptyset$, where i_3 and i_4 are itemsets over I.

(ii) For $q \in QI$, q is a good quantitative item if, and only if, all items in q are associated tolerant. More intuitively, for any two items $i_1, i_2 \in q$ and $i_3 \in I$, $p(i_3|i_1) \approx p(i_3|i_2)$ holds.

(iii) For $q_1, q_2 \in QI$, q_1 and q_2 are not-good quantitative items if, and only if, q_1 and q_2 can be composed into a new quantitative item q_3, and q_3 is a good quantitative item.

Proof: This can be directly proven according to previous definitions. ∇

Certainly, bad quantitative items are not allowed in mining quantitative association rules. And not-good quantitative items are also avoided unless they are specifically required. Accordingly, we now build the decomposition of bad quantitative items and the composition of not-good quantitative items as follows.

Procedure 4.1 *DecComposeQI;*
begin
    Input: *I: set of all items, QI: set of all quantitative items in property;*
    Output: *OQI: set of optimized quantitative items;*
(1) let $OQI \leftarrow \emptyset$;
    let $qset \leftarrow QI$;
    for any element q in $qset$ **do begin**
        if q is a bad quantitative item **then**
            if $i_1, i_2 \in q$ and they are not associated tolerant **then**
beginif
                decompose q into two sub-quantitative items q_1 and
q_2 such that
$$q_1 \cup q_2 = q, \; i_1 \in q_1 \text{ and } i_2 \in q_2;$$
        let $qset \leftarrow (qset - \{q\}) \cup \{q_1, q_2\}$;
      endif;
    enddo;
(2) **for** any two elements q_1 and q_2 in $qset$ **do begin**
      if q_1 and q_2 are property tolerant **then**
        if q_1 and q_2 are associated tolerant **then beginif**
            compose q_1 and q_2 into a new quantitative item q such
that $q = q_1 \cup q_2$
                and q is not a bad quantitative item;
            let $qset \leftarrow (qset - \{q_1, q_2\}) \cup \{q\}$;
      endif;
    enddo;
(3) let $OQI \leftarrow qset$;
    output OQI;
end;

The procedure $DecComposeQI$ is used to generate a set OQI of optimized quantitative items by decomposing 'bad quantitative items' and composing (property or associated) tolerant quantitative items. This work is completed in a three-step process as follows.

Step (1) decomposes 'bad quantitative items' in QI, which is a set of all quantitative items in a property. For example, let $[3500, +\infty)$ for $R(Salary)$ be a bad quantitative item. We need to divide $[3500, +\infty)$ into two quantitative items such as $[3500, 5000)$ and $[5000, +\infty)$ if $[3500, 5000)$ and $[5000, +\infty)$ are not associated tolerant. In other words, this step decomposes each bad quantitative item in QI into two quantitative items which are not associated tolerant.

Step (2) composes any two tolerant quantitative items in QI. For example, let $[0, 1500)$ and $[1500, 2100)$ for $R(Salary)$ be two tolerant quantitative items. We need to merge $[0, 1500)$ and $[1500, 2100)$ as a quantitative item $[0, 2100)$ if $[0, 2100)$ is not a bad quantitative item. That is, this step composes any two tolerant quantitative items in QI into a quantitative item that is not a bad quantitative item.

Then, Step (3) outputs the optimized quantitative items in OQI.

4.3.4 Item Variables

According to our partitioning model, an attribute such as *Education* and *Salary* can be taken as an item variable. For the above item variables X and Y, X is the set of quantitative items *Doctor*, *Master* and *UnderMaster* all with the same attribute, *Education*. That is, any element of X denotes a degree of education. And Y is the set of quantitative items: $[3500, +\infty)$, $[2100, 3500)$ and $[0, 2100)$ with the same attribute — *Salary*. That is, any element of y is denoted as an order of salary. However, an attribute sometimes needs to be divided into several different variables for specific applications according to different properties. For example, let the domain of the attribute 'Weather' in a system be $\{strongsun, middlesun, weaksun, lheavy-rain, middlerain, lightrain, \cdots\}$. In some applications, 'Weather' is sometimes taken as a variable, and sometimes it is divided into different variables such as $X_1, X_2, \cdots$, where the domain of X_1 is $\{strongsun, middlesun, weaksun\}$, the domain of X_2 is $\{heavyrain, middlerain, lightrain\}$, $\cdots$. In this partitioning, item variable X_1 is used for describing the degree of sun, or all elements of X_1 have the same property: sun. Item variable X_2 is used for describing the degree of rain, or all elements of X_2 have the same property: rain. We can now formally define the item variables as follows.

Definition 4.2 *Assume QI is a set of quantitative items. An item variable over QI is a set of all quantitative items satisfying a property (or attribute). A consequence of the item variables $X_1, X_2, \cdots, X_m$ is a partition of QI if it satisfies:*

(1) $QI = X_1 \cup X_2 \cup \cdots \cup X_m$;

(2) the range of X_i is the set $\{q|q \in QI \wedge P1(q)\}$, where P1 is a property (or attribute), and $P1(q)$ indicates that the quantitative item q satisfies the property P1; and

(3) $X_i \cap X_j = \emptyset$ for $i \neq j, 1 \leq i, j \leq m$.

An item variable is the generalization of certain quantitative items with the same properties. From previous examples, $QI = \{q_1, q_2, q_3, q_4, q_5, q_6\}$, and we take X and Y as two item variables with domains $R(X) = \{q_1, q_2, q_3\}$ and $R(Y) = \{q_4, q_5, q_6\}$, respectively. Then the consequence of item variables, X and Y, is a partition of QI according to the above definition. Also, we apply decomposition and composition for item variables to generate a good partition.

4.3.5 Decomposition and Composition for Item Variables

Lemma 4.2 *Let I be the set of all items of a given database, and QI the set of all quantitative items under a partition. And IV is the set of all item variables under a partition.*

(1) For $X \in IV$, X is a bad item variable if, and only if, there are at least two quantitative items q_1 and q_2 in X, such that $q_1 \rightarrow q_3$ and $q_2 \rightarrow q_4$ can all be extracted as valid quantitative rules, and $q_3 \cap q_4 = \emptyset$, where q_3 and q_4 are quantitative itemsets over QI.

(2) For $X \in IV$, X is a good item variable if, and only if, all quantitative items in X are associated tolerant. More intuitively, for any two items $q_1, q_2 \in X$ and $q_3 \in QI$, $p(q_3|q_1) \approx p(q_3|q_2)$ holds.

(3) For $X_1, X_2 \in IV$, X_1 and X_2 are not-good item variables if, and only if, X_1 and X_2 can be composed into a new item variable X_3 and X_3 is a good item variable.

Proof: This can directly be proven according to previous definitions. ∇

Certainly, bad item variables are not permitted in mining causal rules. And not-good item variables are also avoided, unless they are specifically required. Accordingly, we now build a decomposition of bad item variables and a composition of not-good item variables as follows.

> **Procedure 4.2** *DecComposeIV*
> **begin**
>   **Input:** *QI: set of all quantitative items, IV: set of all item variables in property,*
>   **Output:** *OIV: set of optimized item variables;*
> (1) **let** $OIV \leftarrow \emptyset$;
>   **let** $vset \leftarrow IV$;
>   **for** any element X in $vset$ **do begin**

if X is bad item variable **then**
     if $q_1, q_2 \in R(X)$ and they are not associated tolerant
then beginif
         decompose X into two item variable X_1 and X_2
such that
$$R(X_1) \cup R(X_2) = R(X), \ q_1 \in R(X_1) \text{ and } q_2 \in$$
$R(X_2)$;
       let $qset \leftarrow (vset - \{X\}) \cup \{X_1, X_2\}$;
     endif;
  enddo;
(2) **for** any two elements X_1 and X_2 in $vset$ **do begin**
   if X_1 and X_2 are property tolerant **then**
     if X_1 and X_2 are associated tolerant **then beginif**
       compose X_1 and X_2 into a new item variable X such
that
$$R(X) = R(X_1) \cup R(X_2) \text{ and } X \text{ is not bad item vari-}$$
able;
      let $vset \leftarrow (vset - \{X_1, X_2\}) \cup \{X\}$;
    endif;
  enddo;
(3) **let** $OIV \leftarrow vset$;
    output OIV;
end;

The procedure *DecComposeIV* generates a set *OIV* of optimized item variables by decomposing 'bad item variables' and composing (property or associated) tolerant item variables. This procedure is similar to the procedure *DecComposeQI*. This work is also designed to be completed in a three-step process as follows.

Step (1) is to decompose 'bad item variables' in *IV*, which is a set of all item variables in a property. For example, let {*largesnow, middlesnow, smallsnow, largerain, middlerain, smallrain*} for $R(Weather)$ be a bad item variable. We need to divide {*largesnow, middlesnow, smallsnow, largerain, middlerain, smallrain*} into two item variables such as {*largesnow, middlesnow, smallsnow*} and {*largerain, middlerain, smallrain*} if {*largesnow, middlesnow, smallsnow*} and {*largerain, middlerain, smallrain*} are not associated tolerant. In other words, this step decomposes each bad item variable in *QI* into two item variables that are not associated tolerant.

Step (2) is to compose any two tolerant item variables in *IV*. For example, let {*largesnow, middlesnow, smallsnow*} and {*largerain, middlerain, smallrain*} for $R(Weather)$ be two tolerant item variables. We need to merge {*largesnow, middlesnow, smallsnow*} and {*largerain, middlerain, smallrain*} as an item variable {*largesnow, middlesnow, smallsnow, largerain, middlerain, smallrain*} if {*largesnow, middlesnow, smallsnow, largerain, middlerain, smallrain*} is not a bad item variable. That is, the step composes any two tolerant item variables in IQ into an item variable that is not a bad item variable.

And Step (3) outputs the optimized item variables in OIV.

4.3.6 Procedure of Partitioning

We now build an algorithm for a partitioning model as follows. We let D be a given database, and I the set of all items in D.

As we have argued, generating all quantitative items and item variables by partitioning requires the consideration of all data in a given database so as to obtain a 'good partition' on the data. And real databases are often very large. This means that partitioning is a time-consuming procedure. For efficiency, we suggest that the following partitioning procedure is performed on a training set of given data sets. Therefore, it is important to select a set of instances from a database (see [Liu-Motoda 1998]).

Procedure 4.3 *PartitionData*

begin
  Input*: D: database, Table: a concept hierarchy table, I: set of all items in D;*
  Output*: OQI: the set of quantitative items, OIV: the set of item variables;*
  (1) generate S_p the set of properties, S_a the set of attributes by *Table*, and S_c the set of constraint conditions for D;
   $QI \leftarrow \emptyset$;
   $IV \leftarrow \emptyset$;
  (2) **let** $I \leftarrow$ all items in D;
    for $c \in S_c$ **do begin**
     generate q_c **over** I
     if $q_c \neq \emptyset$ **then**
      let $QI \leftarrow QI \cup \{q_c\}$;
    endfor;
    for each item i of I **then**
     if i is not contained in any quantitative item **then begin**
      let $r \leftarrow r \cup \{i\}$;
      let $QI \leftarrow QI \cup \{r\}$;
    endif
  (3) optimize QI by procedure DecComposeQI;
  (4) **for** $a \in S_p \cup S_a$ **do begin**
    generate x_a **over** QI;
    if $x_a \neq \emptyset$ **then**
     let $IV \leftarrow IV \cup \{x_a\}$;
    endfor

for each quantitative item q of QI **do**
    if q is not a value of any item variable **then begin**
        let $z \leftarrow z \cup \{q\}$;
        let $IV \leftarrow IV \cup \{z\}$;
    endif
(5) optimize IV by procedure DecComposeIV;
endall;

The procedure *PartitionData* generates a partition on a given database, and obtains a set of optimized quantitative items OQI and a set of optimized item variables OIV. The initialization of the procedure is carried out in Step (1).

Step (2) generates a set of quantitative items: OQI, from I, which is the set of all items in D. The items in I are divided into subsets according to the conditions (such as in S_c which is a set of constraint conditions for D), where any two subsets are not intersected. Then, each of the remaining items in I is taken as a single subset. For example, let $\{largesnow, middlesnow, smallsnow, largerain, middlerain, smallrain, strongsun, middlesun, weaksun\}$ for $R(Weather)$ be a part of I. These can be divided into three quantitative items such as $q_1 = \{largesnow, middlesnow, smallsnow\}$, $q_2 = \{largerain, middlerain, smallrain\}$, and $q_3 = \{largesun, middlesun, smallsun\}$. This step only partitions the items into rough quantitative items. These rough quantitative items are optimized in Step (3) by calling in the procedure *DecComposeQI*.

Step (4) is to generate a set of item variables, IV, from QI, after the elements in QI are optimized. The quantitative items in QI are divided into subsets according to conditions (such as in S_p which is the set of properties), where any two subsets are not intersected. Each of the remaining quantitative items in QI is then taken as a single subset. For example, let $\{q_1, q_2, q_3, q_4, q_5\}$ for $R(Weather)$ be quantitative items in QI. They can be divided into three item variables such as $v_1 = \{q_1, q_2, q_3\}$, $v_2 = \{q_4\}$, and $v_3 = \{q_5\}$. This step only partitions the quantitative items into rough item variables. These rough item variables are optimized in Step (5) by calling in the procedure *DecComposeIV*.

4.4 Dependency among Variables

In this section, we first present a method for acquiring the conditional probabilities of the point-values (quantitative items) of an item variable given another item variable, and we then propose a way to identify causal rules of interest.

4.4.1 Conditional Probabilities

After quantitative items and item variables are generated, the work of mining causal rules in databases becomes easy. We can calculate the probabilities $p(X = a), p(Y = b)$, and $p(Y = b \wedge X = a)$ for any two item variables X and Y as follows.

$$p(X = a) = N(X = a)/n$$
$$p(Y = a) = N(Y = b)/n$$
$$p(Y = b \wedge X = a) = N(Y = b \wedge X = a)/n$$

where n is the total number of tuples in the database, $N(X = a)$ denotes the number of tuples in the database that contain the quantitative item a, $N(Y = b)$ denotes the number of tuples in the database that contain the quantitative item b, and $N(Y = b \wedge X = a)$ denotes the number of tuples in the database that contain the quantitative items a and b. Now we can solve the conditional probability of $Y = b$, given $X = a$, as

$$p(Y = b | X = a) = \frac{p(Y = b \wedge X = a)}{p(X = a)}$$

In Example 4.2, we illustrate how the above method can be used.

Example 4.2 *Ten tuples are selected from a relational database, as shown in Table 4.2. The supports and probabilities of single quantitative items and sets of quantitative items are shown in the table. Because there are 10 tuples in the database, the support is the number of tuples in which the items or sets of quantitative items occur, divided by 10.*

Table 4.2. Some data in the database

EMP#	Education	salary
25	doctor	5000
26	doctor	4500
27	doctor	3500
28	doctor	3500
29	doctor	4100
30	doctor	3500
31	doctor	4200
32	doctor	5400
33	doctor	2600
34	doctor	2000

Let n be the number of all tuples in the above database, and let $N(a)$ stand for the number of tuples in the database where quantitative items or a set of quantitative items a occurs in. For example, $N(a)$ of quantitative item $[3500, +\infty)$ and the set of quantitative item $\{Doctor, [3500, +\infty)\}$ can be counted as

- $N([3500, +\infty))$: the number of all tuples in the database where its projection on *Salary* is greater than, or equal to, 3500; and
- $N(\{Doctor, [3500, +\infty)\})$: the number of all tuples in the database where its projection on *Education* is *Doctor* and its projection on *Salary* is greater than, or equal to, 3500.

Accordingly, we can obtain the $N(a)$ of quantitative itemsets as shown in Table 4.3.

Table 4.3. Statistical results for Table 4.2

Itemset	Number of Tuples	Support $sup(X)$	Probability $p(X)$
$[3500, +\infty)$	8	80%	0.8
$[2100, 3500)$	1	10%	0.1
$[0, 2100)$	1	10%	0.1
Doctor	10	100%	1
Doctor, $[3500, +\infty)$	8	80%	0.8
Doctor, $[2100, 3500)$	1	10%	0.1
Doctor, $[0, 2100)$	1	10%	0.1

According to previous definitions, we obtain

$$p(Y = [3500, +\infty)|X = Doctor) = \frac{p(Y = [3500, +\infty) \wedge X = Doctor)}{p(X = Doctor)}$$
$$= 0.8$$
$$p(Y = [2100, 3500)|X = Doctor) = \frac{p(Y = [2100, 3500) \wedge X = Doctor)}{p(X = Doctor)}$$
$$= 0.1$$
$$p(Y = [0, 2100)|X = Doctor) = \frac{p(Y = [0, 2100) \wedge X = Doctor)}{p(X = Doctor)}$$
$$= 0.1$$

4.4.2 Causal Rules of Interest

As you will see in Table 5.1, when the item variable X impacts on the item variable Y at only one, or a few, point-values, the conditional probability matrix will contain much unnecessary information. In this case, an association rule (based on items), or a quantitative association rule, would be more efficient than the above causal rule. For this reason, if a causal rule $X \rightarrow Y$ with $M_{Y|X}$ is of interest, it must satisfy three conditions:

(1) there must be sufficient conditional probabilities $p(y_i|x_j)$ in $M_{Y|X}$ that are greater than, or equal to, $minconf$;

(2) for a point-value $p(y_i|x_j) \geq minconf$, $p(x_j \cup y_i) \geq minsupp$ in $M_{Y|X}$; and

(3) these point-values must also match the Piatetsky-Shapiro argument ([Piatetsky 1991]), or $p(y_i|x_j) - p(x_j)$ must be greater than, or equal to, a threshold λ given by users.

This means that, if QI is a set of quantitative items in a database D, X and Y are item variables in D, $R(X) \subset QI$, $|R(X)| = n$, $R(Y) \subset QI$, $|R(Y)| = m$, where $minsupp, minconf, \gamma > 0$, $\alpha > 0$, $\lambda > 0$, and $\eta > 0$, are given by users or experts. Here γ is the minimum number of itemsets with supports greater than or equal to $minsupp$, η is the minimum number of conditional probabilities, α is the minimum number of probabilities satisfying the Piatetsky-Shapiro argument. Then, $X \Rightarrow Y$ is a causal rule of interest if there are enough point-pairs (x_j, y_i) in $M_{Y|X}$ such that $p(x_j \cup y_i) \geq minsupp$, $p(Y = y_i|X = x_j) \geq minconf$ and $(p(Y = y_i|X = x_j) - p(Y = y_i)) \geq \lambda$.

For example, let $minsupp = 0.3$, $minconf = 0.6$, $\gamma > 2$, $\alpha > 2$, $\lambda = 0.1$ and $\eta = 2$. And $QI = \{Doctor, Master, UnderMaster, [3500, +\infty), [2100, 3500), [0, 2100)\}$ as in Example 4.1, and $X = \{Doctor, Master, UnderMaster\}$, $|R(X)| = 3$, $Y = \{[3500, +\infty), [2100, 3500), [0, 2100)\}$, and $|R(Y)| = 3$. On the basis of the above definition, $X \Rightarrow Y$ with $M_{Y|X}$ can be extracted as a causal rule of interest.

Theorem 4.1 *Let QI be a set of quantitative items in a database D, X and Y be item variables in D, $R(X) \subset QI$, $|R(X)| = n$, $R(Y) \subset QI$, $|R(Y)| = m$, and $R(X) \cap R(Y) = \emptyset$. Also, $minsupp, minconf, \gamma > 0$, $\alpha > 0$, $\lambda > 0$ and $\eta > 0$ are given by users or experts. Let*

(1) $S_{support} = \{(x_j, y_i)|p(x_j \cup y_i) \geq minsupp \wedge (1 \leq i \leq m) \wedge (1 \leq j \leq n)\}$,
(2) $S_{conf} = \{(x_j, y_i)|p(Y = y_i|X = x_j) \geq minconf \wedge (1 \leq i \leq m) \wedge (1 \leq j \leq n)\}$, and
(3) $S_{depend} = \{(x_j, y_i)|(p(Y = y_i|X = x_j) - p(Y = y_i)) \geq \lambda \wedge (1 \leq i \leq m) \wedge (1 \leq j \leq n)\}$.

The causal rule $X \Rightarrow Y$ is of interest if, and only if, $|S_{support} \cap S_{conf} \cap S_{depend}| \geq min\{n, m, \gamma, \eta, \alpha\}$.

Proof: We first prove ("$\Rightarrow$"). According to the definition of the rule of interest, there are enough point-pairs (x_j, y_i) in $M_{Y|X}$, such that $p(x_j \cup y_i) \geq minsupp$, $p(Y = y_i|X = x_j) \geq minconf$, and $(p(Y = y_i|X = x_j) - p(Y = y_i)) \geq \lambda$. Or

$$|S_{support} \cap S_{conf} \cap S_{depend}| \geq min\{n, m, \gamma, \eta, \alpha\}$$

Now we prove ("$\Leftarrow$"). Because $|S_{support} \cap S_{conf} \cap S_{depend}| \geq min\{n, m, \gamma, \eta, \alpha\}$, so

$$|S_{support}| \geq min\{n, m, \gamma\}$$
$$|S_{conf}| \geq min\{n, m, \eta\}$$
$$|S_{depend}| \geq min\{n, m, \alpha\}$$

That is, the causal rule $X \to Y$ is of interest. ∇

4.4.3 Algorithm Design

Let D be a given database, and let $minsupp, minconf, \alpha, \lambda, \eta$ be threshold values given by users. Our algorithm for mining causal rules in databases is as follows.

Algorithm 4.1 *CausalityDB*
begin
   Input: *D: database, minsupp, minconf, α, λ, η: threshold values;*
   Output: *$X \to Y$: causal rule, $M_{Y|X}$: the conditional probability matrix of Y given X;*
(1) **call** the procedure PartitionData;
(2) **for** $X, Y \in OIV$ **do**
         for each element a in $R(X)$ and b in $R(Y)$ **do begin**
            let $p(Y = b|X = a) \leftarrow p(Y = b \wedge X = a)/p(X = a)$;
            let $CRSET \leftarrow$ the rule $X \to Y$ as a candidate rule;
                  with conditional probability matrix of Y given X: $M_{Y|X}$;
         endfor
(3) **for** each extracted rules R with $M_{Y|X}$ in $CRSET$ **dogegin**
         let $S_{support} \leftarrow \{(x_j, y_i)|p(x_j \cup y_i) \geq minsupp \wedge (1 \leq i \leq m) \wedge$
         $(1 \leq j \leq n)\}$;
         let $S_{conf} \leftarrow \{(x_j, y_i)|p(Y = y_i|X = x_j) \geq minconf \wedge (1 \leq i \leq$
         $m) \wedge (1 \leq j \leq n)\}$;
         let $S_{depend} \leftarrow \{(x_j, y_i)|(p(Y = y_i|X = x_j) - p(Y = y_i)) \geq$
         $\lambda \wedge (1 \leq i \leq m) \wedge (1 \leq j \leq n)\}$;
         if $|S_{support}| < min\{n, m, \gamma\}$ **then**
            generate item-based rules or quantitative rules for $S_{support}$;
         else if $|S_{conf}| < min\{n, m, \eta\}$ **then**
            generate item-based rules or quantitative rules for S_{conf};
         else if $|S_{depend}| < min\{n, m, \alpha\}$ **then**
            generate item-based rules or quantitative rules for S_{depend};
            else let $NewCRSET \leftarrow$ the rule $X \to Y$ as an interest
rule;
                  with conditional probability matrix of Y given X: $M_{Y|X}$;
      enddo;
(4) **call** RefineRules($NewCRSET, RSET$);
(5) **output** $RSET$;
   endall.

The algorithm *CausalityDB* finds all causal rules of the form $X \to Y$ attached to a conditional probability matrix $M_{Y|X}$, from a given database D.

Step (1) calls in the procedure *PartionData* for data preprocessing so as to generate all possible quantitative items and item variables in D. This has already been discussed in Section 4.3.

Step (2) generates the conditional probability matrix $M_{Y|X}$ for each pair of item variables X and Y by computing the supports of the related quantitative items. Each rule is a candidate causal rule in $CRSET$.

Step (3) determines which of the candidate rules in $CRSET$ are of interest. In fact, the matrices of causal rules of interest contain much unnecessary information. It is not easy to use them in real applications. Therefore, they are optimized in Step (4) by calling in the procedure *RefineRules*, the optimizing technique of which is presented in Chapter 5.

From this algorithm we can obtain a theorem as follows.

Theorem 4.2 *For a given large database, D, minsupp and minconf are given by users. If $A \to B$ is extracted as a rule in Algorithm 4.1, then it is of interest under the partition.*

Proof: There are three kinds of rules extracted in Algorithm 1. We need to prove that each kind of rule is of interest under our partition. We do this in the following way.

(i) If A and B are itemsets, $A \to B$ is of interest under the partition according to Theorem 4.1 and the Piatetsky-Shapiro argument ([Piatetsky 1991]).

(ii) If A and B are quantitative items, $A \to B$ is of interest under the partition according to Theorem 4.1 and the Piatetsky-Shapiro argument ([Piatetsky 1991]).

(iii) If A and B are item variables, it can be directly proven that $A \to B$ is of interest under the partition by Algorithm 4.1 and the Piatetsky-Shapiro argument ([Piatetsky 1991]).

$$\nabla$$

Theorem 4.3 *For a given large database, D, minsupp and minconf are given by users. Let R_I and R_C be the set of item-based rules (or quantitative rules) and the rules in Algorithm 4.1, respectively, then R_I is generalized by R_C.*

Proof: According to Procedure 4.3, the partition on items and the partition on quantitative items are all good partitions. This means that, for any rule $A \to B$ in R_I, it satisfies

(a) A and B are all itemsets, $A \to B$ is in R_C, or generalized in a certain quantitative association rule in R_C under the partition for items, or generalized in a certain causal rule $X \to Y$ under the partition for quantitative items; where A and B are generalized in two particular quantitative items in $R(X)$ and $R(Y)$, respectively.

(b) A and B are all quantitative items, $A \rightarrow B$ is in R_C, or generalized in a certain causal rule $X \rightarrow Y$, under the partition for quantitative items.

Consequently, R_I is generalized by R_C.

∇

4.5 Causality in Probabilistic Databases

Today's database systems must tackle uncertainty in the data they store ([Zhang 2000]). Such uncertainty arises from different sources, such as measurement errors, approximation errors, and the dynamic nature of the real world. In order to perform anything efficiently, some useful dependent patterns in probabilistic databases must be discovered. However, probabilistic data in 1NF (First Normal Form) relations is redundant, with the result that previous mining techniques fail for probabilistic databases. For this reason, an alternative mining model for such databases is established in this section. In this model, the partition proposed in Section 4.3 is applied to preprocess probabilistic data, and Bayesian rules are used to identify causality.

4.5.1 Problem Statement

Recently, there has been much work done on mining special databases. For example, techniques for mining special databases include spatial data mining ([Cai-Cercone-Han 1991, Ester-Kriegel-Sander 1997, Han-KS 1997, Ng-H 1994]), which finds novel and interesting relationships, and characteristics that may exist implicitly in spatial databases; temporal databases mining ([Chen-Park-Yu 1998]); image data mining ([Cromp-Campbell 1993]), for multi-dimensional remotely sensed images; mining time-series databases ([Tsumoto 1999]), text mining ([Feldman-AFLRS 1999]), and Web mining ([Srivastava-CDT 2000]), for the discovery and application of usage patterns from Web data. However, there has been no work done on mining probabilistic databases.

Today's database systems must handle uncertainties in the data they store. For example, in an image retrieval system, an image processing algorithm may fetch images that are similar to a given sample image, and feed the results into a relational database. These results are generally uncertain. In a sensor application, depending on the reliability of the sensor, the data from the sensor is generally associated with a probability.

A model of mining causality among multi-value variables in large databases based on partition has already been proposed in previous sections. This technique can capture the dependencies among multi-value variables in probabilistic databases. Consequently, in this chapter, we propose a model for discovering dependency rules from probabilistic databases, where the probabilistic data model in [Dey 1996] and [Zhang 2000] is adopted. We now illustrate this in Example 4.3.

Example 4.3 *Consider a probabilistic personnel database at a university. The interest data is a set of records concerning 'education', 'salary' and 'pS' (probability) of an employee, as shown in Table 4.4.*

Table 4.4. A probabilistic relation

EMP#	Education	salary	pS
3025	Doctor	4100	0.8
3025	Doctor	2500	0.1
3025	Doctor	1800	0.1
6637	Doctor	3500	0.14
6637	Doctor	2400	0.06
6637	Master	3500	0.1
6637	Master	2400	0.6
6637	Master	1800	0.1
7741	Bachelor	3500	0.1
7741	Bachelor	2400	0.1
7741	Bachelor	1500	0.8

To mine such a database, we first need to partition the domain of *Education* into *Doctor*, *Master*, and *UnderMaster*; and the domain of *Salary* into $[3500, +\infty)$, $[2100, 3500)$ and $[0, 2100)$, using a partition. *Doctor*, *Master*, *UnderMaster*, $[3500, +\infty)$, $[2100, 3500)$, and $[0, 2100)$ are quantitative items. We now compute the probabilities of the quantitative items in the database. Let X and Y stand for Education and Salary, respectively, and let $\tau_1, \tau_2, \cdots, \tau_{10}$ be the sequential tuples in Table 4.4. Then, for $EMP\#3025$,

$$p(X = Doctor) = \tau_1(pS) + \tau_2(pS) + \tau_3(pS) = 0.8 + 0.1 + 0.1 = 1$$
$$p(X = Master) = 0, p(X = UnderMaster) = 0, p(Y = [3500, +\infty))$$
$$= 0.8$$
$$p(Y = [21003500)) = 0.1, p(Y = [0, 2100)) = 0.1;$$

for $EMP\#6637$,

$$p(X = Doctor) = \tau_4(pS) + \tau_5(pS) = 0.14 + 0.06 = 0.2$$
$$p(X = Master) = \tau_6(pS) + \tau_7(pS) + \tau_8(pS)$$
$$= 0.1 + 0.6 + 0.1 = 0.8$$
$$p(X = UnderMaster) = 0, p(Y = [0, 2100)) = 0.1,$$

$$p(Y = [3500, +\infty)) = \tau_4(pS) + \tau_6(pS) = 0.14 + 0.1 = 0.24$$
$$p(Y = [2100, 3500)) = \tau_5(pS) + \tau_7(pS) = 0.06 + 0.6 = 0.66$$

and for $EMP\#7741$,

$$p(X = Doctor) = 0, p(X = Master) = 0$$
$$p(X = UnderMaster) = \tau_9(pS) + \tau_{10}(pS) + \tau_{11}(pS)$$
$$= 0.1 + 0.1 + 0.8 = 1$$
$$p(Y = [3500, +\infty)) = 0.1, p(Y = [2100, 3500)) = 0.1$$
$$p(Y = [0, 2100)) = 0.8$$

That is, $X = (1, 0, 0)$ and $Y = (0.8, 0.1, 0.1)$ for $EMP\# = 3025$; $X = (0.2, 0.8, 0)$ and $Y = (0.24, 0.66, 0.1)$ for $EMP\# = 6637$; and $X = (0, 0, 1)$ and $Y = (0.1, 0.1, 0.8)$ for $EMP\# = 7741$. More are listed in Table 4.5.

Table 4.5. Probabilities of X and Y in the database

EMP#	$p(x_1)$	$p(x_2)$	$p(x_3)$	$p(y_1)$	$p(y_2)$	$p(y_3)$
3025	1	0	0	0.8	0.1	0.1
3125	0	1	0	0.1	0.8	0.1
3225	0	0	1	0.1	0.1	0.8
3335	0.9	0.1	0	0.73	0.17	0.1
3515	0.9	0	0.1	0.73	0.1	0.17
3625	0.1	0.9	0	0.17	0.73	0.1
3820	0	0.9	0.1	0.1	0.73	0.17
4014	0.1	0	0.9	0.17	0.1	0.73
4516	0	0.1	0.9	0.1	0.17	0.73
4725	0.8	0.2	0	0.66	0.24	0.1
5218	0.8	0	0.2	0.66	0.1	0.24
6637	0.2	0.8	0	0.24	0.66	0.1
6714	0	0.8	0.2	0.1	0.66	0.24
6925	0.2	0	0.8	0.24	0.1	0.66
7005	0	0.2	0.8	0.1	0.24	0.66
7313	0.8	0.1	0.1	0.66	0.17	0.17
7516	0.1	0.8	0.1	0.17	0.66	0.17
7741	0.1	0.1	0.8	0.17	0.17	0.66
7913	0.7	0.3	0	0.59	0.31	0.1
8125	0.7	0	0.3	0.59	0.1	0.31

Next, we need to find a conditional probability matrix $M_{Y|X}$ to fit the data as the above probabilities of the item variables. If these data are fitted in a conditional probability matrix $M_{Y|X}$, then the causality between X and Y can be determined by this matrix. Another main goal of this chapter is to build a model which will learn these probabilities. In fact, using the algorithm designed in this section we can acquire a conditional probability matrix $M_{Y|X}$ from the above data as follows.

$$M_{Y|X} = \begin{bmatrix} p_{11} & p_{12} & p_{13} \\ p_{21} & p_{22} & p_{23} \\ p_{31} & p_{32} & p_{33} \end{bmatrix} = \begin{bmatrix} 0.8 & 0.1 & 0.1 \\ 0.1 & 0.8 & 0.1 \\ 0.1 & 0.1 & 0.8 \end{bmatrix}$$

Finally, we extract $X \rightarrow Y$ as a valid rule, which has a conditional probability matrix $M_{Y|X}$ and a support greater than, or equal to, some user specified minimum support (*minsupp*) threshold.

However, previous models used for discovering causality among item variables have only been efficient for traditional databases that have certain data. In order to mine probabilistic databases, in this chapter, we propose a new model for discovering useful causal rules in probabilistic databases, where the probabilistic data of interest is preprocessed by a partition. Of course, after preprocessing the probabilistic data set of interest, statistical techniques can be used straight away to discover patterns in the data sets. For efficiency, a random search model and a partition search method are proposed as improved models to overcome the weaknesses of the statistical model.

4.5.2 Required Concepts

Given an item variable X, all point values of X can construct a *vector* such as $(x_1, x_2, ..., x_n)$. Each state of X can be described by point values associated with probabilities in the vector, that is, $(p(x_1) = a_1, p(x_2) = a_2, ..., p(x_n) = a_n)$, is a *state* of X. This state will be written as $(a_1, a_2, ..., a_n)$. All states of X constructing the *state space* of X, will be denoted by $S(X)$.

For example, let the possible values of item variable X be *red, green, yellow, blue, purple*, then $(p(red) = 0.3, p(green) = 0.25, p(yellow) = 0.05, p(blue) = 0.11, p(purple) = 0.29) \in S(X)$; or $(0.3, 0.25, 0.05, 0.11, 0.29) \in S(X)$ is a state of X.

The problem of mining dependency rules in probabilistic databases is how to generate all rules $X \rightarrow Y$ that have both support and $M_{Y|X}$, where support is greater than, or equal to, some user specified minimum support (*minsupp*) threshold.

4.5.3 Preprocess of Data

The key to mining probabilistic databases is to build an effective partition on the data. This was carried out in Section 4.3. Probabilistic data preprocessing is demonstrated by an example as follows.

In general, probabilistic relations have deterministic keys. That is, each tuple represents a known real entity. Non-key attributes describe the properties of the entities, and may be deterministic or stochastic in nature. For example, Table 4.4 adopts a 1NF view of probabilistic relations. Its N1NF (Non-First Normal Form) view is shown in Table 4.6.

In Table 4.6, $X = (1, 0, 0)$ and $Y = (0.8, 0.1, 0.1)$ for $EMP\# = 3025$; $X = (0.2, 0.8, 0)$ and $Y = (0.24, 0.66, 0.1)$ for $EMP\# = 6637$; and $X = (0, 0, 1)$ and $Y = (0.1, 0.1, 0.8)$ for $EMP\# = 7741$.

Table 4.6. A probabilistic relation

EMP#	Education	salary, pS
3025	doctor	4100, 0.8 2500, 0.1 1800, 0.1
6637	Doctor, 0.2 master, 0.8	3500, 0.24 2400, 0.66 1800, 0.1
7741	bachelor	3500, 0.1 2400, 0.1 1500, 0.8

Though the N1NF models provide a framework for describing intuitively the nature of uncertainty data, they pose the usual implementation problems associated with all N1NF relations. Much of the previous work done on modeling probabilistic data is based on 1NF relations, therefore, our work in this section concentrates on the 1NF probabilistic relational model.

You will note that the techniques for partitioning quantitative attributes are the same as in previous sections. With no loss of generality, an attribute is taken as an item variable in this section. The probabilities of quantitative items are required to satisfy

$$p(Z = a) = \sum_{\tau(K)=k \wedge \tau(Z)=a} \tau(pS)$$

For example, some probabilities of quantitative items in Table 4.4 are as follows. For $EMP\#3025$,

$$p(X = Doctor) + p(X = Master) + p(X = UnderMaster) = 1 + 0 + 0 = 1$$

$$p(Y = [3500, +\infty)) + p(Y = [2100, 3500)) + p(Y = [0, 2100)) = 0.8 + 0.1 + 0.1 = 1$$

for $EMP\#6637$,

$$p(X = Doctor) + p(X = Master) + p(X = UnderMaster) = 0.2 + 0.8 + 0 = 1$$

$$p(Y = [3500, +\infty)) + p(Y = [2100, 3500)) + p(Y = [0, 2100)) = 0.24 + 0.66 + 0.1 = 1$$

and for $EMP\#7741$,

$$p(X = Doctor) + p(X = Master) + p(X = UnderMaster) = 0 + 0 + 1 = 1$$

$$p(Y = [3500, +\infty)) + p(Y = [2100, 3500)) + p(Y = [0, 2100)) = 0.1 + 0.1 + 0.8 = 1$$

We now show the data preprocess using the following procedure.

Procedure 4.4 *Generatedata*
begin
    Input: *D: probabilistic database,* γ: *threshold values;*
    Output: *PS: set of probabilities of interest;*
  (1) **call** the procedure PartitionData;
      let $IV \leftarrow$ all item variables;
      let $PS \leftarrow \emptyset$;
  (2) let $DS \leftarrow \emptyset$,
      for a subset X of set Z of IV **beginfor**
        let $Y \leftarrow Z - X$;
        let $DS \leftarrow DS \cup \{X, Y\}$;
        for each tuple τ in D **beginfor1**
          for each key value $\tau(K) = k$ **beginfor2**
            for each element a in $R(X)$ **do**
              let $p(X = a) \leftarrow \sum_{\tau(K)=k \wedge \tau(X)=a} \tau(pS)$;
            for each element a in $R(Y)$ **do**
              let $p(Y = a) \leftarrow \sum_{\tau(K)=k \wedge \tau(Y)=a} \tau(pS)$;
          endfor2
          if $|X| > 0$ **then**
            let $DS \leftarrow DS \cup \{p(X), p(Y)\}$;
        endfor1
        let $PS \leftarrow PS \cup \{DS\}$;
      endfor
  (3) **output** PS set of probability sets;
  endall.

The procedure *Generatedata* preprocesses the data in a given probabilistic database so as to find all interesting data.

Step (1) calls in the procedure PartionData for data preprocessing so as to generate all possible quantitative items and item variables in D. This has already been discussed in Section 4.3. Initialization is also done in this step.

Step (2) is to standardize the probabilities of quantitative items by the formula

$$p(X = a) = \sum_{\tau(K)=k \wedge \tau(X)=a} \tau(pS)$$

The standardized data set is output in Step (3).

For a given probabilistic database, the preprocess of the database generates a set, PS, of the sets DS which are the probabilities of item variables.

4.5.4 Probabilistic Dependency

We now present a method to calculate a conditional probability matrix $M_{X|Y}$ for a possible rule $X \rightarrow Y$, and we then estimate the support for the rule.

For a given probabilistic database, X and Y are two item variables. Let $R(X) = \{x_1, x_2, ..., x_n\}$, $R(Y) = \{y_1, y_2, ..., y_m\}$, and $DS = \{(a, b) | a \in S(X), b \in S(Y)\} \in PS$ be a set of k data generated by the procedure *Generatedata*. In order to mine the rule of the form $X \to Y$, we need to determine the conditional probability matrix of Y given X: $M_{Y|X}$. The influence of X on Y is the following formula according to the Bayesian rule,

$$P(Y = y_i | X = x) = \sum_{k}^{n} p(y_i | x_k) * p(x_k),$$ (4.1)

where $x \in R(X)$, $i = 1, 2, \cdots, m$.

In the following, $P(Y = y_i | X = x)$ is denoted by b_i, and $p(y_i | x_j)$ is denoted by p_{ji}, where $i = 1, 2, \cdots, m$, $j = 1, 2, \cdots, n$. Now, given $a = (p(x_1) = a_1, p(x_2) = a_2, \cdots, p(x_n) = a_n) \in S(X)$ as an observation, then b_i can be solved in Equation 4.2 as follows

$$\sum_{k}^{n} a_k p_{ki},$$ (4.2)

where $i = 1, 2, \cdots, m$.

Intuitively, there is a relationship between data a and b from Equation 4.2 if (a, b) is an observation. And p_{ji} are invariant, where a_j and b_i are variable factors. Therefore, by using Equation 4.2, we can construct a method for identifying probabilistic causal rules.

In this section, our goal is to find the probability, p_{ji}, from probabilistic databases. So, for DS, the following function is the ideal expectation for all elements of DS to satisfy:

$$f(p_{1i}, p_{2i}, ..., p_{ni}) = \sum_{t \in DS} (\sum_{k}^{n} a_{jk} p_{ki} - b_{ji})^2$$

and the value of $f(p_{1i}, p_{2i}, ..., p_{ni})$ must be the minimum. Or, the above formula can be written as

$$f(p_{1i}, p_{2i}, ..., p_{ni}) = \sum (\sum_{k}^{n} a_{jk} p_{ki} - b_{ji})^2$$

Theorem 4.4 *The minimal solutions to the above formula for constants* $p_{1i}, p_{2i}, ..., p_{ni}$ *are*

$$p_{1i} = \frac{d_1}{d}, p_{2i} = \frac{d_2}{d}, \cdots, p_{ni} = \frac{d_n}{d},$$

where d_i, the determinant of the matrix after ith rank in A, is replaced by the constant rank $\sum(a_{j1} b_{ji})$, $\sum(a_{j2} b_{ji})$, $\cdots$, $\sum(a_{jn} b_{ji})$. And $i = 1, 2, \cdots$, m.

Below, we will show how the above solutions were derived.

Using the principle of extreme values in mathematical analysis, we can find the minimum by taking the partial derivatives over $f(p_{1i}, p_{2i}, \cdots, p_{ni})$ with respect to $p_{1i}, p_{2i}, \cdots, p_{ni}$. We must determine, and then set, these derivatives to 0. That is,

$$
\begin{cases}
\frac{\partial f}{\partial p_{1i}} = 2\sum(\sum_k^n a_{jk}p_{ki} - b_{ji})a_{j1} = 0 \\[2mm]
\frac{\partial f}{\partial p_{1i}} = 2\sum(\sum_k^n a_{jk}p_{ki} - b_{ji})a_{j2} = 0 \\[2mm]
\cdots \\[2mm]
\frac{\partial f}{\partial p_{1i}} = 2\sum(\sum_k^n a_{jk}p_{ki} - b_{ji})a_{jn} = 0
\end{cases}
$$

or,

$$
\begin{cases}
p_{1i}\sum(a_{j1})^2 + p_{2i}\sum(a_{j1}a_{j2}) + \cdots + p_{ni}\sum(a_{j1}a_{jn}) - \sum(a_{j1}b_{ji}) = 0 \\[2mm]
p_{1i}\sum(a_{j1}a_{j2}) + p_{2i}\sum(a_{j2})^2 + \cdots + p_{ni}\sum(a_{j2}a_{jn}) - \sum(a_{j2}b_{ji}) = 0 \\[2mm]
\cdots \\[2mm]
p_{1i}\sum(a_{j1}a_{jn}) + p_{2i}\sum(a_{jn}a_{j2}) + \cdots + p_{ni}\sum(a_{jn})^2 - \sum(a_{jn}b_{ji}) = 0
\end{cases}
$$

Let A be the coefficient matrix of this equation group concerning $p_{1i}, p_{2i}, \cdots, p_{ni}$. If $d = |A| \neq 0$, then this equation group has only one result, which is

$$
p_{1i} = \frac{d_1}{d}, p_{2i} = \frac{d_2}{d}, \cdots, p_{ni} = \frac{d_n}{d},
$$

where d_i is the determinant of the matrix after the ith rank in A is replaced by the constant rank $\sum(a_{j1}b_{ji})$, $\sum(a_{j2}b_{ji})$, $\cdots$, $\sum(a_{jn}b_{ji})$, and $i = 1, 2, \cdots, m$.

In the above, p_{ji} represents the probabilities of $Y = y_i$ under the condition $X = x_j$, $i = 1, 2, \cdots, m$; and $j = 1, 2, \cdots, n$. In order to assure the probabilistic significance, the results should be:

$$
p_{ji} := p_{ji}/(p_{1i} + p_{2i} + \cdots + p_{ni}),
$$

where, $i = 1, 2, \cdots, m$; $j = 1, 2, \cdots, n$.

Another measurement of $X \to Y$ is its degree of support. Because this is a probabilistic dependency rule, we define a metric to check the degree of $M_{Y|X}$ which fits the given fact set. For the fact $(a, b) \in DS$, $a = (a_1, a_2, \cdots, a_n) \in S(X)$ and $b = (b_1, b_2, \cdots, b_m) \in S(Y)$, let $b' = (b'_1, b'_2, \cdots, b'_m) = a \cdot M_{Y|X}$. Then the fitting error is defined as

$$error(b, b') = |b - b'| = \sum_{i=1}^{m} |b_i - b_i'|$$

If $error(b, b')$ is less than, or equal to, some user specified maximum allowance error e, then fact (a, b) supports the conditional probability matrix $M_{Y|X}$. We let N be the size of DS that is the data set of interest, and M be the number of data supporting $M_{Y|X}$ in DS. Then, the support of $X \to Y$ is defined as

$$support(X, Y) = M/N$$

If $support(X, Y) \geq minsupp$, $X \to Y$ with $M_{Y|X}$ can be extracted as valid rule.

Algorithm. We now give the algorithm for the above statistical model.

Algorithm 4.2 *MLP*
   Input: *D: probabilistic database, minsupp and e: threshold values;*
   Output: *$X \to Y$: causal rule, $M_{Y|X}$: the conditional probability matrix of Y given X;*

   Begin
   call *the procedure Generatedata;*
   Let *$DS \leftarrow$ a set of probabilities in D with respect to item variables X and Y;*
   Calculate $M_{Y|X}$;
   For $(a, b) \in DS$ **do**
      Statistics *M the number of data supporting $M_{Y|X}$ in DS for e;*
      If $M/|DS| \geq minsupp$ **then**
         Output $X \to Y$ *with* $M_{Y|X}$ *and support(X, Y);*
   End.

The algorithm MLP generates causal rules of the form $X \to Y$ attached to a conditional probability matrix $M_{Y|X}$, from a given probabilistic database D.

It firstly calls in the procedure *Generatedata* to preprocess the data in D. Then, for each pair of interesting item variables X and Y, the conditional probability matrix $M_{Y|X}$ is obtained from the database by considering each pair of quantitative items of X and Y.

The above method can synthesize the probability meanings of all point values of a sample. We now illustrate the use of this algorithm by Example 4.4.

Example 4.4 *For a given probabilistic database, X and Y are two item variables. Let $R(X) = \{x_1, x_2\}$ and $R(Y) = \{y_1, y_2, y_3\}$. Twenty two probabilities are generated by the procedure Generatedata, as shown in Table 4.7.*

Table 4.7. Probabilities of X and Y

EMP#	$p(x_1)$	$p(x_2)$	$p(y_1)$	$p(y_2)$	$p(y_3)$
01	1	0	0.5	0.3	0.2
02	0	1	0.1	0.6	0.3
03	0.9	0.1	0.46	0.33	0.21
04	0.1	0.9	0.14	0.57	0.29
05	0.8	0.2	0.42	0.36	0.22
06	0.2	0.8	0.18	0.54	0.28
07	0.7	0.3	0.38	0.39	0.23
08	0.3	0.7	0.22	0.51	0.27
09	0.6	0.4	0.34	0.42	0.24
10	0.4	0.6	0.26	0.48	0.26
11	0.5	0.5	0.3	0.45	0.25
12	0.95	0.05	0.48	0.315	0.205
13	0.05	0.95	0.12	0.585	0.295
14	0.85	0.15	0.44	0.345	0.215
15	0.15	0.85	0.16	0.555	0.285
16	0.75	0.25	0.4	0.375	0.225
17	0.25	0.75	0.2	0.525	0.275
18	0.65	0.35	0.36	0.405	0.235
19	0.35	0.65	0.24	0.495	0.265
20	0.55	0.45	0.32	0.435	0.245
21	0.855	0.145	0.3	0.4	0.4
22	0.654	0.346	0.4	0.2	0.4

We can acquire a great deal of probabilistic information for the rule from these data by using the above method. That is, the following equation group can be established from the data as follows,

$$\begin{cases} 8.131241p_{11} + 3.427759p_{21} = 4.3121 \\ 3.427759p_{11} + 7.013241p_{21} = 2.4079 \end{cases}$$

So, we have,

$$\begin{cases} p_{11} = 0.4856369 \\ p_{21} = 0.1059786 \end{cases}$$

In the same way, we can obtain,

$$\begin{cases} 8.131241p_{12} + 3.427759p_{22} = 4.41105 \\ 3.427759p_{12} + 7.013241p_{22} = 5.17395 \end{cases}$$

and we then have,

$$\begin{cases} p_{12} = 0.2793863 \\ p_{22} = 0.595241 \end{cases}$$

Hence,

$$\begin{cases} 8.131241p_{13} + 3.427759p_{23} = 2.92135 \\ 3.427759p_{13} + 7.013241p_{23} = 2.87365 \end{cases}$$

And we have,

$$\begin{cases} p_{13} = 0.4059914 \\ p_{23} = 0.2949115 \end{cases}$$

In order to assure the probability significance level of the prior probabilities, the results should be:

$p_{11} = p_{11}/(p_{11}+p_{12}+p_{13}) = 0.4856369/(0.4856369+0.2793863+0.4059914) = 0.414715$, *and*

$$p_{12} = 0.238585, p_{13} = 0.3467$$
$$p_{21} = 0.10639, p_{22} = 0.597553, p_{23} = 0.296057$$

That is, we acquire a conditional probability matrix $M_{Y|X}$ for the above rule as follows

$$M_{Y|X} = \begin{bmatrix} p_{11} & p_{12} & p_{13} \\ p_{21} & p_{22} & p_{23} \end{bmatrix} = \begin{bmatrix} 0.414715 & 0.238585 & 0.3467 \\ 0.10639 & 0.597553 & 0.296057 \end{bmatrix}$$

If the allowance error e is equal to, or less than, 0.3, then $X \to Y$ (with conditional probability matrix $M_{Y|X}$) can be extracted as a valid probabilistic rule, with a support of 1.

4.5.5 Improvements

As we have seen from algorithm MLP, the statistical model is blind. So the results are very rough. Also, some rules may be lost for allowance error e. We now present two optimal algorithms: random search and partition search.

Random Search Algorithm. In algorithm MLP, Bayesian rules and regression techniques are applied to fit the data set. In fact, if $X \to Y$ with conditional probability matrix $M_{Y|X}$, and a high support, $supp$, can be extracted as a valid probabilistic rule, then there are $supp * N$ data satisfying $M_{Y|X}$ for the allowance error e; where N is the number of data in the interest set. Therefore, we can randomly choose n data in the set to directly solve $M_{Y|X}$, where n is $R(X)$. We now use the data in Example 4.4 to demonstrate this argument.

First, for $n = 2$, let $EMP\# = 3$ and $EMP\# = 13$ be the randomly selected data in Table 4.7. Then the possible $M_{Y|X}$ is solved as follows.

$$\begin{cases} 0.9p_{11} + 0.1p_{21} = 0.46 \\ 0.05p_{11} + 0.95p_{21} = 0.12 \end{cases}$$

So, we have,

$$\begin{cases} p_{11} = 0.5 \\ p_{21} = 0.1 \end{cases}$$

In the same way, we can obtain,

$$\begin{cases} 0.9p_{12} + 0.1p_{22} = 0.33 \\ 0.05p_{12} + 0.95p_{22} = 0.585 \end{cases}$$

We then have,

$$\begin{cases} p_{12} = 0.3 \\ p_{22} = 0.6 \end{cases}$$

Hence,

$$\begin{cases} 0.9p_{13} + 0.1p_{23} = 0.21 \\ 0.05p_{13} + 0.95p_{23} = 0.295 \end{cases}$$

and

$$\begin{cases} p_{13} = 0.2 \\ p_{23} = 0.3 \end{cases}$$

In order to assure the probability significance level of the prior probabilities, the results should be:

$$\begin{aligned} p_{11} &= p_{11}/(p_{11} + p_{12} + p_{13}) \\ &= 0.5/(0.5 + 0.3 + 0.2) \\ &= 0.5 \end{aligned}$$

and

$$p_{12} = 0.3, p_{13} = 0.2$$
$$p_{21} = 0.1, p_{22} = 0.6, p_{23} = 0.3$$

That is, we acquire a conditional probability matrix $M_{Y|X}$ for the above rule as follows

$$M_{Y|X} = \begin{bmatrix} p_{11} & p_{12} & p_{13} \\ p_{21} & p_{22} & p_{23} \end{bmatrix} = \begin{bmatrix} 0.5 & 0.3 & 0.2 \\ 0.1 & 0.6 & 0.3 \end{bmatrix}$$

Then, for Table 4.7, we check how much data fits the matrix $M_{Y|X}$ for the allowance error, e. Let $e = 0.08$, then the former 20 data can fit matrix $M_{Y|X}$ for the allowance error 0.08. We can also apply algorithm MLP to merge the 20 data so as to obtain a better matrix for the data. In this example, the new matrix is the same as the above matrix, $M_{Y|X}$.

Finally, we check how much data fits the new matrix for the allowance error e for Table 4.7. We let M be the number of data fitting the new matrix in Table 4.7, and $minsupp = 0.6$. Then the support is M/N. If $M/N \geq minsupp$, $X \to Y$ with $M_{Y|X}$ and the support of M/N can be extracted as a valid rule. For this example, $M/N = 20/22 = 0.909 > minsupp = 0.6$. So, $X \to Y$ with matrix

$$M_{Y|X} = \begin{bmatrix} 0.5 & 0.3 & 0.2 \\ 0.1 & 0.6 & 0.3 \end{bmatrix}$$

and the support 0.909 can be extracted as a valid rule.

This algorithm for random search is designed as follows.

Algorithm 4.3 *RandomSearch*
   Input: *D: probabilistic database, minsupp and e: threshold values;*
   Output: *X → Y: causal rule, $M_{Y|X}$: the conditional probability matrix;*

   Begin
   Let *DS ← a set of probabilities of item variables X and Y in D;*
   For *n selected random data in DS* **do***;*
      Begin
      Calculate $M_{Y|X}$ *using R;*
      For *(a, b) ∈ DS* **do**
      Statistics *M the number of data supporting $M_{Y|X}$ in DS for e;*
      If *M/|DS| ≥ minsupp* **then**
         Begin
         Output *X → Y with $M_{Y|X}$ and support(X,Y);*
         Goto *LL;*
         end
      end
   LL: **End.**

The algorithm *RandomSearch* is also used to generate causal rules of the form $X \to Y$, attached to a conditional probability matrix $M_{Y|X}$, from a given probabilistic database, D. However, this algorithm is performed on a set of instances (random samples). So it is more efficient than the algorithm MLP.

Partition Search Algorithm. Using the random search algorithm, weaknesses in the algorithm MLP can be overcome. In other words, we can discover all possible rules in a data set of interest, for which the results are more accurate than those in algorithm MLP. However, this model has one fatal problem: its running time in the worst case, is increased exponentially as

$$\frac{C_N^n}{C_M^n} * t,$$

where t is the time taken solving matrix $M_{Y|X}$ by n random data, C_N^n is the number of all possible selections of n random data in DS, and C_M^n is the number of all possible selections of n random data in the data set, where its data supports a matrix $M_{Y|X}$.

To solve this problem, we propose to use heuristic information to reduce the running time to an acceptable level. We first partition the data set into several subsets, where the data in each subset has a specific property. Then, a random search model is applied to these subsets. We now illustrate this method using the data in Table 4.7.

First, we partition the data into groups:

- $Group1 = \{1, 3, 5, 12, 14, 16\}$ with property $p(x_1) > p(x_2)$, $p(y_1) > p(y_2)$ and $p(y_1) > p(y_3)$;
- $Group2 = \{2, 4, 6, 8, 13, 15, 17, 19\}$ with property $p(x_1) < p(x_2)$, $p(y_1) < p(y_2)$ and $p(y_1) < p(y_3)$;
- $Group3 = \{7, 9, 18, 20\}$ with property $p(x_1) > p(x_2)$, $p(y_2) > p(y_1)$ and $p(y_2) > p(y_3)$; and
- $Group4 = \{10, 11, 21, 22\}$ the remaining data.

We can then randomly choose n data in each subset to directly solve $M_{Y|X}$, where n is $R(X)$. Suppose that the data set of interest, DS, is partitioned into k subsets: $DS_1, DS_2, \cdots, DS_k$, with sizes: $N_1, N_2, \cdots, N_k$. The running time in the worst case is

$$(C_{N_1}^n + C_{N_2}^n + \cdots + C_{N_{k-1}}^n + \frac{C_{N_k}^n}{C_{M_k}^n}) * t$$

where $C_{N_i}^n$ is the number of all possible selections of n random data in DS_i, and $C_{M_k}^n$ is the number of all possible selections of n random data in a subset of DS_k, where its data supports a matrix $M_{Y|X}$. Obviously, the partition search is faster than the random search.

The algorithm for partition search is designed as follows.

Algorithm 4.4 *PartitionSearch*
   Input: *D: probabilistic database, minsupp and e: threshold values;*
   Output: *X → Y: causal rule, $M_{Y|X}$: the conditional probability matrix of Y given X;*

Begin
 Let $DS \leftarrow$ *a set of probabilities of item variables X and Y in D;*
 Let $PS \leftarrow$ *all partitioned subsets of DS;*
 For *each subset A in PS* **do**
  Begin
  Let $R \leftarrow$ *select randomly n data in A;*
  Calculate $M_{Y|X}$ *using R;*
  For $(a, b) \in DS$ **do**
  Statistics M *the number of data supporting $M_{Y|X}$ in DS for e;*
  If $M/|DS| \geq minsupp$ **then**
   Begin
    Output $X \rightarrow Y$ *with $M_{Y|X}$ and support(X, Y);*
    Goto *LL;*
   End
  End
 LL: **End**.

The algorithm *PartitionSearch* is an alternative approach for generating causal rules of the form $X \rightarrow Y$, attached to a conditional probability matrix $M_{Y|X}$, from a given probabilistic database D. This algorithm is more effective and efficient than the two former algorithms, *MLP* and *RandomSearch*.

4.6 Summary

In this chapter, we have proposed a new approach for mining causality among multi-value variables in large databases, based on partition, where causality is represented by the form $X \rightarrow Y$, with a conditional probability matrix $M_{Y|X}$ ([Pearl 1988]). To end this chapter, a simple comparison with previous work, and a summary, are presented.

As we have seen, past research into mining association rules ([Agrawal-Imielinski-Swami 1993, Piatetsky 1991]) and quantitative association rules ([Han-Cai-Cercone 1993, Srikant-Agrawal 1996]) is not only useful, but also paves the way for identifying causality ([Silverstein-Brin-Motwani-Ullman 1998]). There has also been significant work done in mining causal relationships using the Bayesian analysis ([Cooper 1997, Heckerman 1995]).

With Bayesian learning techniques (such as described in [Cooper 1997, Heckerman 1995, Pearl 1988]), a user typically specifies a prior probability distribution over a space of possible Bayesian networks. These algorithms then search for that network, which maximizes the posterior probability of the data provided. In general, the algorithms attempt to balance the complexity of the network with its fit to the data.

The main differences between our causality mining model and previous methods are summarized below.

(1) Item-based association rules and quantitative association rules can still be discovered as two special causal forms in our model. In other words, discovering causal rules is a generalization of mining item-based association rules and quantitative association rules. In particular, *good partition* on items as a concept is proposed.

(2) A model for partitioning the quantitative items into item variables has been presented, where each item variable is a set of certain quantitative items with the same property (or attribute). In particular, a *good partition* on quantitative items as a concept is proposed.

(3) Causality in databases is mined, and represented by the form $X \to Y$, with the conditional probability matrix $M_{Y|X}$.

(4) Our model for discovering causality in databases is focused on causal rules of interest, which satisfy three conditions: Piatetsky-Shapiro's argument, minimum support, and minimum confidence.

(5) Another important difference is that our model offers a method for optimizing conditional probability matrices of causal rules (see Chapter 5), which merges unnecessary information in extracted causal rules. It seems that this model might be used to optimize knowledge in intelligent systems.

Mining causality among variables in large databases is very useful for practical applications such as decision-making and planning. It is still an important and prevailing topic in machine learning. Accordingly, some mining models for causality in databases, such as the LCD algorithm ([Cooper 1997]) and the CU-path algorithm ([Silverstein 1998]), which are constraint-based for causal discovery, have been proposed for mining causal relationships in market basket data. However, these methods are of only limited efficiency on causal relationships between items. Discovering causality among variables in large databases still requires further exploration. For this reason, we have built a model for mining such causality in large databases which is based on partitioning. The key points of this chapter are as follows:

(1) Defined 'property tolerant' and 'associated tolerant'.

(2) Presented a new model to partition items into item variables for a given database. This model decomposes the 'bad item variables' and composes the 'not-good item variables'.

(3) Proposed a model for discovering causal rules of interest from databases based on this partition. In particular, item-based association rules and quantitative association rules were also extracted as specific forms.

(4) Proposed a statistical model for discovering causal rules from probabilistic databases using Bayesian rule.

(5) Two improved models, random search algorithm and partition search algorithm, were presented.

5. Causal Rule Analysis

Causal rules attached to matrices can be used to capture causal relationships among multi-value variables in data. However, because the causal relations are represented in a non-linear form (a matrix), it is rather difficult to make decisions using the causal rules. Therefore, one of the main challenges is to reduce the complexity of the representation. As important research into post data mining, this chapter firstly establishes a method of optimizing causal rules which tackles the 'useless' information in the conditional probability matrices of the extracted rules. Then, techniques for constructing polynomial functions for approximate causality in data are advocated. Finally, we propose an approach for finding the approximate polynomial causality between two variables from a given data set by fitting.

This chapter is organized as follows. We begin in Section 5.1 by introducing causal rule analysis. A problem statement is presented in Section 5.2. In Section 5.3, we construct a method for improving causal rules so as to reduce the useless information in their matrices once causal rules are extracted. In Section 5.4, we establish an encoder technique and present a method of constructing a linear approximating function for the simplest causality. We then suggest a method for handling higher-degree polynomial problems in Section 5.5. In Section 5.6, we propose an alternative approach for finding polynomial causality by fitting. This is followed by a summary.

5.1 Introduction

Because causality among multi-value variables is represented in conditional probability matrices, it often suffers from NP-hard implementations ([Cooper 1987]). In particular, the amount of probabilistic information necessary for computation is often overwhelming. Therefore, approximating conditional probability matrices is one of the most important issues we face. Using encoding, this chapter presents an *approximate polynomial function* for non-linear causality.

Though causal rules with matrices have been widely accepted as a suitable, general and natural knowledge representation framework for decision making under uncertainty, the computation has been proven to be NP-hard as might have been expected ([Cooper 1987, Shimony-Charniak 1990]). This has generally prevented problem formulations from utilizing the full representational capabilities of the framework. For example, an $n * m$ conditional probability matrix needs at least $n * m$ storage units to save its $n * m$ probabilities (elements). And operating the causal rules is a non-linear procedure which depends upon the multiplication of matrices. Therefore, the sizes of n and m heavily impact on the efficiency of the framework. This leads to low-efficiency decision making, *although the problems faced may be tractable*. For efficiency, in this chapter, we aim at constructing an approximate polynomial function to replace a non-polynomial causal rule, by encoding. This model requires, at most, $2 * Max\{n, m\}$ storage units.

In order to apply causal rules efficiently, we design a causal rule analysis. This causal analysis consists of a three-phase approach. In the first phase, a technique is proposed for reducing useless (unnecessary) information for the causal rules mined. Obviously, this technique of reducing useless information is extremely useful for optimizing knowledge in intelligent systems. In the second phase, a method for constructing polynomial functions is advocated. This approximates causality in data. In the final phase, we propose an approach for finding approximate polynomial causality by fitting.

5.2 Problem Statement

As described in Chapter 4, because the partition on data is blind, relative to a given database, the point-value space of a variable is difficult to fit in with real-world applications. Or, if only the probabilities of some point-values are greater than, or equal to, $minconf$, then others can be taken as unnecessary information in the conditional probability matrix.

On the other hand, causal rules attached to matrices can be used to capture the causal relations among multi-value variables in data. However, because the causal relations are represented in a non-linear form (matrix), it is rather difficult to make decisions by the rules. We now illustrate this problem by an example.

Example 5.1 *In many cracked criminal cases, suspicious footprints discovered at the scene of a crime are useful for estimating the height and weight of a suspect. Let X denote the length of a footprint of a suspect, and Y the height of the suspect. For simplicity, suppose the domain of X be $\{long, middle, short\}$ and the domain of Y be $\{tall, middle, small\}$. Experience shows that Y is relatively dependent on X. For a data set, D, of the length of footprints and the height of people in a certain town, the conditional probability matrix of Y, given X, is as follows.*

$$M_{Y|X} = \begin{bmatrix} 0.8 & 0.1 & 0.1 \\ 0.1 & 0.8 & 0.1 \\ 0.1 & 0.1 & 0.8 \end{bmatrix}$$

Now, suppose one clue is that 'the probabilities that the length X of a suspicious footprint is long, middle and short are 0.7, 0.2 and 0.1, respectively', then we have,

$$[0.7 \ 0.2 \ 0.1] \begin{bmatrix} 0.8 & 0.1 & 0.1 \\ 0.1 & 0.8 & 0.1 \\ 0.1 & 0.1 & 0.8 \end{bmatrix} = [0.59 \ 0.24 \ 0.17]$$

Therefore, $y = (0.59, 0.24, 0.17)$ is the result that we require. This means, 0.59, 0.24 and 0.17 are the probabilities that the height of the suspect is tall, middle and small, respectively.

In Example 5.1, the operations are obviously non-linear. Let us consider some probabilities of X and the corresponding values of Y, which are listed below.

$p(x_1)$	$p(x_2)$	$p(x_3)$	$p(y_1)$	$p(y_2)$	$p(y_3)$
0.9	0.1	0	0.73	0.17	0.1
0	1	0	0.1	0.8	0.1
0	0.7	0.3	0.1	0.59	0.31
0.6	0	0.4	0.52	0.1	0.38
0.1	0.1	0.8	0.17	0.17	0.66

Intuitively, there is no direct linear relationship between $(p(x_1), p(x_2), p(x_3))$ and $(p(y_1), p(y_2), p(y_3))$ in the above table. Now we encode the results using the following functions:

$$E_X(x) = p(x_1)10^2 + p(x_2)10^4 + p(x_3)10^6$$
$$E_Y(y) = p(y_1)10^2 + p(y_2)10^4 + p(y_3)10^6$$

Then the above table can be transformed into a table of the form:

$E_X(x)$	$E_Y(y)$
1090	101773
10000	108010
307000	315910
400060	381052
801010	661717

Now we take $E_X(x)$ and $E_Y(y)$ as an ordered pair of the form $(E_X(x), E_Y(y))$. In fact, (1090, 101773), (10000, 108010), (307000, 315910), (400060, 381052), and (801010, 661717) are fitted into a line. The line is of the form:

$$E_Y(y) = 0.7E_X(x) + 101010.$$

Once the above formulas are determined, then for all x, we can determine $E_Y(y)$ by those formulas. Further, we can determine $p(y_1), p(y_2)$ and $p(y_3)$ by $E_Y^{-1}(y)$, where $E_Y^{-1}(y)$ is the decorder function of $E_Y(y)$. For example, let $x = (0.1, 0.3, 0.6)$, then $E_X(x) = 603010$. By using the above formulae, $E_Y(y) = 523117$. So, by using $E_Y^{-1}(y)$, $p(y_1) = 0.17$, $p(y_2) = 0.31$ and $p(y_3) = 0.52$. As a matter of fact, this result is the same as the result obtained by using Pearl's inference model (see [Pearl 1988] for this model). Hence, we can replace $M_{Y|X}$ with the above function.

This means that we can represent the causality in Example 5.1 by using a polynomial function. As we have stated in Chapter 1, knowledge representation is an important step in the post data-mining of KDD. Therefore, the above function can be used in causality mining.

As one of the phases of causal rule analysis, we will establish an approximation function similar to the above formulae to close the causal rules with matrices by encoding. More formally, for a causal rule $X \rightarrow Y$, let the domain of X be $R(X) = \{x_1, x_2, ..., x_m\}$, the domain of Y be $R(Y) = \{y_1, y_2, ..., y_n\}$, and the conditional probability matrix be $M_{Y|X}$. Suppose $s = (p(x_1), p(x_2), \cdots, p(x_m))$ be an observation, $P(Y_P) = (p(y_1), p(y_2), \cdots, p(y_n))$ be the result obtained by operating the matrix, and $P(Y_Z) = (p(y_1'), p(y_2'), \cdots, p(y_n'))$ be the result obtained by operating the corresponding approximation function. Our goal is to find the approximate solution $P(Y_Z)$ by using the approximation function such that

$$||P(Y_Z) - P(Y_P)|| \leq \theta$$

where,

$$||P(Y_Z) - P(Y_P)|| = ||p(y_1') - p(y_1)|| + ||p(y_2') - p(y_2)|| + \cdots + ||p(y_n') - p(y_n)||$$

where $\theta > 0$ is small enough.

Once the function is constructed for the above causal rule, $M_{Y|X}$ can be approximated by this function. The storage space of this rule, as part of a node in a belief network, can be reduced from $O(mn)$ to $O(m)$, and its running time can be decreased from $O(mn)$ to $O(m)$. Hence, the task of causality mining should be to find approximate polynomial functions in databases. Or it can be taken as a step of post-data-mining such that causal rules attached to matrices are represented in linear functions after they are discovered.

5.2.1 Related Concepts

Before move on to construct linear functions for causality, we recall some of the concepts that we use. Throughout this chapter, upper case letters, such as $A, B, \cdots$, represent random variables and lower case letters such as $a, b, \cdots$

represent the possible assignments to the associated upper case letter random variable.

Definition 5.1 *Given a random variable A, the set of possible values for A (known as the range of A) will be denoted by $R(A)$. For $x \in R(A)$, x is the point value of A. And $|R(A)|$ denotes the the number of possible values of A.*

For example, let the possible values of the random variable A be *red, green, yellow, blue, purple*. Then, $R(A) = \{$red, green, yellow, blue, purple$\}$, and $|R(A)| = 5$.

Definition 5.2 *Given a random variable A, all point values of A can construct a vector such as $(x_1, x_2, ..., x_n)$. Each state of A can be described by its point values associated with probabilities in the vector. That is, $(P(x_1) = a_1, P(x_2) = a_2, ..., P(x_n) = a_n)$ is a state (or observation) of A. This state will be written as $(a_1, a_2, ..., a_n)$. All states of A construct the state space of A, which will be denoted by $S(A)$.*

For example, let the possible values of the random variable A be *red, green, yellow, blue, purple*, then $(P(red) = 0.3, P(green) = 0.25, P(yellow) = 0.05, P(blue) = 0.11, P(purple) = 0.29) \in S(A)$; or $(0.3, 0.25, 0.05, 0.11, 0.29) \in S(A)$ is a state of A.

There are infinite elements in $S(A)$. In this chapter, we concentrate on a random sample space $\Omega(A)$ of $S(A)$, because it is impossible to give consideration to all elements in $S(A)$. Let the sample space have ℓ elements in $\Omega(A)$, where ℓ as the capacity of $\Omega(A)$, denoted by $\Im(\Omega(A))$.

Definition 5.3 *$\Re$ is a set of rational numbers. $\Re^+$ is a set of positive rational numbers.*

Definition 5.4 *Given a random variable $A \in V$, a one-to-one mapping $E_A : S(A) \to \Re^+$, is referred to as an encoder for A.*

The requirement that an encoder is one-to-one mapping is necessary to assure that the encoder is a reversible mode because we need to be able to recover the original probability values after they have been handled.

Definition 5.5 *Given a causal rule $X \to Y$, let $R(X) = \{x_1, x_2, \cdots, x_n\}$, $R(Y) = \{y_1, y_2, \cdots, y_m\}$, and let $a = (a_1, a_2, \cdots, a_n) \in S(X)$ be an observed value (or state) of X. Then the state $b = (b_1, b_2, \cdots, b_m) \in S(Y)$ of Y can be determined by the observed value and $M_{Y|X}$. That is,*

$$(a_1 \; a_2 \ldots a_n) M_{Y|X} = (b_1 \; b_2 \ldots b_m)$$

or

$$a M_{Y|X} = b \tag{5.1}$$

This is an alternative form of causality that is represented in a non-linear function.

5.3 Optimizing Causal Rules

This section carries out the first phase of causal rule analysis. It presents a method for reducing unnecessary information in matrices after causal rules are mined.

5.3.1 Unnecessary Information

If the probabilities of a row (or a column) of a conditional probability matrix satisfy $p(Y = y_i | X = x_j) < minconf$ for $i = i_0$ and $j = 1, 2, \cdots, m$ (or $i = 1, 2, \cdots, n$ and $j = j_0$), then this row (or column) is referred to as the *unnecessary information* in the matrix. For example, let us partition the domains of *Education* and *Salary* as

$$\{PostDoctor, Doctor, PostMaster, Master, Bachelor, UnderBachelor\}$$

and

$$\{[3500, +\infty), [2400, 3500), [0, 2400)\}$$

respectively, where X and Y stand for *Education* and *Salary*, respectively. The statistical results are from a database as listed in Table 5.1.

Table 5.1. Statistical results of interest data

Education	Salary	Number
PostDoctor	$[3500, +\infty)$	9000
	$[2100, 3500)$	900
	$[0, 2100)$	100
Doctor	$[3500, +\infty)$	8000
	$[2100, 3500)$	1900
	$[0, 2100)$	100
PostMaster	$[3500, +\infty)$	1000
	$[2100, 3500)$	7500
	$[0, 2100)$	1500
Master	$[3500, +\infty)$	3100
	$[2100, 3500)$	3100
	$[0, 2100)$	3800
Bachelor	$[3500, +\infty)$	2400
	$[2100, 3500)$	3800
	$[0, 2100)$	3800
UnderBachelor	$[3500, +\infty)$	2000
	$[2100, 3500)$	4000
	$[0, 2100)$	4000

According to the above model, $X \to Y$ can be extracted as a causal rule with the conditional probability matrix $M_{Y|X}$ as follows.

$$M_{Y|X}^1 = \begin{bmatrix} 0.9 & 0.09 & 0.01 \\ 0.8 & 0.19 & 0.01 \\ 0.1 & 0.75 & 0.15 \\ 0.31 & 0.31 & 0.38 \\ 0.24 & 0.38 & 0.38 \\ 0.2 & 0.4 & 0.4 \end{bmatrix}$$

In this conditional probability matrix, if $minconf = 0.6$, then $p(Y = y_i|X = Master) < minconf$, $p(Y = y_i|X = Bachelor) < minconf$, and $p(Y = y_i|X = Under Bachelor) < minconf$. That is, rows 4, 5 and 6 certainly contain unnecessary information. In fact, when given evidences are $(0,0,0,1,0,0)$, $(0,0,0,0,1,0)$, and $(0,0,0,0,0,1)$, the results propagated by the rule are $(0.31, 0.31, 0.38)$, $(0.24, 0.38, 0.38)$, and $(0.2, 0.4, 0.4)$. These results cannot be useful to applications. They must be reduced if possible. We now define a model to refine the extracted causal rules.

5.3.2 Merging Unnecessary Information

Let $X \longrightarrow Y$ be an extracted causal rule with conditional probability matrix $M_{Y|X}$. Assume the domain of X is $R(X) = \{x_1, x_2, ..., x_m\}$, and the domain of Y is $R(Y) = \{y_1, y_2, ..., y_n\}$. The problems of merging unnecessary information are outlined below:

(1) Finding out all columns $i_1, i_2, \cdots, i_s$, where any column i_k holds $p(y_{i_k}|x_j) < minconf$ for $j = 1, 2, \cdots, m$ and $k = 1, 2, \cdots, s$.
(2) Merging all columns $i_1, i_2, \cdots, i_s$ into column i_1 if $s > 1$, and deleting columns $i_2, \cdots, i_s$ from $M_{Y|X}$.
(3) Finding out all rows $i_1, i_2, \cdots, i_t$ where any row i_k holds $p(y_j|x_{i_k}) < minconf$ for $j = 1, 2, \cdots, n$ and $k = 1, 2, \cdots, t$.
(4) Merging all rows $i_1, i_2, \cdots, i_t$, into row i_1, if $t > 1$, and deleting rows $i_2, \cdots, i_t$ from $M_{Y|X}$.

A procedure for optimizing a given set of causal rules is designed as follows.

Procedure 5.1 *RefineRules*
begin
    Input: *NewCRSET: the set of interest causal rule;*
    Output: *RSET: the set of optimized causal rules;*
(1) **let** $RSET \leftarrow \emptyset$;
        for each rule $X \rightarrow Y$ with $M_{Y|X}$ in $NewCRSET$ **do begin**
(2)   **let** $col \leftarrow \emptyset$;
           for each column i of $M_{Y|X}$ **beginfor**
              for $j := 1$ **to** m **do**
                if $p(y_i|x_j) \geq minconf$ **then**
                    next i

$$\text{let } col \leftarrow col \cup \{i\};$$
$$\textbf{endfor}$$

(3)   **for** $j := 1$ **to** m **do**
               let $p_j \leftarrow 0$;
           for each $i \in col$ **do**
               for $j := 1$ **to** m **do**
                   let $p_j \leftarrow p_j + p(y_i|x_j)$;
           for $j := 1$ **to** m **do**
               let $p_j \leftarrow p_j/|col|$;
           for each $i \in col$ **do**
               delete column i from matrix $M_{Y|X}$;
           add $(p_1, p_2, \cdots, p_m)$ as a new column of $M_{Y|X}$;

(4)   **let** $r \leftarrow \emptyset$;
           for each row i of $M_{Y|X}$ **beginfor**
               for $j := 1$ **to** n **do**
                   if $p(y_j|x_i) \geq minconf$ **then**
                       next i
                   else let $r \leftarrow r \cup \{i\}$;
           endfor

(5)   **for** $j := 1$ **to** n **do**
               let $p_j \leftarrow 0$;
           for each $i \in r$ **do**
               for $j := 1$ **to** n **do**
                   let $p_j \leftarrow p_j + p(y_j|x_i)$;
           for $j := 1$ **to** n **do**
               let $p_j \leftarrow p_j/|r|$;
           for each $i \in r$ **do begin**
               delete row i from matrix $M_{Y|X}$;
               add $(p_1, p_2, \cdots, p_n)$ as a new row of $M_{Y|X}$;
           endfor

(6)   **let** $RSET \leftarrow$ optimized rule $X \rightarrow Y$ with $M_{Y|X}$;
     endfor
   endall;

The procedure *RefineRules* is used to optimize all causal rules of interest in *NewCRSET* by merging unnecessary information into corresponding conditional probability matrices. Step (1) consists of the initialization of the procedure. Optimization is performed in a for-loop as follows.

Step (2) is to find the set, *col*, of columns $i_1, i_2, \cdots, i_s$, where any column i_k holds $p(y_{i_k}|x_j) < minconf$ for $j = 1, 2, \cdots, m$ and $k = 1, 2, \cdots, s$.

Step (3) merges the columns $i_1, i_2, \cdots, i_s$ into a single column i_1, if $s > 1$, and deletes columns $i_2, \cdots, i_s$ from $M_{Y|X}$.

Step (4) is to find the set, r, of rows $i_1, i_2, \cdots, i_t$ where, any row i_k holds $p(y_j|x_{i_k}) < minconf$ for $j = 1, 2, \cdots, n$, and $k = 1, 2, \cdots, t$.

Step (5) is to merge the rows $i_1, i_2, \cdots, i_t$ into a single row i_1 if $t > 1$, and delete rows $i_2, \cdots, i_t$ from $M_{Y|X}$.

The optimized causal rules are saved into $RSET$.

We now demonstrate the use of this model using the above rules. As a matter of fact, when $X = Master$, $X = Bachelor$, and $X = UnderBachelor$, we cannot determine what salary will be earned. In order to reduce this unnecessary information, we can merge these three quantitative items into the quantitative item $M\&U$. Hence, the above data can be reduced, as shown in Table 5.2.

Table 5.2. Statistical results of interest data

Education	Salary	Number
PostDoctor	$[3500, +\infty)$	9000
	$[2100, 3500)$	900
	$[0, 2100)$	100
Doctor	$[3500, +\infty)$	8000
	$[2100, 3500)$	1900
	$[0, 2100)$	100
PostMaster	$[3500, +\infty)$	1000
	$[2100, 3500)$	7500
	$[0, 2100)$	1500
M&U	$[3500, +\infty)$	7500
	$[2100, 3500)$	10900
	$[0, 2100)$	11600

Hence, for the following causal rule $X \to Y$, with the conditional probability matrix $M_{Y|X}$, the domain of X is $R(X) = \{PostDoctor, Doctor, PostMaster, M\&U\}$, and the domain of Y is $R(Y) = \{[3500, +\infty), [2100, 3500), [0, 2100)\}$.

$$
M_{Y|X}^2 = \begin{bmatrix} 0.9 & 0.09 & 0.01 \\ 0.8 & 0.19 & 0.01 \\ 0.1 & 0.75 & 0.15 \\ 0.25 & 0.363 & 0.387 \end{bmatrix}
$$

Theorem 5.1 *Merging of the row for unnecessary information is reasonable.*

Proof: In the above merge, rows $i_1, i_2, \cdots, i_t$ refer to unnecessary information, if all rows satisfy $p(y_j|x_{i_k}) < minconf$ for $j = 1, 2, \cdots, n$, and $k = 1, 2, \cdots, t$. Rows $i_1, i_2, \cdots, i_t$ are all merged as row i_1 with $p(y_j|x_{i_1}) = (p(y_j|x_{i_1}) + p(y_j|x_{i_2}) + \cdots + p(y_j|x_{i_t}))/t$, for $j = 1, 2, \cdots, n$. Certainly,

$$
\sum_{j=1}^{n} p(y_j|x_{i_1}) = (p(y_1|x_{i_1}) + p(y_1|x_{i_2}) + \cdots + p(y_1|x_{i_t}))/t
$$
$$
+ (p(y_2|x_{i_1}) + p(y_2|x_{i_2}) + \cdots + p(y_2|x_{i_t}))/t
$$

$$+ \cdots$$
$$+ (p(y_n|x_{i_1}) + p(y_n|x_{i_2}) + \cdots + p(y_n|x_{i_t}))/t$$
$$= (1 + 1 + \cdots + 1)/t = 1$$

Hence, the merge of the row for unnecessary information is reasonable.

$$\triangledown$$

5.3.3 Merging Items with Identical Properties

As we have seen, this merging of quantitative items can improve the probability matrix. On the other hand, when $X = PostDoctor$ and $X = Doctor$, we can determine that a salary is in $[3500, +\infty)$ with higher confidence. Such quantitative items are called **items with identical property**. For the same reason, we can merge these two quantitative items into a quantitative item $P\&D$. Hence, the above data can be reduced as shown in Table 5.3.

Table 5.3. Statistical results of interest data

Education	Salary	Number
P&D	$[3500, +\infty)$	17000
	$[2100, 3500)$	2800
	$[0, 2100)$	200
PostMaster	$[3500, +\infty)$	1000
	$[2100, 3500)$	7500
	$[0, 2100)$	1500
M&U	$[3500, +\infty)$	7500
	$[2100, 3500)$	10900
	$[0, 2100)$	11600

Hence, the causal rule $X \rightarrow Y$ with the conditional probability matrix $M_{Y|X}$ is as follows, where the domain of X is $R(X) = \{P\&D, PostMaster, M\&U\}$, and the domain of Y is $R(Y) = \{[3500, +\infty), [2100, 3500), [0, 2100)\}$.

$$M_{Y|X}^3 = \begin{bmatrix} 0.85 & 0.14 & 0.01 \\ 0.1 & 0.75 & 0.15 \\ 0.25 & 0.363 & 0.387 \end{bmatrix}$$

Let $X \rightarrow Y$ be an extracted causal rule with conditional probability matrix $M_{Y|X}$. Assume the domain of X is $R(X) = \{x_1, x_2, ..., x_m\}$, and the domain of Y is $R(Y) = \{y_1, y_2, ..., y_n\}$. The problems of merging such quantitative items are formally described below:

(1) finding out all columns $i_1, i_2, \cdots, i_s$ where column i_k holds $p(y_{i_k}|x_j) \geq minconf$ at some j $(1 \leq j \leq m)$ and $k = 1, 2, \cdots, s$.
(2) merging all columns $i_1, i_2, \cdots, i_s$ into column i_1 if $s > 1$, and deleting columns $i_2, \cdots, i_s$ from $M_{Y|X}$.

(3) finding out all rows $i_1, i_2, \cdots, i_t$ where row i_k holds $p(y_j|x_{i_k}) \geq minconf$ at some j $(1 \leq j \leq m)$ and $k = 1, 2, \cdots, t$.

(4) merging all rows $i_1, i_2, \cdots, i_t$ into row i_1 if $t > 1$, and deleting rows $i_2, \cdots, i_t$ from $M_{Y|X}$.

The algorithm for merging quantitative items with identical properties is similar to the above procedure for reducing unnecessary information, so we omit it here.

Theorem 5.2 *Merging of a column for unnecessary information is reasonable.*

Proof: The proof is similar to the proof of Theorem 5.1.

$$\nabla$$

Above, we have illustrated that causal rules are useful for reasoning and decision under uncertainty. When such rules are applied, the probabilities of the merged point-values are added altogether as the probability of a new point-value. This is used as a substitute for the merged point-values. For example, let an evidence be $(0.7, 0.1, 0.08, 0.08, 0.02, 0.02)$ for $M_{Y|X}^1$. If this is used as an inference in $M_{Y|X}^3$, the evidence $(0.7, 0.1, 0.08, 0.08, 0.02, 0.02)$ needs to merge into $(0.8, 0.08, 0.12)$. In this way, we can obtain $Y = (0.718, 0.216, 0.066)$. In other words, 0.718 is the probability that a person can earn a salary within $[3500, +\infty)$, 0.216 is the probability that he/she can earn a salary within $[2100, 3500)$, and 0.066 is the probability that he/she can earn a salary within $[0, 2100)$.

Theorem 5.3 *For a given large database D, minsupp and minconf, if $X \to Y$ is extracted as a rule in our model, then $X \to Y$ is an optimized rule.*

Proof: There are two kinds of causal rules.

(1) If X and Y are either itemsets or quantitative items, $X \to Y$ is certainly an optimized rule.

(2) If X and Y are item variables, then a conditional probability matrix $M_{Y|X}$ is attached to this rule, and unnecessary information in $M_{Y|X}$ is merged in rows and columns of the matrix. Also, items with identical properties in $M_{Y|X}$ are merged in rows and columns of the matrix. Consequently, $M_{Y|X}$ is an optimal matrix after reducing unnecessary information. Or, $X \to Y$ is an optimized rule.

$$\nabla$$

5.4 Polynomial Function for Causality

This section, and the next, tackle the second phase of causal rule analysis. For approximating causality, we first construct a suitable encoding method.

5.4.1 Causal Relationship

As we have seen, the causal relationship between the variables X and Y are described by attaching to a conditional probability matrix $M_{Y|X}$. In our view, the conditional probability matrix $M_{Y|X}$ can also be transformed to an approximation function. For convenience, we focus first on a simple classification for the causal relationships between X and Y.

Generally, for a rule $X \rightarrow Y$, we divide the causality between X and Y into three cases.

Case–I : A linear relationship between X and Y.
   Example 5.1 presents a typical linear relationship between X and
   Y, which constitutes the simplest form of causality.
Case–II : A polynomial relationship between X and Y.
   For example, the total distance, X, traveled by a free-falling object,
   is directly proportional to the square of the time, Y, of travel. There
   is a polynomial relationship between the total distance traveled and
   the time of travel of the object.
Case–III : A non-polynomial relationship between X and Y.
   For example, let X be 'years' and Y be 'the population of China'.
   There is a non-polynomial relationship between the population of
   China and years.

Case-I obviously refers to a class of *tractable problems* in Bayesian networks. Also, there are potential polynomial functions that can be used to approximate some non-polynomial causal relations (Case-II). These non-polynomial causal relations refer, as well, to tractable problems in Bayesian networks. In the remainder of this chapter, we construct polynomial functions for approximating the propagation.

5.4.2 Binary Linear Causality

For simplicity, suppose $X \rightarrow Y$ is a causal rule with a matrix $M_{Y|X}$. In order to establish a 1st-order linear function to replace (1), we construct a function of the form $F(a) = k_1 E_X(a) + k_0$, close to equation 5.1. Ideally, this function should be expected to satisfy $F(a) = E_Y(b)$. That is

$$k_1 E_X(a) + k_0 = E_Y(b)$$

or

$$k_1 E_X(a) + k_0 = E_Y(a M_{Y|X}) \tag{5.2}$$

Equation 5.2 needs to determine the constants k_1 and k_0, and the mappings (encoders) E_X and E_Y. We will first determine the encoders E_X and E_Y.

Let $R(X) = \{x_1, x_2, \cdots, x_k\}$, and $R(Y) = \{y_1, y_2, \cdots, y_m\}$. And let the state space of X be

$$S(X) = \{(p_1, p_2, \cdots, p_k) | 1 \le i \le k, 0 \le p_i \le 1, \sum_{i=1}^{k} p_i = 1\}$$

The encoder E_X is defined as,

$$E_X(p_1, p_2, \cdots, p_k) = 10^d p_1 + 10^{2d} p_2 + \cdots + 10^{kd} p_k$$

where $d > 0$ is a positive integer, and d is determined as (i) $d = r + 1$, if the decimal places demanded is r in an application; otherwise (ii) $d = n + 1$ when $10^{n-1} < Max\{|R(X)|, |R(Y)|\} \le 10^n$.

As a rule, the encoders would naturally capture the sort of the point values of X. For example, assume $R(X) = \{$none-rain, small-rain, middle-rain, heavy-rain$\}$, then we can construct $E_X(1, 0, 0, 0) = 10^d, E_X(0, 1, 0, 0) = 10^{2d}, E_X(0, 0, 1, 0) = 10^{3d}, E_X(0, 0, 0, 1) = 10^{4d}$ as the encoder values of 'none-rain', 'small-rain', 'middle-rain', and 'heavy-rain', respectively. This matches the ordered relationship of the amount of rain. Also, the encoder of X must be determined as an increasing order by the increasing order of the encoder of Y, due to the fact that the encoders directly influence the efficiency of the constructed approximate functions. Hence, it is important to determine an encoder for constructing an approximation function. The following examples in Subsection 5.4.4 will demonstrate this further.

Theorem 5.4 *The above encoder E_X is a one-to-one mapping.*

Proof: *Reduction to absurdity.* Let the encoder of $(p_1, p_2, \cdots, p_k)$ be equal to the encoder of $(p'_1, p'_2, \cdots, p'_k)$. That is

$$E_X(p_1, p_2, \cdots, p_k) = E_X(p'_1, p'_2, \cdots, p'_k)$$

or,

$$10^d p_1 + 10^{2d} p_2 + \cdots + 10^{kd} p_k$$
$$= 10^d p'_1 + 10^{2d} p'_2 + \cdots + 10^{kd} p'_k$$

or,

$$10^d(p_1 - p'_1) + 10^{2d}(p_2 - p'_2) + \cdots + 10^{kd}(p_k - p'_k) = 0.$$

We know, from the above suppositions, that not all of $p_i - p'_i (i = 1, 2, \cdots, k)$ are equal to 0. We assume that when $i = j_1, j_2, \cdots, j_m, p_i - p'_i \ne 0$, where, $j_1 < j_2 < \cdots < j_m$. Then the above formula can be re-written to,

$$10^{j_1 d}(p_{j_1} - p'_{j_1}) + \cdots + 10^{j_m d}(p_{j_m} - p'_{j_m}) = 0$$

or,

$$10^{j_1 d}(p_{j_1} - p'_{j_1}) + \cdots + 10^{j_{m-1} d}(p_{j_{m-1}} - p'_{j_{m-1}})$$
$$= -10^{j_m d}(p_{j_m} - p'_{j_m})$$

In other words,

$$||10^{j_1 d}(p_{j_1} - p'_{j_1}) + \cdots + 10^{j_{m-1} d}(p_{j_{m-1}} - p'_{j_{m-1}})||$$

$$= ||10^{j_m d}(p_{j_m} - p'_{j_m})||$$

or,

$$||10^{j_1 d}(p_{j_1} - p'_{j_1}) + \cdots + 10^{j_{m-1} d}(p_{j_{m-1}} - p'_{j_{m-1}})||$$

$$= 10^{j_m d}||p_{j_m} - p'_{j_m}||$$

Because $0 \leq p_i \leq 1$, so,

$$10^{j_m d}||p_{j_m} - p'_{j_m}||$$

$$\geq 10^{j_m d} 10^{-d}$$

$$= 10^{(j_m - 1)d}$$

On the other hand, according to the suppositions

$$1 \leq i \leq k, 0 \leq p_i \leq 1, \sum_{i=1}^{k} p_i = 1$$

and

$$1 \leq i \leq k, 0 \leq p'_i \leq 1, \sum_{i=1}^{k} p'_i = 1$$

we have, $||p_{j_1} - p'_{j_1}|| + \cdots + ||p_{j_m} - p'_{j_m}|| \leq 1$ and $||p_{j_m} - p'_{j_m}|| \neq 0$. So $||p_{j_1} - p'_{j_1}|| + \cdots + ||p_{j_{m-1}} - p'_{j_{m-1}}|| < 1$. And notice the power of 10 of each operand, when we have,

$$||10^{j_1 d}(p_{j_1} - p'_{j_1}) + \cdots + 10^{j_{m-1} d}(p_{j_{m-1}} - p'_{j_{m-1}})||$$

$$\leq ||10^{j_1 d}(p_{j_1} - p'_{j_1})|| + \cdots + ||10^{j_{m-1} d}(p_{j_{m-1}} - p'_{j_{m-1}})||$$

$$< 10^{j_{m-1} d}.$$

Because $j_{m-1} < j_m$, therefore $j_{m-1} \leq j_m - 1$, and thus the above inequation can be reduced as,

$$||10^{j_1 d}(p_{j_1} - p'_{j_1}) + \cdots + 10^{j_{m-1} d}(p_{j_{m-1}} - p'_{j_{m-1}})||$$

$$< 10^{j_{m-1} d}$$

$$\leq 10^{(j_m - 1)d}$$

Hence,

$$||10^{j_1 d}(p_{j_1} - p'_{j_1}) + \cdots + 10^{j_{m-1} d}(p_{j_{m-1}} - p'_{j_{m-1}})||$$

$$< 10^{j_m d}||p_{j_m} - p'_{j_m}||$$

This contradicts the above suppositions. That is, the above encoder is a one-to-one mapping.   ▽

Intuitively, this theorem shows $E_X(p_1, p_2, \cdots, p_k) = E_X(p'_1, p'_2, \cdots, p'_k)$, iff $p_1 = p'_1$, $p_2 = p'_2$, $\cdots$, $p_k = p'_k$. In this case the encoder of E_Y is the same as E_X.

We now determine the constants k_1 and k_0. Because our goal is to compress (1) to an approximation function, so for all states in $S(X)$, or $a \in S(X)$, the approximation function must satisfy:

$$\|k_1 E_X(a) + k_0 - E_Y(aM_{Y|X})\| < \varepsilon$$

where $\varepsilon > 0$ is small enough. Or, for

$$f'(k_1, k_0) = \sum_{a \in S(X)} (k_1 E_X(a) + k_0 - E_Y(aM_{Y|X}))^2$$

the value of $f'(k_1, k_0)$ must be the *minimum*. Or for $\Omega(A) \subset S(A)$ and

$$f(k_1, k_0) = \sum_{a \in \Omega(X)} (k_1 E_X(a) + k_0 - E_Y(aM_{Y|X}))^2$$

the value of $f(k_1, k_0)$ must be the *minimum*.

Theorem 5.5 *The minimal solution to the above formula for constants* k_1, k_0 *is*

$$k_1 = \frac{\omega_1 - \omega_2}{\omega_3 - \omega_4}$$
$$k_0 = 1/\Im(\Omega(X))(\omega_5 - \omega_6)$$

where,

$$\omega_1 = \sum_{a \in \Omega(X)} E_X(a) \sum_{a \in \Omega(X)} E_Y(aM_{Y|X})$$

$$\omega_2 = \Im(\Omega(X) \sum_{a \in \Omega(X)} (E_Y(aM_{Y|X})E_X(a))$$

$$\omega_3 = (\sum_{a \in \Omega(X)} E_X(a))^2, \quad \omega_4 = \Im(\Omega(X)) \sum_{a \in \Omega(X)} E_X^2(a)$$

$$\omega_5 = \sum_{a \in \Omega(X)} E_Y(aM_{Y|X}), \quad \omega_6 = k_1 \sum_{a \in \Omega(X)} E_X(a))$$

Proof: We now present the proof of Theorem 5.5 by deriving the above solutions as follows.

For the principle of extreme value in mathematical analysis, we can find the *minimum* by taking the partial derivatives over $f(k_1, k_0)$ with respect to k_1, k_0 we must determine, and then set these derivatives to 0. That is,

$$
\begin{cases}
\frac{\partial f}{\partial k_1} = 2 \sum_{a \in \Omega(X)} ((k_1 E_X(a) + k_0 - E_Y(aM_{Y|X}))E_X(a)) = 0 \\
\frac{\partial f}{\partial k_0} = 2 \sum_{a \in \Omega(X)} (k_1 E_X(a) + k_0 - E_Y(aM_{Y|X})) = 0
\end{cases}
$$

Or,

$$
\begin{cases}
k_1 \sum_{a \in \Omega(X)} E_X^2(a) + k_0 \sum_{a \in \Omega(X)} E_X(a) - \sum_{a \in \Omega(X)} (E_Y(aM_{Y|X})E_X(a)) = 0 \\
k_1 \sum_{a \in \Omega(X)} E_X(a) + k_0 \Im(\Omega(X)) - \sum_{a \in \Omega(X)} E_Y(aM_{Y|X}) = 0
\end{cases}
$$

So, we can estimate k_1 and k_0 by solving the above equation group as follows,

$$
\begin{cases}
k_1 = \frac{\omega_1 - \omega_2}{\omega_3 - \omega_4} \\
k_0 = 1/\Im(\Omega(X))(\omega_5 - \omega_6)
\end{cases}
$$

where,

$$
\omega_1 = \sum_{a \in \Omega(X)} E_X(a) \sum_{a \in \Omega(X)} E_Y(aM_{Y|X})
$$

$$
\omega_2 = \Im(\Omega(X) \sum_{a \in \Omega(X)} (E_Y(aM_{Y|X})E_X(a))
$$

$$
\omega_3 = (\sum_{a \in \Omega(X)} E_X(a))^2
$$

$$
\omega_4 = \Im(\Omega(X)) \sum_{a \in \Omega(X)} E_X^2(a)
$$

$$
\omega_5 = \sum_{a \in \Omega(X)} E_Y(aM_{Y|X})
$$

$$
\omega_6 = k_1 \sum_{a \in \Omega(X)} E_X(a))
$$

Then, the above formula $F(a) = k_1 E_X(a) + k_0$ is the approximation function of Equation 5.1.

$\triangledown$

For an observation a, $F(a)$ can be gained from the above formula. Then we can solve $b_1, b_2, ..., b_m$ by $F(a)$. That is,

$$b_i = (INT(F(a)/10^{(i-1)d}) - INT(F(a)/10^{id}) * 10^d)/10^d$$

where $i = 1, 2, \cdots, m$, and $INT()$ is an integer function. In order to assure the probability significance level of the results, the final results are:

$$b_1 := Max\{0, 1 - (b_2 + b_3 + ... + b_m)\}$$
$$b_i := b_i/(b_1 + b_2 + ... + b_m)$$

where, $i = 1, 2, \cdots, m$.

Theorem 5.6 *For rules of the form $X \rightarrow Y$ where the causality is of the form Case-I, the causality can be perfectly fitted by $F(a)$ above.*

Proof: This can be obtained immediately from the above minimization problem, and from Theorem 5.5.   ▽

5.4.3 N-ary Linear Propagating Model

We now discuss the 1st-order linear form of the general rules of the form:

$$X_1 \wedge X_2 \wedge \cdots \wedge X_n \rightarrow Y$$

In order to construct a 1st-order linear function to close the causality of such a rule, we construct a function of the form,

$$F(a) = k_0 + k_1 E_{X1}(a_1) + \cdots + k_n E_{Xn}(a_n)$$

Ideally, it would satisfy the following equation,

$$k_0 + k_1 E_{X1}(a_1) + \cdots + k_n E_{Xn}(a_n) = E_Y(b) \qquad (5.3)$$

In Equation 5.3 we need to determine the constants $k_0, k_1, \cdots, k_n$, and the encoders $E_{X1}, \cdots, E_{Xn}$ and E_Y. The encoders of $E_{X1}, \cdots, E_{Xn}$ and E_Y are determined in the same way as in Subsection 5.4.2. Therefore, we need only determine the constants $k_0, k_1, \cdots, k_n$.

For $a_i \in S(X_i)$, $i = 1, 2, \cdots, n$, the result b can be solved by the non-linear form of causality. Again, b, and the states $a_1, a_2, \cdots, a_n$, can be constructed as a vector of the form $(a_1, a_2, \cdots, a_n, b)$, and the set of all these vectors is written as ST. Then, for $t = (a_1, a_2, \cdots, a_n, b) \in ST$, the function must satisfy:

$$\|k_0 + k_1 E_{X1}(a_1) + \cdots + k_n E_{Xn}(a_n) - E_Y(b)\| < \varepsilon$$

where $\varepsilon > 0$ is small enough. Or, for

$$f'(k_0, k_1, \cdots, k_n) = \sum_{t \in ST} (k_0 + k_1 E_{X1}(a_1) + \cdots + k_n E_{Xn}(a_n) - E_Y(b))^2$$

the value of $f'(k_0, k_1, \cdots, k_n)$ must be the *minimum*. Or letting $S_T \subset ST$, for

$$f(k_0, k_1, \cdots, k_n) = \sum_{t \in S_T} (k_0 + k_1 E_{X1}(a_1) + \cdots + k_n E_{Xn}(a_n) - E_Y(b))^2$$

the value of $f(k_0, k_1, \cdots, k_n)$ must be the *minimum*.

Theorem 5.7 *The minimal solutions to the above formula for the constants* $k_0, k_1, \cdots, k_n$ *are*

$$k_0 = \frac{d_0}{d}; \ k_1 = \frac{d_1}{d}; \cdots; k_n = \frac{d_n}{d}$$

where d is the determinant of the coefficient matrix of the following equation group with respect to $k_0, k_1, \cdots, k_n$ and $d \neq 0$, d_i is the determinant after the ith rank in d is replaced with the constant rank $\sum E_Y(b)$, and $\sum (E_Y(b) E_{X1}(a_1)), \ \cdots, \ \sum (E_Y(b) E_{Xn}(a_n))$.

Proof: Below, we show the proof of Theorem 5.7 by derivation from the above solutions.

In the same way as in the above subsection, we can find the *minimum* by taking the partial derivatives over $f(k_0, k_1, \cdots, k_n)$ with respect to $k_0, k_1, \cdots, k_n$ we must determine, and we then set these derivatives to 0. That is,

$$\begin{cases} \frac{\partial f}{\partial k_0} = 2 \sum_{t \in S_T} (k_0 + k_1 E_{X1}(a_1) + \cdots k_n E_{Xn}(a_n) - E_Y(b)) = 0 \\[2mm] \frac{\partial f}{\partial k_0} = 2 \sum_{t \in S_T} ((k_0 + k_1 E_{X1}(a_1) + \cdots k_n E_{Xn}(a_n) - E_Y(b)) E_{X1}(a_1)) = 0 \\[2mm] \cdots \\[2mm] \frac{\partial f}{\partial k_0} = 2 \sum_{t \in S_T} ((k_0 + k_1 E_{X1}(a_1) + \cdots k_n E_{Xn}(a_n) - E_Y(b)) E_{Xn}(a_n)) = 0 \end{cases}$$

Or,

$$\begin{cases} k_0 \Im(\Omega(S_T)) + k_1 \sum E_{X1}(a_1) + \cdots + k_n \sum E_{Xn}(a_n) = \sum E_Y(b) \\[2mm] k_0 \sum E_{X1}(a_1) + k_1 \sum E_{X1}^2(a_1) + \cdots + k_n \sum (E_{Xn}(a_n)E_{X1}(a_1)) \\ = \sum (E_Y(b)E_{X1}(a_1)) \\[2mm] \cdots \\[2mm] k_0 \sum E_{Xn}(a_n) + k_1 \sum (E_{X1}(a_1)E_{Xn}(a_n)) + \cdots + k_n \sum E_{Xn}^2(a_n) \\ = \sum (E_Y(b)E_{Xn}(a_n)) \end{cases}$$

Let A be the coefficient matrix of this equation group with respect to $k_0, k_1, \cdots, k_n$. If $d = |A| \neq 0$, then this equation group has the following unique solution

$$\begin{cases} k_0 = \frac{d_0}{d} \\[2mm] k_1 = \frac{d_1}{d} \\[2mm] \cdots \\[2mm] k_n = \frac{d_n}{d} \end{cases}$$

where d_i is the determinant of the matrix after the ith rank in A is replaced with the constant rank $\sum E_Y(b), \sum(E_Y(b)E_{X1}(a_1)), \cdots, \sum(E_Y(b)E_{Xn}(a_n))$.

Then the formula $F(a) = k_0 + k_1 E_{X1}(a_1) + \cdots + k_n E_{Xn}(a_n)$ is the approximation function of (3).

$$\triangledown$$

In the same way, $b_1, b_2, \cdots, b_m$ can be determined by $F(a)$ according to the decoder in the above subsection.

Theorem 5.8 *For rules of the form $X_1 \wedge X_2 \wedge \cdots \wedge X_n \to Y$ in Case-I, the causality can be perfectly fitted by the above $F(a)$.*

Proof: The theorem can be proved immediately from the above minimization technique, and from Theorem 5.7.

$$\triangledown$$

5.4.4 Examples

Now two simple examples demonstrate the use of the above approximation function.

Table 5.4. Some data for Example 5.2

$p(x_1)$	$p(x_2)$	$p(x_3)$	$p(y_1)$	$p(y_2)$	$p(y_3)$
0.9	0	0.1	0.73	0.1	0.17
0.1	0.9	0	0.17	0.73	0.1
0	0.1	0.9	0.1	0.17	0.73
0.8	0	0.2	0.66	0.1	0.24
0.2	0	0.8	0.24	0.1	0.66
0	0.2	0.8	0.1	0.24	0.66
0	0.3	0.7	0.1	0.31	0.59
0.7	0.2	0.1	0.59	0.24	0.17
0.1	0.2	0.7	0.17	0.24	0.59
0.4	0.6	0	0.38	0.52	0.1
0	0.6	0.4	0.1	0.52	0.38
0.1	0.3	0.6	0.17	0.31	0.52
0.2	0.6	0.2	0.24	0.52	0.24
0.2	0.2	0.6	0.24	0.24	0.52
0.5	0.3	0.2	0.45	0.31	0.24

Example 5.2 *Example 5.1 demonstrates a typical linear causality between X and Y. We can represent this as a linear function. Suppose the encoders of X and Y are both the same as in Subsection 5.4.2, and d = 2. Some of the data is listed in Table 5.4.*

According to Theorem 5.5, k_0 and k_1 are determined, using the data in Table 5.4 concerning $S(X)$ and $S(Y)$ as follows:

$$k_0 = 101010, k_1 = 0.7$$

Hence, the approximating function is as follows:

$$F(a) = 0.7E_X(a) + 101010$$

Given an observation $a = (p(x_1) = 0.3, p(x_2) = 0.5, p(x_3) = 0.2)$, the probabilities of the point values of Y_P can be gained by the non-linear causality as follows,

$$p(y_1) = 0.31, p(y_2) = 0.45, p(y_3) = 0.24$$

The encoder of this observation is as $E_X(a) = 205030$. If this is substituted into the above approximation function, we have,

$$F(a) = 244531$$

According to the decoder in Subsection 5.4.2, we can obtain the probabilities of the point values of Y_Z from $F(a)$ as follows,

$$p(y_1) = 0.31, p(y_2) = 0.45, p(y_3) = 0.24$$

So, we have

$$||P(Y_Z)-P(Y_P)|| = ||p_Z(y_1)-p_P(y_1)||+||p_Z(y_2)-p_P(y_2)||+||p_Z(y_n)-p_P(y_n)||$$

$$= 0$$

The values of E_{Y_P} and E_{Y_Z} are listed in Table 5.5, for some given random observations on $(p(x_1), p(x_2), p(x_3))$.

Table 5.5. Comparison of E_{Y_P} and E_{Y_Z}

$p(x_1)$	$p(x_2)$	$p(x_3)$	$E_X(a)$	$F(a)$	E_{Y_Z}	E_{Y_P}
0.2	0	0.8	800020	522028	522028	522028
0	0.1	0.9	901000	562420	562420	562420
0.2	0.1	0.7	701020	482428	482428	482428
0.6	0.3	0.1	103060	243244	243244	243244
0.1	0.7	0.2	207010	284824	284824	284824

Note that, if $d = 3$, then k_0 and k_1 are determined according to samples such as: $k_0 = 100100100, k_1 = 0.7$. Then the approximating function is as follows:

$$F(a) = 0.7E_X(a) + 100100100$$

And, if $d = 4$, then k_0 and k_1 are determined according to some samples as: $k_0 = 100010001000, k_1 = 0.7$. Then the approximating function is as follows:

$$F(a) = 0.7E_X(a) + 100010001000$$

This example shows, for rules of the form $X \rightarrow Y$ in Case-I, the causality can be perfectly fitted by the above $F(a)$. In this example, we have directly used the encoder method described in Subsection 5.4.2. However, the encoder of X usually needs to consider the increasing order of the encoder of Y. We illustrate this argument with the following example.

Example 5.3 *For the rule* $X \rightarrow Y$, *let* $d = 2$ *and*

$$M_{X|Y} = \begin{bmatrix} 0.1 & 0.8 & 0.1 \\ 0.1 & 0.1 & 0.8 \\ 0.8 & 0.1 & 0.1 \end{bmatrix}$$

For this matrix, the encoder of X must give consideration to the increasing order of the encoder of Y. Thus, the encoders from Subsection 5.4.2 are not the best choice.

In fact, the *minimum* and *maximum* of E_Y are 101080 and 801010, respectively, according to the encoder method we have used. The *minimum* of E_Y corresponds to the probabilities of point values of Y as

$$p(y_1) = 0.8, p(y_2) = 0.1, p(y_3) = 0.1,$$

and the *minimum* corresponds to the state of X as

$$p(x_1) = 0, p(x_2) = 0, p(x_3) = 1$$

Also, the *maximum* of E_Y corresponds to the probabilities of the point values of Y as

$$p(y_1) = 0.1, p(y_2) = 0.1, p(y_3) = 0.8$$

while the *maximum* corresponds to the state of X as

$$p(x_1) = 0, p(x_2) = 1, p(x_3) = 0$$

Therefore, these encoders are obviously not the best choice for estimating the approximation function of the rule.

Certainly, if the encoder E_X is determined with respect to the increasing order of the encoder of Y (or the encoders of states $(0,0,1)$ and $(0,1,0)$ are the *minimum* and the *maximum* respectively, of the encoder of X), then these encoders are more appropriate for estimating the approximation function. In order to construct this encoder, we must re-arrange the order of the point values as

$$x_3, x_1, x_2$$

and rename them as

$$z_1 = x_3, z_2 = x_1, z_3 = x_2$$

Then, the state space is $S(X) = \{(p(z_1) = a_1, p(z_2) = a_2, p(z_3) = a_3) | a_1 + a_2 + a_3 = 1\}$, and the encoder is

$$E_X(a) = E_X(a_1, a_2, a_3) = 10^d a_1 + 10^{2d} a_2 + 10^{3d} a_3$$

or

$$E_X(a) = 10^d p(x_3) + 10^{2d} p(x_1) + 10^{3d} p(x_2)$$

and

$$E_Y(b) = 10^d p(y_3) + 10^{2d} p(y_1) + 10^{3d} p(y_2)$$

Now we can solve the approximation function with the above encoder as follows:

$$F(a) = 0.7 E_X(a) + 101010$$

Given an observation $a = (p(x_1) = 0.2, p(x_2) = 0.1, p(x_3) = 0.7)$, the probabilities of the point values of Y_P can be gained by the non-linear causality as follows,

$$p(y_1) = 0.59, p(y_2) = 0.24, p(y_3) = 0.17$$

The corresponding state of this observation is (0.7, 0.2, 0.1), and the encoder of the state is $E_X(a) = 107020$. If this is substituted into the above approximation function, we have

$$F(a) = 175924$$

According to the decoder in Section 5.4.2, we can obtain the probabilities of Y_Z from $F(a)$ as follows,

$$p(y_1) = 0.59, p(y_2) = 0.24, p(y_3) = 0.17$$

So, we have

$$||P(Y_Z) - P(Y_P)|| = ||p_Z(y_1) - p_P(y_1)|| + ||p_Z(y_2) - p_P(y_2)|| + ||p_Z(y_n) - p_P(y_n)||$$

$$= 0$$

This example shows that if the causality of rules is of the form $X \to Y$ in Case-I, the causality can be perfectly fitted by $F(a)$ above.

5.5 Functions for General Causality

This section presents a means of constructing a polynomial function close to Equation 5.1, which can be applied to the approximating problem of causality in Case-II and Case-III as defined in Subsection 5.4.1.

If there is no non-polynomial function in Equation 5.1, we can estimate an approximation function. Ideally, this function should be expected to satisfy

$$||k_2 E_X^2(a) + k_1 E_X(a) + k_0 - E_Y(aM_{Y|X})|| < \varepsilon,$$

where $\varepsilon > 0$ is small enough. Or, for

$$f'(k_2, k_1, k_0) = \sum_{a \in S(X)} (k_2 E_X^2(a) + k_1 E_X(a) + k_0 - E_Y(aM_{Y|X}))^2$$

the value of $f'(k_2, k_1, k_0)$ must be the *minimum*. Or for $\Omega(A) \subset S(A)$ and

$$f(k_2, k_1, k_0) = \sum_{a \in \Omega(X)} (k_2 E_X^2(a) + k_1 E_X(a) + k_0 - E_Y(aM_{Y|X}))^2$$

the value of $f(k_2, k_1, k_0)$ must be the *minimum*.

Theorem 5.9 *The minimal solutions to the above formula for the constants* k_2, k_1, k_0 *are*

$$k_2 = \frac{\eta_1(E_Y)\xi_4(E_X) - \eta_2(E_Y)\xi_2(E_X)}{\xi_1(E_X)\xi_4(E_X) - \xi_2(E_X)\xi_3(E_X)}$$

$$k_1 = \frac{\eta_1(E_Y)\xi_3(E_X) - \eta_2(E_Y)\xi_1(E_X)}{\xi_2(E_X)\xi_3(E_X) - \xi_1(E_X)\xi_4(E_X)}$$

$$k_0 = 1/\Im(\Omega(X))(\sum_{a \in \Omega(X)} E_Y(aM_{Y|X}) - k_2 \sum_{a \in \Omega(X)} E_X^2(a)$$

$$- k_1 \sum_{a \in \Omega(X)} E_X(a))$$

Where,

$$\xi_1(E_X) = \Im(\Omega(X)) \sum_{a \in \Omega(X)} E_X^4(a) - (\sum_{a \in \Omega(X)} E_X^2(a))^2$$

$$\xi_2(E_X) = \Im(\Omega(X)) \sum_{a \in \Omega(X)} E_X^3(a) - \Im(\Omega(X)) \sum_{a \in \Omega(X)} E_X^2(a)$$

$$\xi_3(E_X) = \Im(\Omega(X)) \sum_{a \in \Omega(X)} E_X^3(a) - \sum_{a \in \Omega(X)} E_X(a) \sum_{a \in \Omega(X)} E_X^2(a)$$

$$\xi_4(E_X) = \Im(\Omega(X)) \sum_{a \in \Omega(X)} E_X^2(a) - \Im(\Omega(X)) \sum_{a \in \Omega(X)} E_X(a)$$

$$\eta_1(E_Y) = \Im(\Omega(X)) \sum_{a \in \Omega(X)} (E_Y(aM_{Y|X})E_X^2(a)$$

$$- \sum_{a \in \Omega(X)} E_X^2(a) \sum_{a \in \Omega(X)} (E_Y(aM_{Y|X})$$

$$\eta_2(E_Y) = \Im(\Omega(X)) \sum_{a \in \Omega(X)} (E_Y(aM_{Y|X})E_X(a)$$

$$- \sum_{a \in \Omega(X)} E_X(a) \sum_{a \in \Omega(X)} (E_Y(aM_{Y|X})$$

Proof: We now present the proof of Theorem 5.9 by the derivation of the above solutions.

Using the principle of extreme value in mathematical analysis, we can find the *minimum* by taking the partial derivatives over $f(k_2, k_1, k_0)$ with respect to k_2, k_1, k_0 that we must determine. We then set these derivatives to 0. That is,

$$\begin{cases} \frac{\partial f}{\partial k_2} = 2 \sum_{a \in \Omega(X)} ((k_2 E_X^2(a) + k_1 E_X(a) + k_0 - E_Y(aM_{Y|X}))E_X^2(a)) = 0 \\[2em] \frac{\partial f}{\partial k_1} = 2 \sum_{a \in \Omega(X)} ((k_2 E_X^2(a) + k_1 E_X(a) + k_0 - E_Y(aM_{Y|X}))E_X(a)) = 0 \\[2em] \frac{\partial f}{\partial k_0} = 2 \sum_{a \in \Omega(X)} (k_1 E_X(a) + k_0 - E_Y(aM_{Y|X})) = 0 \end{cases}$$

Or,

$$\begin{cases} k_2 \sum_{a \in \Omega(X)} E_X^4(a) + k_1 \sum_{a \in \Omega(X)} E_X^3(a) + k_0 \sum_{a \in \Omega(X)} E_X^2(a) \\ \quad - \sum_{a \in \Omega(X)} (E_Y(aM_{Y|X})E_X^2(a)) = 0 \\[1.5em] k_2 \sum_{a \in \Omega(X)} E_X^3(a) + k_1 \sum_{a \in \Omega(X)} E_X^2(a) + k_0 \sum_{a \in \Omega(X)} E_X(a) \\ \quad - \sum_{a \in \Omega(X)} (E_Y(aM_{Y|X})E_X(a)) = 0 \\[1.5em] k_2 \sum_{a \in \Omega(X)} E_X^2(a) + k_1 \sum_{a \in \Omega(X)} E_X(a) + k_0 \Im(\Omega(X)) \\ \quad - \sum_{a \in \Omega(X)} E_Y(aM_{Y|X}) = 0 \end{cases}$$

Let

$$\xi_1(E_X) = \Im(\Omega(X)) \sum_{a \in \Omega(X)} E_X^4(a) - \left(\sum_{a \in \Omega(X)} E_X^2(a) \right)^2,$$

$$\xi_2(E_X) = \Im(\Omega(X)) \sum_{a \in \Omega(X)} E_X^3(a) - \Im(\Omega(X)) \sum_{a \in \Omega(X)} E_X^2(a),$$

$$\xi_3(E_X) = \Im(\Omega(X)) \sum_{a \in \Omega(X)} E_X^3(a) - \sum_{a \in \Omega(X)} E_X(a) \sum_{a \in \Omega(X)} E_X^2(a),$$

$$\xi_4(E_X) = \Im(\Omega(X)) \sum_{a \in \Omega(X)} E_X^2(a) - \Im(\Omega(X)) \sum_{a \in \Omega(X)} E_X(a),$$

$$\eta_1(E_Y) = \Im(\Omega(X)) \sum_{a \in \Omega(X)} (E_Y(aM_{Y|X})E_X^2(a)$$

$$\quad - \sum_{a \in \Omega(X)} E_X^2(a) \sum_{a \in \Omega(X)} (E_Y(aM_{Y|X}),$$

$$\eta_2(E_Y) = \Im(\Omega(X)) \sum_{a \in \Omega(X)} (E_Y(aM_{Y|X})E_X(a)$$

$$\quad - \sum_{a \in \Omega(X)} E_X(a) \sum_{a \in \Omega(X)} (E_Y(aM_{Y|X})$$

We can gain the following solutions by solving the above equation group as follows:

$$\begin{cases} k_2 = \frac{\eta_1(E_Y)\xi_4(E_X)-\eta_2(E_Y)\xi_2(E_X)}{\xi_1(E_X)\xi_4(E_X)-\xi_2(E_X)\xi_3(E_X)} \\[2mm] k_1 = \frac{\eta_1(E_Y)\xi_3(E_X)-\eta_2(E_Y)\xi_1(E_X)}{\xi_2(E_X)\xi_3(E_X)-\xi_1(E_X)\xi_4(E_X)} \\[2mm] k_0 = 1/\Im(\Omega(X))(\displaystyle\sum_{a \in \Omega(X)} E_Y(aM_{Y|X}) \\[2mm] -k_2 \displaystyle\sum_{a \in \Omega(X)} E_X^2(a) - k_1 \displaystyle\sum_{a \in \Omega(X)} E_X(a)) \end{cases}$$

$$\nabla$$

Theorem 5.10 *For rules of the form $X \to Y$ in Case-II or Case-III, and the encoders can be constructed in increasing order, these causality relationships can be perfectly fitted by $F(a)$ above.*

Proof: This can be obtained immediately from the above minimization problem, and from Theorem 5.9.

$$\nabla$$

The approximation function $f(k_3, k_2, k_1, k_0) = k_3 E_X^3(a) + k_2 E_X^2(a) + k_1 E_X(a) + k_0$, or other higher order functions, can be constructed in the same way as above. Generally, polynomial approximating functions for the rules of the form $X_1 \wedge X_2 \wedge \cdots \wedge X_n \to Y$, can also be constructed in the same way. Now we demonstrate this with an example.

Let the conditional probability matrix of a node be

$$M_{Y|X} = \begin{bmatrix} 0.5 & 0.2 & 0.3 \\ 0.3 & 0.4 & 0.3 \\ 0.2 & 0.4 & 0.4 \end{bmatrix}$$

Suppose the encoders of X and Y are the same as those in Subsection 5.4.2, and $d = 2$. The appropriate data is listed in Table 5.6.

According to the method above, k_0, k_1, and k_2 are determined by the above probabilities in $S(X)$ and $S(Y)$ as follows:

$$k_0 = 302693.63, k_1 = 0.10128629, k_2 = -1.26717 \times 10^{-10}$$

Then the approximating function is as follows:

$$F(a) = -1.26717 \times 10^{-10} E_X^2(a) + 0.10128629 E_X(a) + 302693.63$$

Given an observation $a = (p(x_1) = 0.3, p(x_2) = 0.5$, and $p(x_3) = 0.2)$, the probabilities of the point values of Y_P can be gained by non-linear causality as follows,

$$p(y_1) = 0.34, p(y_2) = 0.34, p(y_3) = 0.32$$

Table 5.6. Some probabilities for $X \to Y$

$p(x_1)$	$p(x_2)$	$p(x_3)$	$p(y_1)$	$p(y_2)$	$p(y_3)$
0	0.9	0.1	0.29	0.4	0.31
0.1	0	0.9	0.23	0.38	0.39
0.2	0.8	0	0.34	0.36	0.3
0.8	0.1	0.1	0.45	0.24	0.31
0.1	0.8	0.1	0.31	0.38	0.31
0	0.3	0.7	0.23	0.4	0.37
0.7	0.1	0.2	0.42	0.26	0.32
0.1	0.2	0.7	0.25	0.38	0.37
0	0.4	0.6	0.24	0.4	0.36
0.6	0.1	0.3	0.39	0.28	0.33
0.1	0.6	0.3	0.29	0.38	0.33
0.1	0.3	0.6	0.26	0.38	0.36
0.2	0.2	0.6	0.28	0.36	0.36
0.5	0.5	0	0.4	0.3	0.3
0	0.5	0.5	0.25	0.4	0.35

The encoder of this observation is $E_X(a) = 205030$. If it is substituted into the above approximation function, we have,

$$F(a) = 323455.04$$

According to the decoder in Subsection 5.4.2, we can obtain the probabilities of the point values of Y_Z from $F(a)$ as follows,

$$p(y_1) = 0.55, p(y_2) = 0.34, p(y_3) = 0.32$$

To assure the probability significance level of the results, we note that the final results would be

$$p(y_1) = 0.34, p(y_2) = 0.34, p(y_3) = 0.32$$

where $p(y_1) = max\{0, 1 - (p(y_2) + p(y_3))\} = 1 - 0.34 - 0.32 = 0.34$.
So, we have

$$||P(Y_Z)-P(Y_P)|| = ||p_Z(y_1)-p_P(y_1)||+||p_Z(y_2)-p_P(y_2)||+||p_Z(y_n)-p_P(y_n)||$$

$$= 0$$

Now, given another observation $a = (p(x_1) = 0.1, p(x_2) = 0$, and $p(x_3) = 0.9)$, the probabilities of the point values of Y_P can be gained by the propagating model of Bayesian networks as follows,

$$p(y_1) = 0.23, p(y_2) = 0.38, p(y_3) = 0.39$$

The encoder of this observation is as $E_X(a) = 900010$. If this is substituted into the above approximation function, we have,

$$F(a) = 393749.66$$

According to the decoder in Subsection 5.4.2, we can obtain the probabilities of the point values of Y_Z from $F(a)$ as follows,

$$p(y_1) = 0.49, p(y_2) = 0.37, p(y_3) = 0.39$$

In order to assure the probability significance level of the results, we note that the final results would be

$$p(y_1) = 0.24, p(y_2) = 0.37, p(y_3) = 0.39$$

So, we have

$$||P(Y_Z)-P(Y_P)|| = ||p_Z(y_1)-p_P(y_1)||+||p_Z(y_2)-p_P(y_2)||+||p_Z(y_n)-p_P(y_n)||$$

$$= 0.02$$

For some given random observations on $(p(x_1), p(x_2), p(x_3))$, the results of E_{Y_P} and E_{Y_Z} are listed as follows.

Table 5.7. Comparison of E_{Y_P} and E_{Y_Z} for general cases

$p(x_1)$	$p(x_2)$	$p(x_3)$	$E_X(a)$	$F(a)$	E_{Y_Z}	E_{Y_P}
0.3	0.5	0.2	205030	323455	323434	323434
1	0	0	100	302703	302743	302050
0	0	1	1000000	403853	403822	404020
0.1	0.8	0.1	108010	313632	313633	313831
0.4	0.2	0.4	402040	343394	343333	343234
0.5	0	0.5	500050	353310	353332	353035
0.1	0.2	0.7	702010	373735	373726	373825

Again, we can construct an approximate function for $d = 3$ with the same samples:

$$k_0 = 300246064, k_1 = 0.1002169, k_2 = -6.69927 \times 10^{-14}$$

Then the approximating function is as follows:

$$F(a) = -6.69927 \times 10^{-14} E_X^2(a) + 0.1002169 E_X(a) + 300246064$$

Now, given an observed value as $p(x_1) = 0.1$, $p(x_2) = 0$, and $p(x_3) = 0.9$, the probabilities of the point values of Y_P can be gained from Pearl's plausible inference model as follows,

$$p(y_1) = 0.23, p(y_2) = 0.38, p(y_3) = 0.39$$

The encoder of this observed value is $E_X(a) = 900000100$. If it is substituted into the above approximation function, we have,

$$F(a) = 390386000$$

According to the decoder, we can obtain the probabilities of the point values of Y_Z from $F(a)$ as follows,

$$p(y_1) = 0.00, p(y_2) = 0.386, p(y_3) = 0.39$$

In order to assure the probability significance level of the results, the final results are:

$$p(y_1) = 0.224, p(y_2) = 0.386, p(y_3) = 0.39$$

So, we have

$$||P(Y_Z)-P(Y_P)|| = ||p_Z(y_1)-p_P(y_1)||+||p_Z(y_2)-p_P(y_2)||+||p_Z(y_3)-p_P(y_3)||$$

$$= 0.012$$

These results show that $||P(Y_Z) - P(Y_P)||$ has decreased from 0.02 to 0.012 for the observation ($p(x_1) = 0.1$, $p(x_2) = 0$, and $p(x_3) = 0.9$). However, the impact range of the computing error is not reduced with d enlarged.

5.6 Approximating Causality by Fitting

This section presents the final phase of causal rule analysis.

As we have seen, we can discover approximate polynomial causality in data by encoding. In scientific research, we often need to find a causal relationship in a function, from numerical data. For example, let the numerical values of X and Y be $x_1, x_2, \cdots, x_n$, and $y_1, y_2, \cdots, y_n$ as listed below:

X	x_1	x_2	$\cdots$	x_n
Y	y_1	y_2	$\cdots$	y_n

In this section, we propose a method for finding the approximate linear causality between X and Y from the given numerical data, by fitting.

5.6.1 Preprocessing of Data

Suppose $D = \{(x_i, y_i), 1 \le i \le n\}$ indicates a set of all numerical data. We need a preprocess for this data.

First, a set D is divided along the y-axis into k groups of data as follows:

$$D_1, D_2, \cdot, D_k$$

This should satisfy the three conditions below.

(1) $\forall (x_{ij}, y_{ij}) \in D_i$, $y_{ij} \in [\underline{y_i}, \overline{y_i}]$, where $\underline{y_i}$ and $\overline{y_i}$ are the *supremum* and *infimum* of y_{ij} in D_i, respectively, $j = 1, 2, \cdots, n_i$, where n_i is the observed point numbers in D_i; and $n = \sum_{i=1}^{k} n_i$. And, for $y \in [\underline{y_i}, \overline{y_i}]$ and $\forall y' \in [\underline{y_{i+1}}, \overline{y_{i+1}}]$, it must hold that $y \leq y'$.

(2) If D_i border D_j and $j = i + 1$, then $[\underline{y_i}, \overline{y_i}] \cap [\underline{y_j}, \overline{y_j}]$ exists at most at one point, $\underline{y_j} = \overline{y_i}$.

(3) y and x have an approximate polynomial relationship on $[\underline{y_i}, \overline{y_i}]$. That is, there exist two constants, a and b, so that $y = a + bx$ can close at the point where $y \in [\underline{y_i}, \overline{y_i}]$.

In fact, we can adopt a linear-relational coefficient as a measure to divide the set D.

After D is divided, the data in D_i becomes a polynomial relationship. Hence, we can use the extreme points of each set D_i as its deputy points. In other words, we select the points $y'_1, \overline{y'_1}, y'_2, ..., \overline{y'_k}$ as deputy points. Let m be the number of deputy points, renamed as $y_1, y_2, ..., y_m$. The corresponding point values of X will be $x_1, x_2, \cdots, x_m$, and we write the point values of Y as $G_1(x_1), G_1(x_2), ..., G_1(x_m)$. Therefore, we have constructed a deputy value set $U = (x_i, G_1(x_i))$, or

X	x_1	x_2	$\cdots$	x_m
Y	$G_1(x_1)$	$G_1(x_2)$	$\cdots$	$G_1(x_m)$

5.6.2 Constructing the Polynomial Function

We now present a method for finding approximate polynomial causality between X and Y, from the above numerical data, by fitting. This is performed by the following theorem.

Theorem 5.11 *For U, the approximate polynomial function for fitting the data can be constructed as*

$$F(x) = F_1(x) + \sum_{i=1}^{N} (F_{i+1}(x)(\prod_{j=1}^{2i}(x - x_j)))$$

where,

$$F_k(x) = \frac{(x - x_{2k})}{(x_{2k-1} - x_{2k})} G_k(x_{2k-1}) + \frac{(x - x_{2k-1})}{(x_{2k} - x_{2k-1})} G_k(x_{2k})$$

and $k = 1, 2, \cdots, N$; N is the fitting times; and G_k is the fitted data.

Proof: As the proof of Theorem 5.11, we will now show how we construct this approximating polynomial function. For U, suppose the polynomial function is

$$F(x) = F_1(x) + (x - x_1)(x - x_2)G_2(x)$$

where

$$F_1(x) = \frac{(x - x_2)}{(x_1 - x_2)}G_1(x_1) + \frac{(x - x_1)}{(x_2 - x_1)}G_1(x_2)$$

and where the values of $G_1(X) = F(x)$ are listed in the above table. Now $(x - x_1)(x - x_2)G_2(X)$ represents a remainder term, and the values of $G_2(x)$ at the other points can be solved as,

$$G_2(x_i) = \frac{G_1(x_i) - F_1(x_i)}{(x_i - x_1)(x_i - x_2)}$$

where $i = 3, 4, \cdots, m$.

If $|(G_2(x_3) + G_2(x_4) + ... + G_2(x_m))(x - x_1)(x - x_2)| < \delta$, where $\delta > 0$ is a small value determined by an expert, or, $m - 2 \le 0$, then we end the procedure, and we obtain $F(x) = F_1(x)$. The term $G_2(x)$ is neglected. Otherwise, we go on to the above procedure for the remaining data as follows. For the data,

E_X	x_3	x_4	$\cdots$	x_m
$G_2(x)$	$G_2(x_3)$	$G_2(x_4)$	$\cdots$	$G_2(x_m)$

let

$$G_2(x) = F_2(x) + (x - x_3)(x - x_4)G_3(x)$$

where

$$F_2(x) = \frac{(x - x_4)}{(x_3 - x_4)}G_2(x_3) + \frac{(x - x_3)}{(x_4 - x_3)}G_2(x_4)$$

And $(x - x_1)(x - x_2)(x - x_3)(x - x_4)G_3(x)$ is the remainder term. Then the values of $G_3(x)$ at the other points can be solved as,

$$G_3(x_i) = \frac{G_2(x_i) - F_2(x_i)}{(x_i - x_3)(x_i - x_4)}$$

where $i = 5, 6..., m$.

If $(G_3(x_5) + G_3(x_6) + ... + G_3(x_m))(x - x_1)(x - x_2)(x - x_3)(x - x_4) < \delta$, where $\delta > 0$ is a small value determined by expert; or if $m - 4 \le 0$, then the procedure is ended, and obtain $F(x) = F_1 + (x - x_1)(x - x_2)F_2(x)$, where the term $G_3(x)$ is neglected. Otherwise, we carry on with the above procedure for the remaining data.

We can obtain a function after repeating the above procedure several times. However, the above procedure is repeated N times ($N \le [m/2]$) at most. Finally, we can gain an approximating function as follows.

$$F(x) = F_1(x) + G_2(x)(x - x_1)(x - x_2)$$
$$= F_1(x) + (F_2(x) + G_3(x)(x - x_3)(x - x_4))(x - x_1)(x - x_2)$$
$$\cdots$$
$$= F_1(x) + \sum_{i=1}^{m}(F_{j+1}(x)(\prod_{j=1}^{2i}(x - x_j)))$$

$$\nabla$$

$F(X)$ is the approximating function of Y that we require. It is a polynomial function for which the order is not over $2N + 1$.

In fact, if $F(x)$ fits the data of X and Y perfectly, then $F(x)$ must be an increasing function. So we have the following theorem.

Theorem 5.12 $F(x)$ *is an increasing function under the above encoders, or for* $\forall x', x''(x' > x'') \rightarrow F(x') > F(x'')$.

Proof: First, we prove that $F_i(x)$ $(i = 1, 2, \cdots, m)$ are increasing functions. We apply induction to $F_i(x)$.

(1) When $i = 1$,

$$F_1(x) = \frac{(x - x_2)}{(x_1 - x_2)}G_1(x_1) + \frac{(x - x_1)}{(x_2 - x_1)}G_1(x_2)$$

For $\forall x', x'', x' > x''$,

$$F_1(x') - F_1(x'') = \frac{(x' - x_2)}{(x_1 - x_2)}G_1(x_1) + \frac{(x' - x_1)}{(x_2 - x_1)}G_1(x_2)$$
$$- (\frac{(x'' - x_2)}{(x_1 - x_2)}G_1(x_1) + \frac{(x'' - x_1)}{(x_2 - x_1)}G_1(x_2))$$
$$= \frac{(x' - x'')(G_1(x_2) - G_1(x_1))}{(x_2 - x_1)}$$
$$> 0$$

That is, $F_1(x') > F_1(x'')$, or $F_1(x)$ is an increasing function.

(2) Suppose $F_{k-1}(x)$ is an increasing function, we want to prove that $F_k(x)$ is also an increasing function. Because

$$F_k(x) = \frac{(x - x_{2k})}{(x_{2k-1} - x_{2k})}G_k(x_{2k-1}) + \frac{(x - x_{2k-1})}{(x_{2k} - x_{2k-1})}G_k(x_{2k})$$

and $F_{k-1}(x)$ is an increasing function, according to the method of constructing $G_k(x)$, G_k is an increasing function; or, for $\forall x', x''(x' > x'') \rightarrow G_k(x') > G_k(x'')$, so for $\forall x', x'', x' > x''$ we have

$$F_k(x') - F_k(x'') = \frac{(x' - x_{2k})}{(x_{2k-1} - x_{2k})} G_k(x_{2k-1}) + \frac{(x' - x_{2k-1})}{(x_{2k} - x_{2k-1})} G_k(x_{2k})$$

$$- (\frac{(x'' - x_{2k})}{(x_{2k-1} - x_{2k})} G_k(x_{2k-1}) + \frac{(x'' - x_{2k-1})}{(x_{2k} - x_{2k-1})} G_k(x_{2k}))$$

$$= \frac{(x' - x'')(G_k(x_{2k}) - G_k(x_{2k-1}))}{(x_{2k} - x_{2k-1})}$$

$$> 0$$

That is, $F_k(x') > F_k(x'')$, or $F_k(x)$ is an increasing function. Hence, $F_i(x)$ $(i = 1, 2, \cdots, m)$ are increasing functions.

▽

Because $H_i(x) = \prod_{j=1}^{2i}(x - x_j)$ $(i = 1, 2, \cdots, m)$ are increasing functions, so $H_i(x)F_i(x)$ $(i = 2, 3, \cdots, m)$ are increasing functions. That is, $F(x)$ is an increasing function, or for $\forall x', x''(x' > x'') \rightarrow F(x') > F(x'')$.

Furthermore, we have the following theorem.

Theorem 5.13 Let a_1, a_2, $a_3 \in S(X)$, $b_1 = a_1 M_{Y|X}, b_2 = a_2 M_{Y|X}, b_3 = a_3 M_{Y|X}$, and $(E_X(a_1) > E_X(a_2) > E_X(a_3)) \wedge (E_Y(b_1) > E_Y(b_2) > E_Y(b_3))$. Then $F(E_X(a_1)) > F(E_X(a_3)) > F(E_X(a_3))$.

Proof: This can be proved immediately from the procedure of constructing $F(x)$ and from Theorem 5.12.

▽

Suppose $\delta = 0.1$ in the following examples. It is important to demonstrate that the above function fits a given data set, D, efficiently. Now we select a data set from function $x^2 + x + 2$ as,

X	0	1	2	3	4	5	6	7	8	9
Y	2	4	8	14	22	32	44	58	74	92

For the above data, the approximation function is

$$F(x) = F_1(x) + (x - 0)(x - 1)G_2(x)$$

where

$$F_1(x) = \frac{(x-1)}{(0-1)}2 + \frac{(x-0)}{(1-0)}4$$
$$= 2x + 2$$

and $G_2(2) = 1, G_2(3) = 1, G_2(4) = 1, G_2(5) = 1, G_2(6) = 1, G_2(7) = 1, G_2(8) = 1, G_2(9) = 1$.

Because

$$(2 - 0)(2 - 1)G_2(2) + (3 - 0)(3 - 1)G_2(3)$$
$$+ (4 - 0)(4 - 1)G_2(4) + (5 - 0)(5 - 1)G_2(5)$$
$$+ (6 - 0)(6 - 1)G_2(6) + (7 - 0)(7 - 1)G_2(7)$$
$$+ (8 - 0)(8 - 1)G_2(8) + (9 - 0)(9 - 1)G_2(9)$$
$$> 1$$

and $10 - 2 > 0$. So, for the following results:

X	2	3	4	5	6	7	8	9
$G_2(x)$	1	1	1	1	1	1	1	1

let

$$G_2(x) = F_2(x) + (x - 2)(x - 3)G_3(x)$$

where

$$F_2(x) = \frac{(x - 3)}{(2 - 3)}1 + \frac{(x - 2)}{(3 - 2)}1$$
$$= 1$$

and $G_3(4) = 0$, $G_3(5) = 0$, $G_3(6) = 0$, $G_3(7) = 0$, $G_3(8) = 0$, $G_3(9) = 0$.
Because

$$(4 - 0)(4 - 1)(4 - 2)(4 - 3)G_3(4) + (5 - 0)(5 - 1)(5 - 2)(5 - 3)G_3(5)$$
$$+ (6 - 0)(6 - 1)(6 - 2)(6 - 3)G_3(6) + (7 - 0)(7 - 1)(7 - 2)(7 - 3)G_3(7)$$
$$+ (8 - 0)(8 - 1)(8 - 2)(8 - 3)G_3(8) + (9 - 0)(9 - 1)(9 - 2)(9 - 3)G_3(9)$$
$$= 0$$

so

$$G_2(x) = F_2(x) + (x - 2)(x - 3)G_3(x)$$
$$= F_2(x)$$
$$= 1$$

Furthermore, we can obtain the polynomial function

$$F(x) = F_1(x) + (x - 0)(x - 1)G_2(x)$$
$$= 2x + 2 + x(x - 1)1$$
$$= x^2 + x + 2$$

This means that the constructed function can fit real polynomial functions.

5.6.3 Algorithm Design

In this subsection, we design an algorithm for constructing an approximate function by fitting. Let the data in a data set be listed as follows:

X	$X[1]$	$X[2]$	$\cdots$	$X[n]$
Y	$Y[1]$	$Y[2]$	$\cdots$	$Y[n]$

After the data is preprocessed, the table becomes

X	$X[1]$	$X[2]$	$\cdots$	$X[m]$
Y	$Y[1]$	$Y[2]$	$\cdots$	$Y[m]$

An algorithm for discovering causal relational functions in data sets is constructed below.

Algorithm 5.1 *PFCPI*

> **begin**
> *(1)*   **readln**(δ);
> *(2)*   **for** $i \rightarrow 1$ **to** n **do**
>   **begin**
>   **readln**$(X[i])$;
>   **readln**$(Y[i])$
>   **end**;
> *(3)*   **preprocess** *the data*;
>   **let** $N1 \leftarrow 0$;
>   **for** $i \rightarrow 1$ **to** n **do**
>   **for** $j \rightarrow 1$ **to** n **do**
>   **let** $GG[i,j] \leftarrow 0; FF[i,j] \leftarrow 0$;
> *(4)*   **for** $j \rightarrow 1$ **to** m **do**
>   **begin**
>   **let** $X[j] \leftarrow encoder\ X[j]$;
>   **let** $Y[j] \leftarrow encoder\ Y[j]$;
>   **let** $GG[1,j] \leftarrow Y[j]$;
>   **end**;
> *(5)*   **if** $2N + 1 \geq m$ **then goto** *(6)*;
> *(6)*   **for** $j \rightarrow 2N + 1$ **to** m **do**
>   **begin**
>   **let**
> $FF[N,j] \leftarrow \frac{X[j]-X[2N]}{X[2N-1]-X[2N]}GG[N,2N-1] + \frac{X[j]-X[2N-1]}{X[2N]-X[2N-1]}GG[N,2N]$
>   **let** $GG[N+1,j] \leftarrow \frac{GG[N,j]-FF[N,j]}{(X[j]-X[2N-1])(X[j]-X[2N])}$;
>   **end**;
> *(7)*   **if** $\sum |GG[N+1,j]| > \delta$ **then**
>   **begin**
>   **let** $N \leftarrow N + 1$;

          goto *(5);*
         end;
(8)   **output** *the result* $F(x);$
(9)   **end** *of all.*

The algorithm $PFCPI$ is to generate a polynomial function $F(x)$ for a given data set, where the function $FF[i,j]$ is the same as F_j, as described in Theorem 5.11. Also, function $GG[i,j]$ is the same as G_j, as described in Theorem 5.11. The algorithm is initialized in Steps (1) and (2); Step (3) preprocesses the given data; Step (4) encodes the given data; Step (5) checks the condition $2N+1 \geq m$; Step (6) calculates Nth function; Step (7) checks the condition $\sum |GG[N+1,j]| > \delta$; and Step (8) outputs the result $F(x)$.

5.6.4 Examples

We now demonstrate the efficiency of the approximation function by an example.

It is important to demonstrate the efficiency with which the above function fits a given data set D. The following data set is taken directly from a real application.

Consider a simple probabilistic table consisting of only one random variable, say A, where $R(A) = \{$ red, green, yellow, blue, purple $\}$. And the probabilities are:

$$P(A = red) = 0.02$$

$$P(A = green) = 0.50$$

$$P(A = yellow) = 0.00$$

$$P(A = blue) = 0.37$$

$$P(A = purple) = 0.11$$

To find a function for fitting the above data, we first encode the data. The encoders of the data of A and $P(A)$ are $(E_A(yellow) = 1, E_A(red) = 2, E_A(blue) = 3, E_A(purple) = 4, E_A(green) = 5,$ and $E_{P(A=yellow)} = 0, E_{P(A=red)} = 6, E_{P(A=blue)} = 16, E_{P(A=purpl)} = 30,$ and $E_{P(A=green)} = 48)$. That is,

E_A	1	2	3	4	5
$E_{P(A)}$	0	6	16	30	48

For the above data, the procedure for finding an approximate fitting function is as

$$F(x) = F_1(x) + (x-1)(x-2)G_2(x)$$

where

$$F_1(x) = \frac{(x-2)}{(1-2)}0 + \frac{(x-1)}{(2-1)}6$$
$$= 6x - 6$$

and $G_2(3) = 2, G_2(4) = 2, G_2(5) = 2$.

Because $G_2(3) + G_2(4) + G_2(5) > 1$, therefore we have the following results

E_X	3	4	5
$G_2(x)$	2	2	2

Let

$$G_2(x) = F_2(x) + (x-3)(x-4)G_3(x)$$

where

$$F_2(x) = \frac{(x-4)}{(3-4)}2 + \frac{(x-3)}{(4-3)}2$$
$$= 2$$

and $G_3(5) = 0$.

Because $G_3(5) = 0$, so

$$G_2(x) = F_2(x) + (x-2)(x-3)G_3(x)$$
$$= F_2(x)$$
$$= 2$$

Furthermore, we can gain a polynomial function as,

$$F(x) = F_1(x) + (x-1)(x-2)G_2(x)$$
$$= 6x - 6 + (x-1)(x-2)2$$
$$= 2x^2 - 2$$

Therefore, $E_{P(A)}(x) = 2E_A^2(x) - 2$ and $P(A = a) = E_{P(A)}^{-1}(a) = E_{P(A)}(a)/100$.

As we have seen, we need only twice the approximation procedures to acquire the final result, and this result fits the above data completely. On the other hand, this method does not require the encoders to be constructed in a sophisticated way.

Also, the approach in this section can be used to find a linear function to replace a non-linear causality in a matrix. We now demonstrate how the data of a given rule with a matrix is fitted by this approach. Let a conditional probability matrix of a rule be

$$M_{Y|X} = \begin{bmatrix} 0.2 \ 0.4 \ 0.4 \\ 0.3 \ 0.4 \ 0.3 \\ 0.5 \ 0.2 \ 0.3 \end{bmatrix}$$

According to our encoder method, the order of the point variables must be rearranged as x_3, x_2, x_1. Then they are renamed as $z_1 = x_3, z_2 = x_2, z_3 = x_1$. Now we select a random data set as follows

E_Z	1090	2080	8020	9010	800020	900010	1000000
E_Y	302248	302446	303634	303832	383626	393823	404020

For the above data, an approximation function is found as follows.

$$F(x) = F_1(x) + (x - 1090)(x - 2080)G_2(x)$$

where

$$F_1(x) = \frac{(x - 2080)}{(1090 - 2080)}302248 + \frac{(x - 1090)}{(2080 - 1090)}302446$$
$$= 0.2x + 302030$$

and $G_2(8020) = 0$, $G_2(9010) = 0$, $G_2(800020) = -1.229933 * 10^{-7}$, $G_2(900010) = -1.092822 * 10^{-7}$, $G_2(1000000) = -9.83214561 * 10^{-8}$.

Because

$$||G_2(8020)(8020 - 1090)(8020 - 2080)||$$
$$+ ||G_2(9010)(9010 - 1090)(9010 - 2080)||$$
$$+ ||G_2(800020)(800020 - 1090)(800020 - 2080)||$$
$$+ ||G_2(900010)(900010 - 1090)(900010 - 2080)||$$
$$+ ||G_2(1000000)(1000000 - 1090)(1000000 - 2080)||$$
$$> 1$$

and $7 - 2 > 0$. Therefore we obtain the following data:

E_Z	800020	900010	1000000
$G_2(x)$	$-1.229933E - 7$	$-1.092822E - 7$	$-9.83214561E - 8$

Notice that, because $G_2(8020) = 0$ and $G_2(9010) = 0$, they do not need to be fitted.

Let

$$G_2(x) = F_2(x) + (x - 800020)(x - 900010)G_3(x)$$

where

$$F_2(x) = \frac{(x - 900010)}{(800020 - 900010)}(-1.229933E - 7)$$
$$+ \frac{(x - 800020)}{(900010 - 800020)}(-1.092822E - 7)$$
$$= 1.37124 * 10^{-13}x - 2.326947 * 10^{-7}$$

and $G_3(1000000) = -1.375653 * 10^{-19}$.

Because $\|G_2(1000000)(1000000{-}1090)(1000000{-}2080)(1000000{-}800020)$
$(1000000 - 900010)\| > 1$ and $7 - 6 > 0$, so for the following data:

E_Z	900010	1000000
$G_2(x)$	0	$-1.375653E - 19$

let

$$G_3(x) = F_3(x) + (x - 900010)(x - 1000000)G_4(x)$$

where

$$F_2(x) = \frac{(x - 1000000)}{(900010 - 1000000)}0$$

$$+ \frac{(x - 900010)}{(1000000 - 900010)}(-1.375653E - 19)$$

$$= 1.37579 * 10^{-24}x + 1.238225 * 10^{-18}.$$

Because $7 - 7 = 0$ and $G_4(x)$ can be neglected, we can obtain the polynomial function as

$$\begin{aligned}
F(x) = {} & 0.2x + 302030 \\
& + (x - 1090)(x - 2080)(1.37124 * 10^{-13}x - 2.326947 * 10^{-7}) \\
& + (x - 1090)(x - 2080)(x - 800020) \\
& * (x - 900010)(1.37579 * 10^{-24}x \\
& + 1.238225 * 10^{-18})
\end{aligned}$$

5.7 Summary

There are still some limitations involved when using causal rules with matrices, which prevent their general use. For example, its complexity has been proven to be NP-hard. The techniques in this chapter have been used for causal rule analysis. First a method was proposed for optimizing matrices for causal rules. Secondly, we constructed 'by encoding' approximate polynomial functions to replace non-linear causality. In particular, we presented a new approach for finding approximate polynomial causality from numerical data, by fitting. The key points of this work are as follows.

(1) Established a method of purifying causal rules, which reduces unnecessary information in their matrices once the rules were extracted.
(2) Presented a means for constructing an encoder and a decoder.
(3) Constructed an method of propagating probabilities in Bayesian networks when causality in Case-I.
(4) Suggested a method of constructing an approximation function for Bayesian networks when causality in Case-II and Case-III.
(5) Proposed a new approach for finding approximate linear causality from numerical data by fitting.

6. Association Rules in Very Large Databases

Dealing with very large databases is one of the defining challenges in data mining research and development. Some databases are simply too large (e.g., with terabytes of data) to be processed at one time. An ideal way of mining very large databases would be by using paralleling techniques. This system employs hardware technology, such as parallel machines, to implement concurrent data mining algorithms. However, parallel machines are expensive, and less widely available, than single processor machines. This chapter presents some techniques for mining association rules in very large databases, using instance selection.

The chapter is organized as follows. In Section 6.1, we spell out our motivation. In Section 6.2, we present a way of selecting instances from a very large database. In Section 6.3, we present a method of finding all approximate association rules of interest based on instance selection. In Section 6.4, we advocate an approach which searches true association rules by a one-pass over a database. This method depends upon approximate association rules. An incremental mining technique is developed in Section 6.5. In Section 6.6, an improved method of incremental mining is advocated. Finally, we summarize the chapter in Section 6.7.

6.1 Introduction

One of the main challenges in data mining is to identify association rules in very large databases that are comprised of millions of transactions and items. The main limitation of these approaches, however, is that multiple passes over the database are required. For very large databases that are typically disk resident, this requires reading the database completely for each pass, resulting in a large number of disk I/Os. The larger the size of a given database, the greater the number of disk I/Os. Therefore, more efficient mining models are being exploited. Accordingly, many variants of the Apriori algorithm (such as the hash based algorithm (see [Park-Chen-Yu 1997]), sampling (see [Toivonen 1996]) and the OPUS_AR algorithm (see [Webb 2000]) have been reported.

To mine huge databases, there are three approaches possible: (1) the use of feature selection based algorithms, (2) the use of parallel mining techniques, and (3) mining by sampling.

The method of mining very large databases based on feature selection (DMFS) selects only the features that are so-called 'relevant' to goal patterns, or functions ([Kohavi-John 1997, Liu-Setiono 1998, Seshadri-Weiss-Sasisekharan 1995]). Although it is often efficient to reduce the searched space by eliminating all irrelevant features, the selected features still make up a huge data set.

An ideal way of mining very large databases would appear to be by using paralleling techniques ([Agrawal-John-Shafer 1996, Chattratichat-etc 1997, Cheung 1996, Park-Chen-Yu 1995b, Parthasarathy-Zaki-Li 1998, Shintani-Kitsuregawa 1998]). This method employs hardware technology, such as parallel machines, to implement concurrent data mining algorithms. Hence, some developers have endeavored to scale up data mining algorithms by changing existing sequential techniques into parallel versions. Certainly, these algorithms are effective and efficient, and play an important role in mining very large databases.

However, parallel machines are expensive, and less widely available than single processor machines. Moreover, parallel data mining algorithms usually require more than just the availability of massive parallel machines. For example, they need extra software to distribute the components of parallel algorithms among the processors of the parallel machines. Also, this strategy does not work with all existing data mining algorithms. Some are sequential in nature, and can not make use of parallel hardware. And finally, it is usually a huge enterprise to re-implement existing software, and is often not worth the effort.

Recently, a sampling model for mining very large databases has been investigated. This model is also known as 'instance selection based mining' ([Toivonen 1996]). Sampling consists of selecting a small data set, RD, from a very large database D, such that, for any pattern P of D, an existing pattern P' in RD is approximate to P.

Sampling models (also known as 'instance selection based models') for mining very large databases do not require high-performance computers, and can be run on some personal computers. On the other hand, many applications, such as marketing and stock investment, may work under time constrains with little requirement for accuracy where the supports of itemsets are concerned. Indeed, for a short-term stock investor, time can cost money. Therefore, if an investor is able to obtain all approximate frequent itemsets from the data in his stock databases in a short time, those itemsets might be sufficient to enable an optimal decision to be made on a specific investment so that a quick profit can be made. On the other hand, if a stock investor were to attempt to extract all the accurate supports of frequent itemsets from his database it would be time-consuming. By the time a decision could be made, the best time for investment might have passed. To satisfy these applications, faster approximating mining models must be developed.

On the other hand, most users work in environments with bounded computational resources. For example, many people use personal computers or work stations without access to powerful compute servers. This means that if algorithms for mining very large databases were designed to work within bounded resources, then the techniques could be used by more people.

For the above reasons, we present some techniques for mining very large databases when resources are bounded. The techniques focus on instance selection by sampling, and include: mining approximate association rules of interest; searching real association rules by one pass over a database, depending on approximate association rules, an incremental mining model; and an anytime incremental mining algorithm.

A database, D, is considered in a trial as follows. Any itemset A in D can be taken as a random variable. If the itemset A occurs in a transaction T in D (written as $T(A)$), it is 1; otherwise, it is 0 (written as $\neg T(A)$). Let P be the set of all transactions in which the itemset A occurs, and let Q be the set of all transactions in which the itemset A does not occur. Then P and Q form a partition of D as follows:

$$P = \{T | T(A)\}$$
$$Q = \{T | \neg T(A)\}$$

Thus, each transaction has two possible outcomes for itemset A. They are 1 and 0. Suppose the probability of A occurring in the database is p, and the probability of A not occurring is $q = 1 - p$. Then, the itemset A in this database has a Bernoulli distribution according to the definition in [Durrett 1996]. In particular, an itemset with a Bernoulli distribution can also be taken as having a binomial distribution.

Such trials (data sets) generally involve large amounts of data. Problem solving involving these trials typically relies on approximate results. The earliest method discovered, was approximation by the 'large number law'. However, the results are very crude using this method. Some better approaches, such as *Chernoff bounds* ([Hagerup 1989]) and the *central limit theorem* ([Durrett 1996]) have been proposed.

Recently, the 'Chernoff bounds' technique has been applied to instance selection for mining very large databases in [Srikant-Agrawal 1997, Toivonen 1996]. In this instance selection, each database is taken with a binomial distribution.

Our work in this chapter focuses on applying the central limit theorem to select instances for mining association rules in very large databases. The instance selection we propose is a faster mining model, especially when the database is viewed as following a Bernoulli distribution, or a binomial distribution.

6.2 Instance Selection

In probability theory it is usually called a *trial*, when a situation is such that only two outcomes (for example, success and failure) are possible. The variable element in a trial is described by a probability distribution on a sample space of two elements, 0 representing failure and 1 success; this distribution assigns the probability $1 - \theta$ to 0 and θ to 1, where $0 \leq \theta \leq 1$. Suppose we consider n independent repetitions of a given trial. The variable element is described by the probability distribution on a sample space of 2^n points, the typical point being $x = (x_1, x_2, \cdots, x_n)$, where each x_i is 0 or 1, and x_i represents the result of the ith trial. The appropriate probability distribution is defined by

$$p_\theta(x) = \theta^{m(x)}(1 - \theta)^{n-m(x)}$$

where $m(x) = \sum_{i=1}^{n} x_i$ is the number of 1s within the results of the n trials. This is the case because the trials are independent.

Given an x in this situation, it seems reasonable to estimate θ by using $m(x)/n$, the proportion of successes obtained. This appears, in a sense, to be a 'good' estimate of θ.

In this way, a database D can be taken as a trial. Any itemset A is 1 if that itemset occurs in a transaction T (written as $T(A)$), or else it is 0 (written as $\neg T(A)$). Suppose the probability of A occurring in the database is p, and the probability of A not occurring is $q = 1 - p$. Then, the database can be taken as a Bernoulli trial, according to the definition in [Durrett 1996]. We can approximate the probability, p, of A by using the central limit theorem.

6.2.1 Evaluating the Size of Instance Sets

As we have seen, some applications require only approximate frequent itemsets. There are already many techniques designed to deal with such approximations, including the large number law, Chernoff bounds ([Hagerup-Rub 1989]), and the central limit theorem ([Durrett 1996]) — all for tackling large data sets. In our method, for efficiency, the central limit theorem is applied to estimate the size of samples, or instance sets.

The central limit theorem has been one of the most remarkable results of work on applications involving probability theory. Loosely put, it states that the sum of a large number of independent random variables has a distribution that is approximately normal. Hence, it not only provides a simple method for computing approximating probabilities for sums of independent random variables, but it also helps explain the remarkable fact that the empirical frequencies of so many natural populations exhibit bell-shaped (normal) curves. In its simplest form the central limit theorem is as follows.

Let $X_1, X_2, \cdots$ be a sequence of independent and identically distributed random variables, each having finite mean $E(X_i) = \mu$ and $Var(X_i) = \sigma^2$. Then the distribution of

$$\frac{X_1 + \cdots + X_n - n\mu}{\sigma\sqrt{n}}$$

tends to the standard normal as $n \to \infty$. That is,

$$P\{\frac{X_1 + \cdots + X_n - n\mu}{\sigma\sqrt{n}} \le a\} \to \frac{1}{\sqrt{2\pi}} \int_{-\infty}^{a} e^{-x^2/2} dx \quad as \quad n \to \infty \quad (6.1)$$

This means that we can approximate probabilities of random variables by applying the central limit theorem. (Readers are referred to [Durrett 1996] for other relevant concepts and theorems.)

In this chapter, we will set up some mining techniques based on instance selection by sampling. The first step is to apply the central limit theorem to generate instance sets from a sample from a large database. We estimate the sample size below.

Theorem 6.1 *Let D be a large database, $T_1, T_2, \cdots, T_m$ be the transactions in D, X be an itemset in D, $\eta > 0$ be the degree of asymptotic to frequent itemsets, and $\xi \ge 0$ be the upper probability of $P[|Ave(X_n) - p| \le \eta]$, where $Ave(X_n)$ is the average of X occurring in n transactions in D. Suppose the records in D are matched Bernoulli trials. If n random records of D are sufficient to determine the approximate frequent itemsets in D, according to the central limit theorem, n must be as follows:*

$$n \ge \frac{z^2_{(1+\xi)/2}}{4\eta^2} \tag{6.2}$$

where z_x is a standard normal distribution function. (See the Appendix in [Durrett 1996].)

Proof: From the given conditions in this theorem, we take

$$P(|Ave(X_n) - p| \le \eta) = \xi$$

Clearly,

$$P(|Ave(X_n) - p| \le \eta) = P(-\eta \le (Ave(X_n) - p) \le \eta)$$
$$= P(\frac{-\eta}{1/(2\sqrt{n})} \le (\frac{Ave(X_n) - p)}{1/(2\sqrt{n})} \le \frac{\eta}{1/(2\sqrt{n})})$$
$$\approx N(2\eta\sqrt{n}) - N(-2\eta\sqrt{n})$$
$$= 2N(2\eta\sqrt{n}) - 1$$

and for this probability to equal ξ we need

$$N(2\eta\sqrt{n}) = \frac{1}{2}(1 + \xi)$$

which is satisfied by

$$2\eta\sqrt{n} = z_{(1+\xi)/2}$$

Then, the required value for n is

$$n \geq \frac{z^2_{(1+\xi)/2}}{4\eta^2}$$

∇

We now illustrate the use of this theorem in Example 6.1.

Example 6.1 *Suppose a new process is available for doping the silicon chips used in electronic devices, and p (unknown) is the probability that each chip produced in this way is defective. We assume that the defective chips are independent of each other. How many chips, n, must we produce and test so that the proportion of defective chips found ($Ave(X_n)$) does not differ from p by more than 0.01, with probability at least 0.99? That is, we want n such that*

$$P(|Ave(X_n) - p| < 0.01) > 0.99$$

where $\eta = 0.01, \xi = 0.995$, and $z_{0.95} = 2.57$. Thus we have

$$n = \frac{2.57^2}{4 * 0.01^2} = 16513$$

which is considerably smaller than the value $n = 27000$ that is required when using the approximating model in Chernoff bounds ([Srikant-Agrawal 1997, Toivonen 1996]).

The procedure for applying the central limit theorem to estimate the size of an instance set is designed as in Procedure 6.1.

Procedure 6.1 *SampleSize*

> *Input: η: accuracy of results, ξ: probability of requirements*
> *Output: n: estimated sample size*
>
> *Begin*
> **read** *accuracy of results η;*
> **read** *probability of requirements ξ;*
> **let** $n \leftarrow \frac{z^2_{(1+\xi)/2}}{4\eta^2} + 1;$
> **output** *the size of instance set n;*
> **end**.

Procedure *SampleSize* is to estimate the size of an instance set for given accuracy of results and probability of requirements using the central limit theorem.

6.2.2 Generating Instance Set

Based on Theorem 6.1, we can obtain a random instance set from the database in two steps: (1) we generate n random numbers, where n is determined by the central limit theorem; and (2) we choose n transactions in the database according to the random numbers. In this subsection, we present a procedure for generating random databases (instance sets).

Generally, it is difficult to apply absolutely random numbers when choosing tuples from a database. Therefore, pseudo-random numbers are used so as to control the selection of the random data subset generated.

There are many methods for generating pseudo-random numbers. We choose one from the following pseudo-random number generators.

Suppose the pseudo-random numbers are:

$$x_0, x_1, x_2, \cdots$$

Then the ith pseudo-random number ($i > 0$) can be determined as

$$x_i = (ax_{i-1} + b) \; MOD \; m \tag{6.3}$$

where a, b, and m are constants. The sequence $x_0, x_1, x_2, \cdots$ is a sequence of integers between 0 and $m - 1$.

In the above formula, if $a = 1$, the other linear pseudo-random number generator is:

$$x_i = (x_{i-1} + b) \; MOD \; m \tag{6.4}$$

and, if $b = 0$, a simple linear pseudo-random number generator is:

$$x_i = ax_{i-1} \; MOD \; m \tag{6.5}$$

It appears that the first generator, (6.3), is the best. It has a higher stochastic degree when x_0, a, b, m are mutually prime numbers. Therefore, for simplicity, we only present an algorithm for that generator, and we generate pseudo-random numbers as in Procedure 6.2.

Procedure 6.2 *RandomNumber*

begin
Input: a: integer constant, b: integer constant, m: real database size,
*   n: random database size, x_0: first pseudo-random number;*
Output: X: set of pseudo-random numbers;

(1) let $X \leftarrow \emptyset$;
    let $a \leftarrow$ a bigger prime number;
    let $b \leftarrow$ a prime number which is different from a;
    read x_0 a prime number which is different from a and b;
    let $c \leftarrow x_0$;
    let $X \leftarrow X \cup \{x_0\}$;
(2) **while** $|X| \neq n$ **do begin**
        let $x_i \leftarrow (a * c + b) \; MOD \; m$;
        if $x_i \notin X$ **then**
         let $X \leftarrow X \cup \{x_i\}$;
        let $c \leftarrow x_i$;
   end
(3) **for** $i = 1$ **to** n **do**
        output random number x_i in X;
  end;

The procedure *RandomNumber* generates n random numbers, where n is equal to the sample size. We can apply these numbers to select n instances as a sample. Step (1) carries out initialization. To generate m different random numbers, a, b, and x_0 are three different prime number, where m is equal to the size of a given large database. Step (2) generates n random numbers and saves them into set X, where each random number is less than m, according to the operator 'MOD'. Step (3) outputs the generated random numbers.

Note that m is required to be equal to, or greater than, the size of a given very large database, such that each transaction in the database has the same probability to be selected.

The method for generating random instance sets from real database is as follows: (1) generating a set X of pseudo-random numbers, where $|X| = n$; and (2) generating the random database RD (instance set) from D, using the pseudo-random number set X. That is, for any $x_i \in X$, we obtain the $(x_i + 1)$th record of D and append it into RD. The generation of a random index database from a real database is demonstrated in Procedure 6.3.

Procedure 6.3 *RandomDatabase*

begin
Input: D: original real database;
Output: RD: random database;
(1) let $RD \leftarrow \emptyset$;
    call procedure SampleSize to estimate the size of instance set;
    call procedure RandomNumber to generate the set X of n random numbers;
(2) **for** any numbers x_i in X **do begin**
        let $j \leftarrow x_i + 1$;
        let *record* $\leftarrow$ the jth record in D;

>   **let** $RD \leftarrow RD \cup \{record\}$;
>   **end**
> (3) **output** the random database RD;
> **end;**

The procedure *RandomDatabase* generates a sample RD from the given large database D by a set of random numbers. In Step (1), an initial value $\emptyset$ is first assigned to the sample RD; then the size of an instance set is estimated by calling in the procedure *SampleSize*; finally, the set X of n random numbers is generated by calling in the procedure *RandomNumber*. Step (2) generates the random data subset RD of D by using the numbers in X. The ith transaction in RD is the x_ith record in the database D. Because the random numbers required must be different from each other when they are generated, each record in the database D can be dealt with, at most, one time. And the records in RD consist of random instances selected from the database D. In Step (3), the sample RD is output.

Note that generating the random database RD of the given database D does not mean that a new database RD is established. It only serves to build a view RD over D.

6.3 Estimation of Association Rules

In this section, we first present a procedure for identifying frequent itemsets in an instance set (sample set) by pruning. Then we construct an algorithm for searching approximate association rules.

6.3.1 Identifying Approximate Frequent Itemsets

As we have seen, we require only the instance set of a given large database to find approximate frequent itemsets. We now construct an algorithm for mining frequent itemsets in the generated random database RD (instance set). The algorithm is similar to that constructed in Chapter 2, and the use of the algorithm is the same as for the Apriori algorithm designed in Chapter 2.

Procedure 6.4 *ApproximateItemsets*

begin
Input: D: data set; minsupp: minimum support; mininterest: minimum interest;
Output: ApproximateISet: approximate frequent itemsets;
(1) **let** large set *ApproximateISet* $\leftarrow \emptyset$;
   call procedure RandomDatabase to generate the instance set RD;

(2) **let** $L_1 \leftarrow$ {frequent 1-itemsets};
   let $ApproximateISet \leftarrow ApproximateISet \cup L_1$;
(3) **for** $(k = 2; L_{k-1} \neq \emptyset; k++)$ **do**
    begin
   //Generate all possible k-itemsets of interest in RD.
      let $C_k \leftarrow \{\{x_1, \ldots x_{k-2}, x_{k-1}, x_k\} \mid \{x_1, \ldots x_{k-2}, x_{k-1}\} \in L_{k-1} \wedge$
 $\{x_1, \ldots x_{k-2}, x_k\} \in L_{k-1}\}$;
      for any transaction t in RD **do**
        begin
   //Check which k-itemsets are included in transaction t.
          let $C_t \leftarrow$ the k-itemsets in t that are contained by C_k;
          for any itemset A in C_t **do**
            let $A.count \leftarrow A.count + 1$;
        end
      let $L_k \leftarrow \{c \mid c \in C_k \wedge (p(c) = (c.count/|RD|) >= minsupp)\}$;
   //Prune all uninteresting k-itemsets in L_k
      for any itemset i in L_k **do**
        if an itemset i is uninteresting **then**;
          let $L_k \leftarrow L_k - \{i\}$;
    end
      let $ApproximateISet \leftarrow ApproximateISet \cup L_k$;
(4) **output** the frequent/large itemsets $ApproximateISet$ in RD;
end;

The procedure *ApproximateItemsets* generates all approximate frequent itemsets in a sample RD. It is a Apriori-like algorithm. The initialization and generating sample RD of a given database, D, are carried out in Step (1). In Step (2), set L_1 of all frequent 1-itemsets in RD is generated in the first pass of the algorithm.

Step (3) generates all sets L_k for $k \geq 2$ by a loop, where L_k is the set of all frequent k-itemsets in RD generated in the kth pass of the algorithm, and the end-condition of the loop is $L_{k-1} = \emptyset$. For $k >= 2$, we need to prune all uninteresting k-itemsets from the set C_k. That is, for any itemset i in C_k, if $|p(X \cup Y) - p(X)p(Y)| < mininterest$ for any expressions $i = X \cup Y$ of i, then i is an uninteresting frequent itemset, and it must be pruned from C_k. Each subsequent pass in Step (3), say pass k, consists of three phases. The first phase is to generate the set C_k of all k-itemsets in RD where each k-itemset contains at least a subset of L_{k-1}. This means that a k-itemset in RD is pruned from C_k if the k-itemset does not contain any subsets of L_{k-1}. The second phase is a loop, which adds the occurrences up for itemsets of C_k in RD. The final phase is to determine the frequent k-itemsets L_k by the k-itemset with $c.count/|RD|) >= minsupp$ in C_k, where $|RD|$ is the number of transactions in the sample RD. And then the set L_k is appended into *ApproximateISet*.

Step (4) outputs the frequent itemsets *ApproximateISet* in *RD*, where each itemset, *i*, in *ApproximateISet* must be with its support $p(i)$ greater than, or equal to, the minimum support *minsupp*.

Obviously, the above algorithm is efficient for discovering the approximate frequent itemsets in a given large database. However, if the support of an itemset A is in the neighbour of *minsupp*, then A can sometimes be treated as a frequent itemset and sometimes not as a frequent itemset, due to approximation errors. In other words, some such itemsets are frequent itemsets in D but not in RD, and some such itemsets are not frequent itemsets in D but are frequent itemsets in RD. This is a weakness of approximating models. For example, consider a random subset RD of a given large database D. Let *minsupp* $= 0.2$ and the probability of error be tolerated at 0.05. Let two itemsets be A and B in D, with probabilities (supports) 0.18 and 0.23 respectively. Assume also that A and B are generated with probabilities 0.21 and 0.194 respectively, in the random database RD. This means that A is a frequent itemset in RD, and B is not a frequent itemset in RD, due to an approximating error of 0.05. These are undesirable results.

In fact, the neighbour of *minsupp* does not effect the goal of discovering high-support itemsets in databases. In applications such as marketing and stock investment, all the high-support itemsets in databases are sufficient to enable users to make correct decisions. Thus, the above approximating error might be tolerated in some applications to save time and cost. However, if we must reduce approximation errors, we can control the process by lowering the upper probability of $P[|Ave(X_n) - p| \leq \eta]$ when we estimate the size of a sample for certain applications. Studies in this section focus on applications that work well under approximate results.

6.3.2 Measuring Association Rules of Interest

For an association rule $X \rightarrow Y$, let $p(X)$, $p(Y)$, and $p(X \cup Y)$ denote the fraction of rows satisfying condition X, Y, XY, respectively, and let $p(Y|X) = p(X \cup Y)/p(X)$ ($X \cup Y$ being the conjunction of X and Y). Note that $p(X \cup Y)$ and $p(Y|X)$ are the support and confidence of a rule $X \rightarrow Y$. We will consider an interestingness, *J-measure*, used in [Smyth-Goodman 1992], which is defined as

$$J(X,Y) = p(X)[p(Y|X)\log_2\frac{p(Y|X)}{p(Y)} + (1 - p(Y|X))\log_2\frac{1 - p(Y|X)}{1 - p(Y)}]$$

The first term '$p(X)$' measures the generality of the rule. The term inside the square bracket measures the 'discrimination power' of X on Y, i.e., how dissimilar the priori $p(Y)$ and the posteriori $p(Y|X)$ are about Y. The dissimilarity is 'two-sided' in that $p(Y|X)$ could be either larger or smaller than $p(X)$, due to $p(Y|X)\log_2\frac{p(Y|X)}{p(Y)}$ and $(1 - p(Y|X))\log_2\frac{1-p(Y|X)}{1-p(Y)}$, respectively.

The rule is useful as it implies a high degree of dissimilarity. In our framework of association rules $X \rightarrow Y$, however, the larger the confidence $p(Y|X)$, the more interesting the rule. Therefore, for association rules we will use the 'one-sided' J-measure equation:

$$I^J(X,Y) = p(X)p(Y|X)\log_2\frac{p(Y|X)}{p(Y)}$$

for measuring the interestingness. Because $p(Y|X) = p(X \cup Y)/p(X)$,

$$I^J(X,Y) = p(X \cup Y)\log_2\frac{p(X \cup Y)}{p(X)p(Y)}$$

We now use an example to demonstrate how to find this model when discovering association rules. Let $minsupp = 0.2$, $minconf = 0.4$ and $mininterest = 0.05$.

Example 6.2 *For an itemset $A \cup C$, let $p(A) = 0.5$, $p(C) = 0.4$; and $p(A \cup C) = 0.36$, and we have $p(A \cup C) - p(A)p(C) = 0.16 > mininterest = 0.05$. According to the above definition, rule $A \rightarrow C$ may be extracted as a rule of interest. Furthermore,*

$$p(C|A) = \frac{p(A \cup C)}{p(A)} = \frac{0.36}{0.5} = 0.72$$

and

$$I^J(A,C) = p(A \cup C)log_2\frac{p(A \cup C)}{p(A)p(C)} = 0.36log_2\frac{0.36}{0.5*0.4} = 0.3053$$

According to our model, $A \rightarrow C$ can be extracted as a rule of interest due to the fact that the confidence $p(C|A) = 0.72 > minconf$, the interestingness $I^J(A,C) = 0.3053 > mininterest$, and the support $p(A \cup C) = 0.36 > minsupp$.

6.3.3 Algorithm Designing

Let D be a very large database, $|D|$ the total number of transactions in D, I the set of all items in D and, for $X \subseteq I$, $|X|$ is the number of transactions in D that contain itemset X, $minsupp, minconf, mininterest$ and γ as given by users. The algorithm for discovering association rules in our probability ratio model is constructed as in Algorithm 6.1.

Algorithm 6.1 *ApproximatingM*

begin
Input: *D: database, $minsupp, minconf, mininterest$ and γ: threshold values;*
Output: *approximate rules;*

(1) **determine** the sample size, n, based on the central limit theorem;
    let $RD \leftarrow$ generating the sample database with n transactions;
    call the procedure *ApproximateItemsets* for RD;
    let $L \leftarrow ApproximateISet$;
    let $T \leftarrow false$;
(2) **for** any frequent itemset $A \subset L$ **do**
    begin
      for any itemset $X \subset A$ **do**
        begin
          if $I^J(X, (A - X)) \geq mininterest$ **then**
          if $p((A - X)|X) \geq minconf$ **then**
            output the rule $X \rightarrow (A - X)$
              with confidence $p((A - X)|X)$ and support $p(A)$;
        end;
    end;
(3) **if** certain rules are required **then**
    begin
      call *FinalFrequentItemset*;
      let $L \leftarrow LL$;
      let $T \leftarrow true$;
    end;
(4) **if** T **then**
      goto step (2);
end.

The algorithm *ApproximatingM* is to generate a set of approximate association rules by sampling. It can also generate accurate association rules in D, based on approximations. This is accomplished by calling in two procedures, as shown below in Section 6.4.

In Step (1) of the above algorithm, the sample database and the frequent itemsets in the sample are generated; Step (2) creates all association rules of interest. That is, all rules of the form $X \rightarrow (A - X)$ if the interestingness $I^J(X, (A - X)) \geq mininterest$, the confidence $p((A - X)|X) \geq minconf$, and the support $p(X) \geq minsupp$; Step (3) deals with certain rules using the procedure *FinalFrequentItemset*, as presented in Section 6.4, to generate all hopeful itemsets and certain rules are extracted from them.

6.4 Searching True Association Rules Based on Approximations

Certainly, if only approximate rules are required by applications, then the algorithm *ApproximatingM* can satisfy such applications. However, some applications need real rules. This requirement can be met by the model of 'assisting knowledge discovery' below.

As has been shown, our model is efficient in discovering approximate association rules in large databases. However, if the support of an itemset A is in the neighbourhood of *minsupp*, then A can sometimes be treated as a frequent itemset, and sometimes not as a frequent itemset, according to approximation errors. In other words, some such itemsets are frequent itemsets in D but not in RD, and some such itemsets are not frequent itemsets in D, but are frequent itemsets in RD. This is a weakness of our model.

On the other hand, if we cannot compromise the validity of mined rules, or if the true support and confidence of a rule are necessary for some applications, $\eta > 0$ can be expected to be much smaller. This implies that we must end up with a very large sample from the database, which diminishes the gains achieved by sampling.

However, because of the randomness of data in a given database, we can first roughly generate a possible set of frequent itemsets. Then this set is used as heuristic information to obtain frequent itemsets with only one pass through the database. In this way, we can use such heuristic information to (1) assist knowledge discovery where accuracy is important or certain support and confidence is desirable, and (2) determine whether an itemset in the neighbourhood of *minsupp*, in the random subset of a given database, is a frequent itemset. However, for significance of probability, $minsupp > \eta$ would hold.

Definition 6.1 *If an itemset A in RD is greater than, or equal to, $minsupp - \eta$, then it is reasonable from probabilistic significance to conjecture that A is a frequent itemset in the database D. An itemset such as A is called a hopeful frequent itemset in D. Reversely, if an itemset A in RD is less than $minsupp - \eta$, then it is reasonable and comprehensive from probabilistic significance to believe that it is impossible for A to be a frequent itemset in the database D.*

Apparently, assessing hopeful frequent itemsets is not only useful to the itemsets in the neighbourhood of *minsupp*, but also efficient in assisting non-approximate knowledge discovery in databases. We now present an algorithm for accomplishing two such tasks.

Procedure 6.5 *TFrequentItemset*

begin
Input: η: accuracy of results, minsupp: minimum support,
        D: original database, HLIsSet: set of hopeful frequent itemsets;
Output: LI: frequent itemsets D;
(1) let $LI \leftarrow \emptyset$;
    let $HLIsSet \leftarrow$ all hopeful frequent itemsets with support $\geq minsupp - \eta$ in the sample;
    for $i = 1$ **to** N **do**

```
            let L_i ← ∅;
    for A ∈ HLIsSet do
            let L_{|A|} ← L_{|A|} ∪ {A};
(2) for each tuple τ of D do
        begin
            let Q ← τ;
            let k ← 0;
            while Q ≠ ∅ do
                begin
                    let P ← ∅;
                    let k ← k + 1;
                    for each i_k ⊂ Q the k-itemsets do
                        if i_k ∈ L_k then
                            begin
                                let Count_{i_k} ← Count_{i_k} + 1;
                                let P ← P ∪ i_k;
                            end;
                    let Q ← P;
                end;
        end;
(3) for each itemset α of HLIsSet do
        if Count_α ≥ minsupp then
            let LI ← LI ∪ {α};
(4) output the set LI of all frequent itemsets in D;
end;
```

Here, the initialization is carried out in Step (1); Step (2) generates the sets L_k of k-itemsets in the original database D; Step (3) finds all frequent itemsets in D and stores them into LI; Step (4) outputs the frequent itemsets LI.

This algorithm requires less running time and space than previous algorithms for generating frequent itemsets. (We will discuss its complexity in the next section.) We now demonstrate this in a simple way in Example 6.3.

Example 6.3 Let $\tau = \{A, B, C, F, E, H\}$ be a transaction in D, and the subsets of τ be in $HLIsSet$ as

$$\{A\}, \{B\}, \{E\}, \{H\}$$
$$\{A, B\}, \{A, E\}, \{B, E\}, \{A, H\}, \{B, H\}, \{E, H\}$$
$$\{A, B, E\}, \{A, B, H\}, \{B, E, H\}$$
$$\{A, B, E, H\}$$

For the tuple τ, the procedure works as follows.

First loop, $Q = \tau$ and $k = 1$. Next each of $Count_A$, $Count_B$, $Count_E$, and $Count_H$ adds 1, and $P = \{A, B, E, H\}$.

Second loop, $Q = P = \{A, B, E, H\}$ *and* $k = 2$. *Then each of* $Count_{AB}$, $Count_{AE}$, $Count_{AH}$, $Count_{BE}$, $Count_{BH}$, *and* $Count_{EH}$ *adds 1, and* $P = \{A, B, E, H\}$.

Third loop, $Q = P = \{A, B, E, H\}$ *and* $k = 3$. *Then* $Count_{ABE}$, $Count_{ABH}$, *and* $Count_{BEH}$ *each adds 1, and* $P = \{A, B, E, H\}$.

Fourth loop, $Q = P = \{A, B, E, H\}$ *and* $k = 4$. *Then* $Count_{ABEH}$ *adds 1, and* $P = \{A, B, E, H\}$.

Fifth loop, $P = \emptyset$; *and this loop ends.*

In this procedure, 28 units are used to store the names of 14 different itemsets and their counts. However, it requires $2*6! = 1440$ *units to store the names of 720 different itemsets and their counts from previous algorithms for generating frequent itemsets. Thus, our algorithm requires less running time and space.*

Again, if the confidence of a rule $A \rightarrow B$ is in the neighbourhood of $minconf$, then $A \rightarrow B$ can sometimes be extracted as a valid rule, and sometimes not as a valid rule, depending upon the approximate error. The problem of the neighbourhood $(minconf - \xi, minconf + \xi)$ of $minconf$ can be addressed using a similar method as that used for the neighbourhhood of $minsupp$. However, for significance of probability, $minconf > \xi$ would hold. We now illustrate how to handle the neighbourhood of $minconf$ in Procedure 6.6.

Procedure 6.6 *FinalFrequentItemset*

begin
Input: *LI: set of frequent itemsets, minconf: minimum confidence,*
ξ: *probability of requirements,*
Output: *LL: final frequent itemsets;*
(1) let $LL \leftarrow \emptyset$;
(2) **for** any frequent itemset $A \subset LI$ **do**
    begin
      for any itemset $X \subset A$ **do**
      begin
        if $p(X \cup (A - X)) - p(X)p(A - X) \geq mininterest$ **then**
          if $PR((A - X)|X) \geq minconf - \xi$ **then**
            let $LL \leftarrow LL \cup A \cup X \cup (A - X)$;
      end;
(3) **output** LL;
    end;

Here, LL is the set of all hopeful itemsets with respect to both neighbourhoods of $minsupp$ and $minconf$.

Now, we can describe a model for applying our method to assist non-approximate knowledge discovery in databases. For a given large database

D, and the user specified *minsupp* and *minconf*, the following steps are performed. We:

(1) generate a random subset RD of D according to our model;
(2) generate the set $HLIsSet$ of all hopeful frequent itemsets in RD with support greater than, or equal to, $max\{0, minsupp - approximate\ error\}$;
(3) generate all final frequent itemsets in D with support greater than or equal to *minsupp* by Procedure 6.6;
(4) generate all the rules with both support and confidence greater than, or equal to, minimum support and minimum confidence, respectively, according to the final frequent itemsets in the database.

It is obvious that, applying approximate results to assist knowledge discovery requires only a rough estimation, such as $\eta = 0.01$ and $\xi = 0.9$, which is enough to generate all hopeful frequent itemsets.

In order to handle the problem caused by both the neighbourhood of *minsupp* and the neighbourhood of *minconf*, we can use two methods as follows. One method is to take $max\{0, minsupp - \eta\}$ and $max\{0, minconf - \xi\}$ as the minimum support and minimum confidence respectively. This is for applications that require only approximate results. Another method requires more accurate results, or true support and confidence, and the following method can be performed.

Algorithm 6.2 *NeighbourRules*

begin

(1) Generate a random subset RD of D;

(2) Generate all hopeful frequent itemsets in RD with support greater than, or equal to, $max\{0, minsupp - approximate\ error\}$;

(3) Generate the set RSET of all the rules with both support and confidence greater than or equal to minimum support ($max\{0, minsupp - \eta\}$) and minimum confidence ($max\{0, minconf - \xi\}$) respectively, according to the hopeful frequent itemsets in RD;

(4) For the subset PS of RSET with both support and confidence in the neighbourhood of minsupp and the neighbourhood of minconf respectively, generate the set VRS of all rules in PS that is valid in D;

(5) Output $(RSET - PS) \cup VRS$.

end

The algorithm *NeighbourRules* also considers that the supports (or confidences) of association rules are in the neighbourhood of *minsupp* (or the neighbourhood of *minconf*). Because they may be valid rules in the original database, we would compute their supports and confidences when true association rules are searched for.

Theorem 6.2 *For a given large database D, minsupp and minconf are given by users. $A \to B$ can be extracted as an approximate rule in Algorithm NeighbourRules if $A \to B$ is a valid rule in D.*

Proof: We first prove ("$\Rightarrow$"). According to the above assumption, if

(1) $support(A \cup B) \geq max\{0, minsupp - \eta\}$, and
(2) $confidence(A \to B) \geq max\{0, minconf - \xi\}$,

hold in a random subset RD of D, by (4) and (5) in Algorithm *NeighbourRules*, we can obtain

(i) $support(A \cup B) \geq minsupp$, and
(ii) $confidence(A \to B) \geq minconf$.

This means that $A \to B$ is still a valid rule in D.

The proof of ("$\Leftarrow$") can be directly obtained from the above definition.

So, $A \to B$ can be extracted as an approximate rule in the algorithm *NeighbourRules* if, and only if, $A \to B$ is a valid rule in D. $\qquad \nabla$

In the real-world, many applications, such as catalog design, store layout, product placement, marketing, stock investment, supermarket management and planning, need only approximate frequent itemsets for goals such as aiming at the shortest time and resource bounded. It is a good idea when mining frequent itemsets to select a sample from a given database for estimating the support of candidates ([Srikant-Agrawal 1997, Toivonen 1996]). (For convenience, the following comparison is on frequent itemsets.) Thus, if we choose a random subset RD of D as the operating object for mining the frequent itemsets of a very large database, D, for example, over 10^6 transactions, the running time can be minimized. Such a random subset would maintain the support of an itemset in RD as approximately equal to that in D. This requires that the transactions of a given database are randomly appended into the database so as to hold a binomial distribution. In [Srikant-Agrawal 1997, Toivonen 1996], the Chernoff bounds technique has been applied to mine approximate frequent itemsets, where the database is taken as with a binomial distribution. The method of mining approximate frequent itemsets in Chernoff bounds is as follows. First, the formula

$$n = \frac{1}{2\eta^2} ln \frac{2}{1 - \xi}$$

is used to estimate the size of a subset RD of a given D, where ξ is the degree of approximate frequent itemsets asymptotic to frequent itemsets, and η is the upper probability of approximate frequent itemsets with error ξ. Then we mine all approximate frequent itemsets in RD. If true association rules are required, one scan of D is able to discover all real frequent itemsets using the approximate frequent itemsets. In our opinion, there are two ways to improve the above algorithms. One is to reduce the sample size. As a matter of fact, it can be cut down by about half by using the central limit theorem under the same conditions. Another way is to narrow the search space by using a pruning technique. To solve this problem, in this chapter, we construct a new algorithm for identifying approximate frequent itemsets.

6.5 Incremental Mining

As we have seen, approximate association rules can be identified in very large databases by sampling. We can also identify real association rules by only one pass over the database upon the discovered approximations. But this still requires scanning all data in the database. Therefore, it is still impossible to mine a very large database on a personal computer. For efficiency, this section presents an incremental mining technique. This incremental mining is based on weighting. The following techniques are generalized for application purposes. As we will see shortly, if only the sizes of data sets are considered when assigning weights, the real association rules in the database can be generated.

Incremental mining firstly generates an instance set D from a given very large database TD, using the sampling techniques in Section 6.2. D is mined by the algorithm *ApproximatingM*. Secondly, an incremental data set D^+ is generated from TD using the sampling techniques. (Note that all transactions in D do not appear in the incremental data set.) Then D^+ is mined by the algorithm *ApproximatingM*. Thirdly, the mined rules in D^+, and old rules in D, are synthesized by weighting. Fourthly, we let $D \rightarrow D \cup D^+$, and the second step and third step are repeated until all transactions in TD are dealt with.

To mine very large databases incrementally, a key point is the reusing technique. That is, some promising itemsets are kept for reuse and some infrequent itemsets may become frequent. We now illustrate this in Example 6.4.

Example 6.4 *Suppose we have a market basket data set, D, from a grocery store, consisting of n baskets, and an incremental data set D^+ with m baskets (where $m = n/100$, minsupp $= 0.01$, and minconf $= 0.4$). Let us focus on the purchase of tea (t), sugar (s) and coffee (c), where (1) $p(t) = 0.25$, $p(t \cup s) = 0.001$ and $p(t \cup c) = 0.2$ in D; and (2) $p(t) = 0.5$, $p(t \cup s) = 0.48$ and $p(t \cup c) = 0.001$ in D^+.*

We now apply the support-confidence model ([Agrawal-Imielinski-Swami 1993]) to the potential association rules $t \rightarrow c$ and $t \rightarrow s$. The support for rule $t \rightarrow c$ is 0.2, which is fairly high. The confidence is of the conditional probability that a customer buys coffee, given that he/she buys tea, i.e., $p(t \cup c)/p(t) = 0.2/0.25 = 0.8$, which too is fairly high. At this point, we may conclude that the rule $t \rightarrow c$ is a valid rule in D. The support for rule $t \rightarrow s$ is 0.001, which is lower. Then $t \rightarrow s$ cannot be extracted as a valid rule in D.

However, the data in the incremental data set D^+ strongly supports that $t \rightarrow s$ can be found to be a valid rule because its support with 0.5, and its confidence with $p(t \cup s)/p(t) = 0.48/0.5 = 0.96$, are very high in D^+. And $t \rightarrow c$ cannot be extracted as a valid rule in D^+ due to the fact that its support with 0.001 is lower.

Although the data in $D \cup D^+$ still supports that $t \rightarrow c$ can be extracted to be a valid rule (because its support with 0.198 and its confidence with $p(t \cup s)/p(t) = 0.198/0.2525 = 0.784$ are higher) and $t \rightarrow s$ cannot be extracted to be a valid rule (because its support with 0.00579 is lower), when a decision is made for this grocery store, $t \rightarrow s$ may be also taken as a valid rule by using competition.

In the above example, $t \rightarrow s$ represents new behavior of a purchaser in the incremental data set. This behavior would be captured during incremental mining by using competition.

Let D be a given database, D^+ the incremental data set to D, and A an itemset that occurs in D. And let A^+ stand for A occurring in D^+. Then A is a frequent itemset in $D \cup D^+$ only if the support of A is greater than, or equal to, $minsupp$. The support-confidence framework is defined below for the above data sets (see Chapter 2).

Definition 6.2 *An association rule $A \rightarrow B$ can be extracted as a valid rule in $D \cup D^+$ only if it has both support and confidence greater than, or equal to, minsupp and minconf respectively. Or if*

$$supp(A \cup B) = \frac{t(A \cup B) + t(A^+ \cup B^+)}{c(D) + c(D^+)} \geq minsupp$$

$$conf(A \rightarrow B) = \frac{supp(A \cup B)}{supp(A)} \geq minconf$$

where $c(D)$ and $c(D^+)$ are the cardinalities of D and D^+, respectively; and $t(A)$ and $t(A^+)$ denote the number of tuples that contain itemset A in D, and the number of tuples that contain itemset A in D^+, respectively.

6.5.1 Promising Itemsets

For efficiency, we reuse the information from the old frequent itemsets. This means, some old frequent itemsets must be retained. For example, let D be a given database with 100 transactions, and D^+ be an incremental data set with 20 transactions. Assume $minsupp = 0.55$, and A is an itemset with support 0.5 in D, and with support 1 in D^+. This means that A is an infrequent itemset in D, and A becomes a frequent itemset with support 0.5833 after the incremental data set D^+ is added to D. To improve performance, the support of itemset A should be kept to avoid re-mining the whole data set. This itemset is called a promising itemset. We now present the conditions that determine promising itemsets.

Let D be a given database, D^+ be an incremental data set, and A be an itemset that occurs in D. And let A^+ stand for A occurring in D^+. Then, A is a frequent itemset only if the support of A in $D \cup D^+$ is greater than, or equal to, *minsupp*, or:

$$\frac{t(A) + t(A^+)}{c(D) + c(D^+)} \geq minsupp$$

where $c(D)$ and $c(D^+)$ are the cardinalities of D and D^+, respectively; and $t(A)$ and $t(A^+)$ denote the number of tuples that contain the itemset A in D and the number of tuples that contain the itemset A in D^+, respectively. According to the confidence-support framework, $supp(A) = t(A)/c(D)$ and $supp(A^+) = t(A^+)/c(D^+)$. Accordingly, we have the following theorems.

Theorem 6.3 *It is possible that an old infrequent itemset A ($supp(A) <$ minsupp) will become a frequent itemset in the incremental database only if*

$$supp(A^+) > minsupp$$

Proof: If an old infrequent itemset A is to become frequent in the incremental database, the following formula must hold:

$$\frac{t(A) + t(A^+)}{c(D) + c(D^+)} \geq minsupp$$

That is,

$$\frac{c(D) * supp(A) + c(D^+)supp(A^+)}{c(D) + c(D^+)} \geq minsupp$$

So,

$$c(D^+)supp(A^+) \geq c(D) * minsupp + c(D^+) * minsupp - c(D) * supp(A)$$

Or,

$$c(D^+)(supp(A^+) - minsupp) \geq c(D) * (minsupp - supp(A))$$

Because $c(D^+) > 0$, and $supp(A) < minsupp$ or $minsupp - supp(A) > 0$, the following condition must hold:

$$supp(A^+) - minsupp > 0$$

That is,

$$supp(A^+) > minsupp$$

$\triangledown$

For convenience, the condition $supp(A^+) > minsupp$ is sometimes replaced with $t(A^+) > c(D^+) * minsupp$ in our algorithms.

Now, the promising itemsets in D must satisfy the following theorem.

Theorem 6.4 *An infrequent itemset A is kept if*

$$supp(A) > minsupp + \frac{n_0}{c(D)}(minsupp - 1)$$

where n_0 is the maximum among the sizes of incremental databases.

Proof: Because an old infrequent itemset A will become frequent in the updated database, then

$$\frac{t(A) + t(A^+)}{c(D) + c(D^+)} \geq minsupp$$

The minimum condition is as:

$$\frac{c(D) * supp(A) + c(D^+)supp(A^+)}{c(D) + c(D^+)} = minsupp$$

So,

$$c(D) * supp(A) = c(D) * minsupp + c(D^+) * minsupp - c(D^+)supp(A^+)$$

Or,

$$supp(A) = minsupp + \frac{c(D^+)}{c(D)}(minsupp - supp(A^+))$$

$$> minsupp + \frac{n_0}{c(D)}(minsupp - 1)$$

$\triangledown$

6.5.2 Searching Procedure

We now propose a new model for mining very large databases incrementally. The model is illustrated in Figure 6.1.

In Figure 6.1, DB stands for a database to be mined; DB_i ($i = 1, 2, \cdots, n, \cdots$) are incremental data sets; RB_{1i} is the set of itemsets in DB_i, where $i = 1, 2, \cdots, n, \cdots$; $RB1$ is the set of itemsets in DB; RB_j is the set of results weighted from RB_{j-1} and $RB_{1(j-1)}$, where $j = 2, 3, \cdots, n, \cdots$.

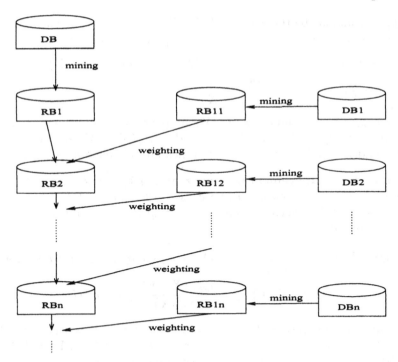

Fig. 6.1. Incremental Databases Mining.

In this approach, a given database DB is firstly mined and all frequent itemsets and promising itemsets are stored in $RB1$. Secondly, each incremental data set DB_i is mined and all frequent itemsets are stored in RB_{1i}. According to the requirements given by users, we can assign a weight to each set DB_i. Thirdly, we can synthesize all rules in RB_i and RB_{1i} by weighting. Finally, we select the high rank itemsets in RB_{i+1} as our output.

To implement the above procedure, we build a two phase approach for mining association rules from incremental data sets. In the first phase, a weighting model of mining association rules is presented. Many factors reflecting properties of data can be fused into the weighted model. To engage the new frequent itemset problem, some infrequent itemsets, or new itemsets, may be changed into frequent itemsets. To deal with this problem, we advocate a competitive set approach in the second phase. Using a competitive set method, some itemsets can became frequent itemsets by competing within our incremental mining model.

In this subsection, we construct only the weighted model. The competitive set method and assignment of weights are dealt with in the next subsection.

To mine rules incrementally, we construct an incremental mining model by weighting to highlight some of the properties of data.

Let w_1 and w_2 be the weights of D and D^+, respectively. Then, for any association rules $X \to Y$, we define the support and confidence as

$$supp_w(X \cup Y) = w_1 * supp_1(X \cup Y) + w_2 * supp_2(X \cup Y),$$
$$conf_w(X \to Y) = \frac{supp_w(X \cup Y)}{supp_w(X)}$$

where $supp_1(X \cup Y)$ and $supp_2(X \cup Y)$ are the supports of $X \to Y$ in D and D^+, respectively; and $supp_w(X \cup Y)$ and $conf_w(X \to Y)$ are the support and confidence of $X \to Y$ in $D \cup D^+$, which are the weighted results.

Definition 6.3 (Incremental mining model by weighting): *An association rule $A \to B$ can be extracted as a valid rule in $D \cup D^+$ if it has both support and confidence greater than, or equal to, minsupp and minconf, respectively. Or*

$$supp_w(X \cup Y) = w_1 * supp_1(X \cup Y) + w_2 * supp_2(X \cup Y) \geq minsupp$$

$$conf_w(X \to Y) = \frac{supp_w(X \cup Y)}{supp_w(X)} \geq minconf$$

Example 6.5 *Let $c(D) = 80$, $c(D^+) = 20$, a rule $X \to Y$ is with $supp_1(X \cup Y) = 0.4$ and $conf_1(X \to Y) = 0.5$ in D, and $supp_2(X \cup Y) = 0.3$ and $conf_1(X \to Y) = 0.6$ in D^+. Then we can take weights as*

$$w_1 = \frac{c(D)}{c(D) + c(D^+)} = \frac{80}{80 + 20} = 0.8,$$

$$w_2 = \frac{c(D^+)}{c(D) + c(D^+)} = \frac{20}{80 + 20} = 0.2$$

So,

$$supp_w(X \cup Y) = w_1 * supp_1(X \cup Y) + w_2 * supp_2(X \cup Y)$$
$$= 0.8 * 0.4 + 0.2 * 0.3 = 0.38$$

Because

$$supp_1(X) = \frac{supp_1(X \cup Y)}{conf_1(X \to Y)} = \frac{0.4}{0.5} = 0.8$$

$$supp_2(X) = \frac{supp_2(X \cup Y)}{conf_2(X \to Y)} = \frac{0.3}{0.6} = 0.5$$

$$supp_w(X) = w_1 * supp_1(X) + w_2 * supp_2(X)$$
$$= 0.8 * 0.8 + 0.2 * 0.5 = 0.74$$

Hence

$$conf_w(X \to Y) = \frac{supp_w(X \cup Y)}{supp_w(X)} = \frac{0.38}{0.74} = 0.5135$$

In fact, according to the assumption in the above example, we can obtain $t(X \cup Y) = 32$, $t(X) = 64$, $t(X^+ \cup Y^+) = 6$, $t(X^+) = 10$, by the support-confidence framework,

$$
\begin{aligned}
supp(X \cup Y) &= \frac{t(X \cup Y) + t(X^+ \cup Y^+)}{c(D) + c(D^+)} \\
&= \frac{32 + 6}{80 + 20} \\
&= 0.38 \\
supp(X) &= \frac{t(X) + t(X^+)}{c(D) + c(D^+)} \\
&= \frac{64 + 10}{80 + 20} \\
&= 0.74 \\
conf(X \to Y) &= \frac{supp(X \cup Y)}{supp(X)} \\
&= \frac{0.38}{0.74} = 0.5135.
\end{aligned}
$$

This means, the results obtained in the incremental mining model by weighting are the same as those obtained in the support-confidence framework if the weights only take into account the sizes of D and D^+. Indeed, the weights can also take into account other cases, such as the novelty of the data, or both the size of the database and the novelty of the data.

Thus, if we consider only the sizes of data sets when we assign weights, the true association rules in the database can be generated. In other words, the support-confidence framework is a special case of incremental mining model by weighting. Therefore, we have a theorem as follows.

Theorem 6.5 *Previous mining models, such as the support-confidence framework, are special cases in the incremental mining model.*

Proof: We need to prove that $supp$ and $conf$ in support-confidence framework are special cases of $supp_w$ and $conf_w$, respectively. Certainly, we can take the assignment of weights as follows:

$$
w_1 = \frac{c(D)}{c(D) + c(D^+)}, \qquad w_2 = \frac{c(D^+)}{c(D) + c(D^+)}
$$

We first prove that $supp$ in the support-confidence framework is a special case of $supp_w$. For $X \to Y$, $supp_1(X \cup Y) = c_1(X \cup Y)/c(D)$ and $supp_2(X \cup Y) = c_2(X \cup Y)/c(D^+)$. According to the definition of $supp_w$ we have

$$
\begin{aligned}
supp_w(X \cup Y) &= w_1 * supp_1(X \cup Y) + w_2 * supp_2(X \cup Y) \\
&= \frac{c(D)}{c(D) + c(D^+)} \frac{c_1(X \cup Y)}{c(D)} + \frac{c(D^+)}{c(D) + c(D^+)} \frac{c_2(X \cup Y)}{c(D^+)} \\
&= \frac{c_1(X \cup Y) + c_2(X \cup Y)}{c(D) + c(D^+)}
\end{aligned}
$$

This means that the weighted support, $supp_w(X \cup Y)$, is equal to the support of the rule $X \to Y$ in $D \cup D^+$. Hence, $supp$ in the support-confidence framework is a special case of $supp_w$.

We now prove that $conf$ in the support-confidence framework is a special case of $conf_w$. For $X \to Y$, $conf_1(X \cup Y) = supp_1(X \cup Y)/supp_1(X)$ and $conf_2(X \cup Y) = supp_2(X \cup Y)/supp_2(X)$. According to the definition of $conf_w$ we have

$$
\begin{aligned}
conf_w(X \to Y) &= \frac{supp_w(X \cup Y)}{supp_w(X)} \\
&= \frac{\frac{c_1(X \cup Y) + c_2(X \cup Y)}{c(D) + c(D^+)}}{\frac{c_1(X) + c_2(X)}{c(D) + c(D^+)}} \\
&= \frac{c_1(X \cup Y) + c_2(X \cup Y)}{c_1(X) + c_2(X)}
\end{aligned}
$$

This means that the weighted confidence, $conf_w(X \to Y)$, is equal to the confidence of the rule $X \to Y$ in $D \cup D^+$. Or, $conf$ in the support-confidence framework is a special case of $conf_w$. Hence, the support-confidence framework is a special case of the incremental mining model.   ▽

Directly, for any association rules $X \to Y$, we can define its support and confidence as

$$supp_w(X \cup Y) = w_1 * supp_1(X \cup Y) + w_2 * supp_2(X \cup Y),$$
$$conf_w(X \to Y) = w_1 * conf_1(X \to Y) + w_2 * conf_2(X \to Y)$$

where $conf_1(X \to Y)$ and $conf_2(X \to Y)$ are the confidences of $X \to Y$ in D and D^+, respectively.

Definition 6.4 (direct incremental mining model by weighting): *An association rule $A \to B$ can be extracted as a valid rule in $D \cup D^+$ if it has both support and confidence greater than, or equal to, minsupp and minconf, respectively. Or*

$$supp_w(X \cup Y) = w_1 * supp_1(X \cup Y) + w_2 * supp_2(X \cup Y) \geq minsupp$$

$$conf_w(X \to Y) = w_1 * conf_1(X \to Y) + w_2 * conf_2(X \to Y) \geq minconf$$

For the data in the above example, $conf_w(X \to Y) = w_1 * conf_1(X \to Y) + w_2 * conf_2(X \to Y) = 0.8 * 0.5 + 0.2 * 0.6 = 0.52$.

Generally, for $D, D_1, \cdots, D_n$ with weights $w_1, w_2, \cdots, w_{n+1}$, we define the weighted $supp_w(X \cup Y)$ and $conf_w(X \to Y)$ for a rule $X \to Y$ as follows

$$
\begin{aligned}
supp_w(X \cup Y) = &\, w_1 * supp(X \cup Y) + w_2 * supp_1(X \cup Y) \\
&+ \cdots + w_{n+1} * supp_n(X \cup Y) \\
conf_w(X \to Y) = &\, w_1 * conf(X \to Y) + w_2 * conf_1(X \to Y) \\
&+ \cdots + w_{n+1} * conf_n(X \to Y)
\end{aligned}
$$

where $supp(X \cup Y)$, and $supp_1(X \cup Y)$, $\cdots$, $supp_n(X \cup Y)$ are the the supports of the rule $X \to Y$ in D, and D_1, $\cdots$, D_n respectively; and $conf(X \to Y)$, $conf_1(X \to Y)$, $\cdots$, $conf_n(X \to Y)$ are the confidences of the rule $X \to Y$ in D, D_1, $\cdots$, D_n respectively;

6.5.3 Competitive Set Method

As has been shown, our model is efficient in reflecting the changes of association rules in incremental databases. Indeed, some infrequent itemsets, or new itemsets, may be changed into frequent itemsets. This is referred to as *the problem of infrequent itemsets*. To deal with this problem, we advocate a competitive set approach. In this subsection, we construct a competitive model. In the next subsection we will present the assignment of weights.

To tackle the problem of infrequent itemsets, a *competitive set CS* is used to store all promising itemsets, where each itemset in CS can become a frequent itemset by competition. We now define some operations on CS.

Let D be a given database, D^+ the incremental data set to D, A an itemset, $supp(A)$ the support of A in D, and $supp(A^+)$ the relative support of A in D^+. Firstly, all promising itemsets in D are appended into CS.

Secondly, when an itemset might become invalid after an incremental mining is carried out, it would be appended into CS if the weighted support is greater than, or equal to, *mincruc*.

Thirdly, some frequent itemsets in D^+ would be appended into CS after an incremental mining if the weighted supports are greater than, or equal to, *mincruc*. These itemsets are neither in the set of frequent itemsets, nor in CS. But their supports are fairly high in D^+. This means, their supports in D are unknown. For unknown itemsets, a compromise proposal seems reasonable. So we can regard their supports in D as $mincruc/2$. For any such itemset X, $supp_w(X) = w_1 * mincruc/2 + w_2 * supp(X^+)$ according to the weight model. And, for $supp_w(X) \geq mincruc$, itemset X is appended into CS. In other words, if

$$supp(A^+) \geq \frac{mincruc(2 - w_1)}{2w_2}$$

in D^+, itemset X is appended into CS; otherwise, itemset X is appended into CS' if the weighted support is greater than, or equal to, $mincruc/2$, of which CS' is an extra competitive set. And CS' is used to record another kind of promising itemset. The operations on CS' are similar to those on CS. The main use of CS' is to generate a category of itemset with middle supports in D^+. For example, let $mincruc = 0.3$ and $minsupp = 0.6$. Assume the support of an itemset A is less than 0.3 in a given database D, and that the supports of A in the incremental data sets D_1, D_2, $\cdots D_9$ are all 0.64. Because the support of A is less than 0.3 in D, A is not kept in the system. Let $w_1 = 0.75$ be the weight of the old database, and $w_2 = 0.25$ the weight of the new incremental data set. According to the operations on CS, $supp_w(A) = w_1*mincruc/2+w_2*supp(A^+) = 0.75*0.15+0.25*0.64 = 0.2725$. This means that itemset A cannot be appended into CS. However, the support is greater than $mincruc/2 = 0.15$. From the changes of data, the itemset can become a frequent itemset if there are enough incremental data sets. Accordingly, we use CS' to capture this feature of the data in the incremental data sets. The changes for the support of the itemset A are listed as follows.

$$supp(A) < 0.3 \rightarrow 0.15 * 0.75 + 0.64 * 0.25 = 0.2725$$
$$\rightarrow A \text{ with } supp(A) = 0.2725 \Rightarrow CS'$$
$$\rightarrow 0.2725 * 0.75 + 0.64 * 0.25 = 0.364375$$
$$\rightarrow A \text{ with } supp(A) = 0.2725 \Rightarrow CS$$
$$\rightarrow 0.364375 * 0.75 + 0.64 * 0.25 = 0.43328$$
$$\rightarrow 0.43328 * 0.75 + 0.64 * 0.25 = 0.48496$$
$$\rightarrow 0.48496 * 0.75 + 0.64 * 0.25 = 0.52372$$
$$\rightarrow 0.52372 * 0.75 + 0.64 * 0.25 = 0.55279$$
$$\rightarrow 0.55279 * 0.75 + 0.64 * 0.25 = 0.57459$$
$$\rightarrow 0.57459 * 0.75 + 0.64 * 0.25 = 0.590945$$
$$\rightarrow 0.590945 * 0.75 + 0.64 * 0.25 = 0.60321$$

Fourthly, some itemsets in CS' are appended into CS after each mining if the weighted supports are greater than, or equal to, $mincruc$

Finally, some itemsets are deleted from CS after each mining of association rules is completed. By the weighted model, for any $A \in CS$, $supp_w(A) = w_1 * supp(A) + w_2 * supp(A^+)$. If $supp_w(A) < mincruc$, A is deleted from CS; otherwise, A is kept in CS with the new support $supp_w(A)$.

6.5.4 Assigning Weights

After defining the competition, we can present the assignment of weights. We have seen that the weighting in the above model is generally straightforward once weights are reasonably assigned. Before assigning weights, we briefly discuss how to determine weights. Obviously, the assignment of weights would be determined by the degree of belief of users on new data.

Considering Requirements of Users To assign weights, we consider the sizes of the old data sets and sizes of the incremental data sets.

Sometimes users might give certain requirements for mining new rules which have arisen from incremental data sets. For example, a new, or infrequent item, can be expected to be competed for as a frequent item when it is strongly supported n times continually by incremental data sets. We can assign weights to data sets according to this requirement.

Let $minsupp$ and $mincruc$ be given by users. Assume that A is an infrequent item (or a new item) in a database D. The support of A in incremental data sets are all taken as 1, and $supp(A) = minsupp$ after n increments. For simplicity, we assume that D is assigned a weight w_1 and all incremental data sets are assigned the same weight, w_2. According to the above competition, we can obtain $supp(A) = w_1^n * (mincruc/2) + w_2$ after 1 increment. And $supp(A) = w_1^n * (mincruc/2) + (w_1^{n-1} + w_1^{n-2} + \cdots + 1) * w_2$ after n increments, because A can be changed as a frequent item. That is,

$$w_1^n * (mincruc/2) + (w_1^{n-1} + w_1^{n-2} + \cdots + 1) * w_2 = minsupp$$

or

$$w_1^n * (mincruc/2) + (w_1^{n-1} + w_1^{n-2} + \cdots + 1) * (1 - w_1) = minsupp$$

Therefore,

$$w_1^n * (mincruc/2) + w_1^{n-1} + w_1^{n-2} + \cdots + 1 - (w_1^n + w_1^{n-1} + \cdots + 1_2) = minsupp$$

or

$$w_1^n * (mincruc/2) - w_1^n + 1 = minsupp$$

Hence,

$$w_1 = \left(\frac{1 - minsupp}{1 - mincruc/2} \right)^{\frac{1}{n}}$$

And $w_2 = 1 - w_1$.

Example 6.6 Let $mincruc = 0.3$, $minsupp = 0.6$ and $n = 4$. Then

$$w_1 = \left(\frac{1 - minsupp}{1 - mincruc/2} \right)^{\frac{1}{n}}$$
$$= \left(\frac{1 - 0.6}{1 - 0.3/2} \right)^{\frac{1}{4}}$$
$$= 0.8282$$

and $w_2 = 1 - w_1 = 1 - 0.8282 = 0.1718$.

Considering Many Factors Sometimes, many factors must be considered by applications. For this reason, we must first assign weights to data sets according to each factor. Then, the final weights are synthesized from all the weights.

Consider m factors. Let $w_{11}, w_{12}, \cdots, w_{1m}$ be assigned to a given database, D, according to m factors, and let $w_{21}, w_{22}, \cdots, w_{2m}$ be assigned to the incremental data set D^+ according to m factors. Then we can take the average of the above weights as the weights of the data sets. That is, the weight w_1 of D is

$$w_1 = (w_{11} + w_{12} + \cdots + w_{1m})/m$$

and the weight w_2 of D^+ is

$$w_2 = (w_{21} + w_{22} + \cdots + w_{2m})/m$$

Example 6.7 *Consider Example 6.5. Let $c(D) = 90$ and $c(D^+) = 10$. Then D and D^+ are assigned weights according to the sizes of the data sets. For example, $w_{12} = 90/(90 + 10) = 0.9$ and $w_{22} = 10/(90 + 10) = 0.1$. Now we consider two factors: the requirements of users and the sizes of data sets. D and D^+ are assigned weights according to the two factors $w_1 = (w_{11} + w_{12})/2 = (0.8282 + 0.9)/2 = 0.8641$ and $w_2 = (w_{21} + w_{22})/2 = (0.1718 + 0.1)/2 = 0.1359$, respectively.*

We can, of course, construct more complicated models to assign weights to data sets by combining the above methods. For example, we can construct a method for assigning different weights to different incremental data sets.

6.5.5 Algorithm of Incremental Mining

Incremental mining generates all valid association rules and a competitive set (CS). Each valid rule $A \rightarrow B$ has both support and confidence that are greater than, or equal to, the minimum support ($minsupp$) and minimum confidence ($minconf$) thresholds. That is, for regular associations,

$$supp_w(A \cup B) \geq minsupp$$

$$conf_w(A \rightarrow B) \geq minconf$$

We now present an algorithm for an incremental mining model by weighting.

Let $VLDB$ be a given very large database. Let D be the first incremental data set (random instance set), D^+ the incremental data set, $supp$ and $conf$ the support and confidence functions of rules in D, $supp^+$ and $conf^+$ the support and confidence functions of rules in D^+, and $minsupp$, $minconf$, $mincruc$ the threshold values; where $mincruc$ ($< Min\{minsupp, minconf\}$) is the crucial value. Algorithm 6.3 is our incremental mining algorithm for mining association rules in very large databases.

Algorithm 6.3 *Miningrules*

begin
Input: *VLDB: very large database; n_0, minsupp, minconf, mincruc: threshold values;*
Output: *$X \rightarrow Y$: weighted association rule;*
(1) **generate** an instance set of $VLDB$;
    let $R \leftarrow$ all rules mined in D;
    let $CS \leftarrow \emptyset$; $CS' \leftarrow \emptyset$; $TD \leftarrow \emptyset$; $i \leftarrow 0$;
(2) **for** any itemset A in D **do**
        if $supp(A) \geq mincruc$ **then**
           if A don't occur in any rule in R **then**
               let $CS \leftarrow CS \cup \{A\}$;

(3) **for** all incremental data sets from $VLDB$ **do**
      begin
          let $D^+ \leftarrow$ an incremental data set;
          mine data set D^+;
          call procedure $weight$;
      end

end.

The algorithm $Miningrules$ is to discover a very large database incrementally by weighting. The initialization is carried out in Steps (1) and (2). Step (3) performs the incremental mining of rules. And the procedure, $weight$, is called in to synthesize the old association rules and the new rules in an incremental data set. The elements in R, CS, and CS' are all the results of the latest mining. The procedure $weight$ is as in Procedure 6.7.

Procedure 6.7 $weight$

begin
Input: D^+: database; minsupp, minconf, mincruc: threshold values;
      R: rule set; CS, CS': sets of itemsets;
Output: $X \rightarrow Y$: rule; CS, CS': sets of itemsets;
(1) **input** $w_1 \leftarrow$ the weight of D;
   input $w_2 \leftarrow$ the weight of D^+;
   let $RR \leftarrow R$; $R \leftarrow \emptyset$; $temp \leftarrow \emptyset$;
   let $Itemset \leftarrow$ all itemsets in D^+;
   let $CS_{D+} \leftarrow$ all frequent itemsets in D^+;
   let $i \leftarrow i + 1$;
(2) **for** any $X \rightarrow Y \in RR$ **do**
      begin
         let $supp(X \cup Y) \leftarrow w_1 * supp(X \cup Y) + w_2 * supp(X^+ \cup Y^+)$;
         let $conf(X \rightarrow Y) \leftarrow w_1 * conf(X \rightarrow Y) + w_2 * conf^+(X \rightarrow Y)$;
         if $supp \geq minsupp$ and $conf \geq minconf$ **then**
           begin
              let $R \leftarrow$ rule $X \rightarrow Y$;
              output $X \rightarrow Y$ as a valid rule of ith mining;
           end;
         else let $temp \leftarrow temp \cup \{X, X \cup Y\}$;
      end;
(3) **for** any $B \in CS$ **do**
      begin
         let $supp(B) \leftarrow w_1 * supp(B) + w_2 * supp(B^+)$;
         if $supp(B) \geq minsupp$ **then**
         for any $A \subset B$ **do**

```
        begin
          let supp(A) ← w₁ * supp(A) + w₂ * supp(A⁺);
          let conf(A → (B − A)) ← supp(B)/supp(A);
          if conf(A → (B − A)) ≥ minconf then
            begin
              let R ⇐ rule A → (B − A);
              output A → (B − A) as a valid rule of ith minings;
            end;
          else let temp ← temp ∪ {B, A};
        end
      end;
  (4) call competing;
end;
```

The Procedure *weight* is responsible for weighting the old association rules and the new rules in an incremental instance set. The initialization is done in Step (1). In Step (2), the weighting operations are performed on the rules in RR, where RR is the set of valid rules in the last maintenance. In this Step, all valid rules are appended into R, and the itemsets of all invalid rules weighted are temporarily stored in *temp*. In Step (3), all rules from the competitive set CS are extracted, and all invalid itemsets weighted in CS are temporarily stored in *temp*. (Note that any itemset in CS' can become a promising itemset and may be appended into CS by competition. However, it cannot become a frequent itemset. In other words, CS' can be ignored when rules are mined.) In Step (4), the procedure, *competing*, is called in to tackle the competing itemsets for CS and CS' as shown in Procedure 6.8.

Procedure 6.8 *competing*

```
begin
Input: mincruc: threshold values; temp, Itemset, CS_{D+}, CS': sets
of itemsets; w₁, w₂: weights;
Output: CS, CS': competitive sets;;
(1) let temp1 ← ∅; temp2 ← ∅;
(2) for A ∈ temp do
        if suupp(A) ≥ mincruc then
          let temp1 ← A;
        else if suupp(A) ≥ mincruc/2 then
          let temp2 ← A;
(3) for A ∈ CS' do
        begin
          let supp(A) ← w₁ * supp(A) + w₂ * supp(A⁺);
          if suupp(A) ≥ mincruc then
            let temp1 ← A;
          else if suupp(A) ≥ mincruc/2 then
```

```
            let temp2 ← A;
         end
(4) for A ∈ CS_{D+} do
      begin
         let supp(A) ← w_1 * mincruc/2 + w_2 * supp(A^+);
         if suupp(A) ≥ mincruc then
            let temp1 ← A;
         else if suupp(A) ≥ mincruc/2 then
            let temp2 ← A;
      end
   (5) let CS ← temp1; let CS' ← temp2;
   end;
```

The procedure *competing* considers the competition of infrequent item-sets. The initialization is done in Step (1). In Step (2), all itemsets in *temp* are handled, and all itemsets with supports in the interval $[mincruc, minsupp)$ are appended into CS and the itemsets with supports in interval $[mincruc/2, mincruc)$ are appended into CS'. Steps (3) and (4) are similar to Step (2) and deal with the itemsets in CS' and CS_{D+}, respectively.

6.6 Improvement of Incremental Mining

As we have seen, the incremental mining technique allows for very large databases to be searched on a personal computer. And, if we consider only the sizes of data sets to assign weights, the real association rules in the database can be generated. Though the first data set is a random instance set with $P[|Ave(X_n) - p| \leq \eta]$ for each itemset X, there are still error problems in the neighborhoods of *minsupp* and *minconf* (see Section 6.5), where $Ave(X_n)$ is the average of X occurring in n transactions of a database TD. For this reason, the incremental mining algorithm is terminated only after all data in a given very large database is processed.

In fact, the following two cases are possible: (1) the first N high-ranking frequent itemsets are supported by m instance sets and, (2) the support and confidence of each such frequent itemset are almost identical (or contain very small differences) in the m instance sets. If one of them occurs, we would certainly terminate the algorithm at once and output the N frequent itemsets if we require only the first N frequent itemsets.

There can also be other requirements proposed by users. To accommodate this, in this section we design an improved algorithm — an anytime algorithm — for searching association rules in databases.

6.6.1 Conditions of Termination

Let TD be a very large database. And $D, D_1, D_2, \cdots, D_n$ are $n+1$ random instance sets generated from TD. $TD = D \cup D_1 \cup D_2 \cup \cdots \cup D_n$, and each transaction of TD is contained by only one instance set. For any frequent itemset X mined by incremental mining,

$$|Ave(X_i) - p| \to 0, \text{ when } i \to n$$

It is typically a time-consuming procedure to deal with all incremental data sets when we mine. For some applications, we may wish to terminate the algorithm. For example, when someone requires only approximate association rules, the algorithm can be terminated, and support results produced at any time. We detail two conditions for terminating the incremental mining algorithm below.

(1) A request for approximate association rules at a certain time t is received.
(2) Existing N high-ranking association rules are supported by m incremental data sets; and the support and confidence of each of their rules have very small differences in the m incremental data sets.

Condition (1) is used as a response to outside requests for current results. The system may not be terminated when the condition occurs. For example, a stock investor may require approximate results at time t_1 for rough decision making, and more accurate results at time t_2 for confirmation of the decision. The user gets some results at time t_1 without implementing the stop instruction. Therefore, the system is not stopped at time t_1.

If Condition (2) occurs, the identified results are confirmed by enough instance sets. And the system is automatically terminated. In this case, the remaining data in a given database is no longer processed. And the data in the database is in a well-distribution.

Let $N_0 > 1$ and *minratio* be *minimum number* and *minimum ratio*, respectively, as given by users or experts. For the database TD, assume each of the first N high-ranking frequent itemsets discovered are practically identical in all the instance sets $D, D_1, D_2, \cdots, D_{N_0-1}$. This means that the number of instance sets is equal to the minimum number N_0, and the ratio of support of the first N high-ranking frequent itemsets is 1 ($\geq$ *miniratio*). Also, the first N high-ranking frequent itemsets are confided. Hence, the system is stopped, and the first N high-ranking frequent itemsets are output as the final results.

When Conditions (1) and (2) are not satisfied, the system takes a great deal of time to discover patterns in a very large database.

6.6.2 Anytime Search Algorithm

An anytime algorithm is a class of algorithm whose quality of results improves gradually as computation time increases ([Zilberstein,1996]). It is particularly useful for solving problems where the search space is very large and the quality of the results can be compromised.

For very large databases, we can also design an anytime search algorithm such that users can ask for the current association rules at anytime while the mining system is autonomously searching the database. Obviously, users would expect that association rules would become increasingly closer to true rules in a database with the passing of time. With this algorithm, users can make a decision on time, and the accuracy of association rules, depending upon application requirements. A short-term stock investor might be happy to terminate the mining process early and thus obtain less accurate patterns from stock databases, and a long-term stock investor might run the mining system slightly longer to obtain more accurate patterns.

To support result inquiries at anytime, we design two tables to save the mined results at different times while the mining process is still running.

Table 6.1. WR: the weighted results

name of rule	support	confidence	rank
r_1	$supp_1$	$conf_1$	1
r_2	$supp_2$	$conf_2$	2
...	...	...	...
r_m	$supp_m$	$conf_m$	m

In Table 6.1 (WR table), 'r_i' is a rule, '$supp_i$' is the weighted support of the rule r_i, '$conf_i$' is the weighted confidence of the rule r_i, and r_i is ranked in the ith row by the weighted supports of rules from large to small. It lists the current weighted information for all valid association rules. Users may access information at a time t_0.

Table 6.2. FR: the frequencies of rules

name of rule	support	confidence	frequency
R_1	$Supp_1$	$Conf_1$	f_1
R_2	$Supp_2$	$Conf_2$	f_2
...	...	...	...
R_m	$Supp_m$	$Conf_m$	f_m

In Table 6.2 (FR table), 'R_i' is a rule, '$Supp_i$' is the weighted support of the rule R_i, '$Conf_i$' is the weighted confidence of the rule R_i, 'f_i' is the number of instance sets from which R_i is extracted as a valid rule in the f_i instance sets, and R_i is ranked in the ith row by the supports of rules from high to low. It lists the current support information concerning all valid association rules in the mined instance sets. (Again, users might be interested in asking for it at a time t_0.)

We now design the anytime search algorithm.

Algorithm 6.4 *AnytimeSearch*

begin
Input: *VLDB: very large database; n_0, minsupp, minconf, mincruc: threshold values;*
Output: *$X \rightarrow Y$: weighted association rule;*
(1) **let** the table of the weighted rules $WR \leftarrow \emptyset$;
   let the table of the frequencies of rules $FR \leftarrow \emptyset$;
   let $CS \leftarrow \emptyset$; $CS' \leftarrow \emptyset$; $TD \leftarrow \emptyset$; $i \leftarrow 0$;
   let *Number* $\leftarrow 0$;
(2) **generate** an instance set of *VLDB*;
   let $R \leftarrow$ all rules mined in D;
   let $WR \leftarrow R$, where rules in WR are ranked by support;
   let $FR \leftarrow R$, where rules in FR are ranked by support and the frequency of each rule is 1;
   let *Number* $\leftarrow$ *Number* $+ 1$;
(3) **output** the first instance set is mined;
   output tables WR and FR;
(4) **for** any itemset A in D **do**
      if $supp(A) \geq mincruc$ **then**
        if A don't occur in any rule in R **then**
         let $CS \leftarrow CS \cup \{A\}$;
(5) **for** all incremental data sets from *VLDB* **do**
      begin
         let $D^+ \leftarrow$ an incremental data set;
         let *Number* $\leftarrow$ *Number* $+ 1$;
         mine the *Number*th instance set D^+;
         for all rules in D^+ **do**
            call weight;
         for all weighted rules of interest **do**
            begin
               update WR by new results, where rules in WR are ranked by support;
               update FR by new results, where rules in FR are ranked by support;
               output the *Number* instance sets are mined;
               output tables WR and FR;
               if $i \geq N_0$ **then**
                  if Condition 2 is satisfied **then**
                     terminate the incremental mining;
            end
      end
end.

The algorithm *AnytimeSearch* is designed for mining very large databases incrementally. Users can ask for the current association rules at anytime while the mining system is autonomously mining a database. The initialization is done in Step (1).

Step (2) firstly generates an instance set D from $VLDB$ by sampling. Secondly, D is mined to obtain all valid and approximate association rules in the data set. The results are saved in a set, R. Finally, the rules in R are used to form two tables, WR and FR.

Step (3) is to output the tables WR and FR as the results of the first incremental data set so as to answer any inquiry at this time point.

Step (4) is to set up the competition set for the first incremental data set, D.

Step (5) consists of two parts. The first part is to process an incremental data set D^+ by the procedure *weight*. The second part is to process the tables WR and FR. In this part, tables WR and FR are firstly updated by the new results from the data set D^+ and then, in answer to any inquiry at this point, the tables WR and FR are output as results. This occurs, just after the *Number*th incremental data set has been processed.

An important process in Step 5 is the checking of whether or not Condition 2 is satisfied. Obviously, the earlier Condition 2 is satisfied, the more the running time is saved.

6.7 Summary

Mining association rules is an expensive process. Mining approximate association rules on a sample from a large database can reduce computation costs significantly. Srikant and Agrawal have suggested a method for selecting the sample of a given large database when estimating the support of candidates using Chernoff bounds ([Srikant-Agrawal 1997]). Also, Toivonen has applied Chernoff bounds to discover frequent itemsets in large databases ([Toivonen 1996]). However, previous approximate models based on Chernoff bounds may require sample sizes larger than our model based on the central limit theorem, when searching for frequent itemsets in large databases. For many applications, such as marketing and stock investment, there may be time and cost constraints and little requirement for total accuracy. To satisfy such applications, faster approximating mining models need to be developed.

Also, as we have argued, most users work under resource-bounded. They often work on personal computers or work stations, rarely having the chance to work on a parallel environment. This means that if algorithms for mining very large databases are designed to work under resource-bounded, rather than on specific environments, then the techniques can be shared by more people.

In this chapter, we have presented techniques for mining very large databases, which can work well when resources are bounded. The key points of this chapter are as follows.

(1) Presented a method of applying the theorems to estimate the size of random database that enables us to mine approximate association rule.
(2) Proposed an efficient algorithm to discover approximate association rules of interest by pruning.
(3) Discussed the neighbourhood of *minsupp* and estimated the complexity of both previous models, and our model. The complexity of mining frequent databases can be computationally and physically decreased to an acceptable amount by pruning and approximation.
(4) Advocated an incremental mining technique by weighting.
(5) Constructed an anytime search algorithm for mining very large databases.

It is worth while to point out that the proposed incremental mining techniques can be used to mine dynamic databases. To deal with a dynamic database, we can take the first data set as the old database in the incremental mining algorithm, and the new data from the applications as the incremental data set.

7. Association Rules in Small Databases

Accidents in nuclear power plants can cause environmental disasters and create personal, economical and ecological damage. Therefore, research into automatic surveillance and early nuclear accident detection has received much attention. To reduce nuclear accidents, reliable information is needed for controlling, and/or preventing, such accidents. Hence, extracting useful patterns from limited data in nuclear power plants is very important, and is imperative for the purpose of safety. This kind of knowledge is generally obtained from theoretical, experimental, and real data. However, nuclear accidents rarely occur, and we may discover nothing from the accident database in a plant. Therefore, reliable mining of an accident database in a nuclear power plant would require dependence upon external data as well.

Utilizing external data collected from external data-sources via the Internet for small database mining provides a feasible way to deal with the small database problem.

A company that has a large database may also wish to utilize external data, in addition to internal data, when making decisions for high-profit purposes. Therefore, employing external data has become a challenging topic. Successful decision-making usually depends upon expert analysts and the utilization of all possible information.

This chapter presents a new model for mining association rules in small databases, utilizing external data. This model might also be appropriate for certain large database mining.

This chapter is organized as follows. We begin by describing why we need to utilize external data in Section 7.1. Section 7.2 outlines the problems of utilizing external data. In Section 7.3, we discuss how to collect information from the media. Section 7.4 advocates a framework for sharing external data. Section 7.5 presents a model for synthesizing the collected patterns. Section 7.6 designs an algorithm for improving mined patterns using quality external data. We summarize in the last section.

7.1 Introduction

As we have seen in previous chapters, there are many approaches for mining very large databases. Some have become accepted tools and technology, and some are already playing important roles in diverse applications.

An association rule describes a strong correlation between two frequent itemsets in a database. Because the objects mined occur frequently in databases, association rules are useful for real-world applications. In particular, frequent itemsets are beneficial for determining association rules in large scale databases. But it is unrealistic to extract association rules from small databases by way of identifying frequent itemsets. For example, if a boy wants to win the love of a girl and get married, he may not be able to form a pattern from his limited knowledge of the girl. He must learn how to obtain common-sense, experience, and models from other people. If this information is synthesized into his data, he can have a successful marriage.

As mentioned above, nuclear accidents rarely occur and, if current mining techniques are applied to the accident database in a given nuclear power plant, nothing may be discovered that will reduce future accidents. In other words, current mining techniques cannot work well when databases are very small. However, it is imperative for the purpose of safety that useful patterns are extracted from data in nuclear power plants, however limited the data might be. Accordingly, an efficient model for mining small databases must be explored, and utilizing external data collected from other data-sources by way of the Internet provides a feasible way to deal with the problem.

Fortunately, individuals and organizations can take advantage of the remarkable possibilities of access to information and knowledge that the Internet provides. Web technologies such as HTTP and HTML have dramatically changed enterprise information management. A corporation can benefit from intranets and the Internet to gather, manage, distribute, and share data, inside and outside their business.

As techniques for the use of the Internet advance into a mature stage, sources and information sharing become easier. This means that a company can take into account both internal and external data when making decisions. However, it is very important that the external data is analyzed, confirmed, judged, and synthesized before it is used, so that reasonable results can be obtained. For example, the value of a rule may be changed when the rule is delivered, the external data itself might not be true, and the data-source might not be trustworthy.

As we examine these problems, we keep in mind that a company that does have a very large database might also want to collect external data for lucrative decision making. Therefore, the employment of external data for applications has become a challenging topic in the web era.

In this chapter, breaking away from the traditional data mining framework that deals with internal and external data equally, we argue that the first step for utilizing external data is to identify believable data-sources for given mining tasks. A framework for utilizing external data is thus built for data preprocessing. In this framework, we advocate pre- and post-analysis techniques for dealing with external data. Due to the fact that only relevant, uncontradictable and high veridical data-sources are used, this process not only reduces the search costs, but also generates quality patterns. This approach is particularly useful for companies or organizations such as nuclear power plants and earthquake bureaus, which often have very small databases but require further reliable knowledge for their applications.

Our main target in this chapter is to present techniques for mining association rules in databases by synthesizing possible external data. Our model is a four-phase approach as listed below.

- The first phase is responsible for collecting external data potentially useful to the mining goal.
- The second phase selects the believable external data from the data collected.
- The third phase synthesizes the external data selected.
- The last phase applies the believable external data to enhance the rules mined in the small database.

7.2 Problem Statement

The process of knowledge discovery in databases (KDD) is defined as an iterative sequence consisting of the following steps: defining the problem, data preprocessing, data mining, and post processing ([Han 1999, Liu 1998, Wu 1995]). Data preprocessing may be more time consuming, and presents more challenges, than data mining (see [Fayyad-Simoudis 1997]).

Generally, data preprocessing includes data collecting, data cleaning, data selection, and data transformation ([Han 1999]). Therefore, data collection is an important part of knowledge discovery in databases. In the process, necessary data from various internal and external sources must be joined together to create a huge homogeneous dataset. In existing techniques, internal and external data are combined into a single dataset for mining tasks, and both play an equal role in the dataset. However, because external data collected may be untrustworthy, even fraudulent, it has the potential to disguise really useful patterns. If external data is not preprocessed before it is applied, it can cause identified patterns which conduct high-risk applications. This section clarifies some of the problems involving when utilizing external data.

7.2.1 Problems Faced by Utilizing External Data

Traditional data collecting among various data-sources directly borrows data from external sources to create a huge dataset suitable for a given mining task. Thus, internal and external data can play equally important roles in the mining task. The process of KDD, using external data, is depicted in Figure 7.1.

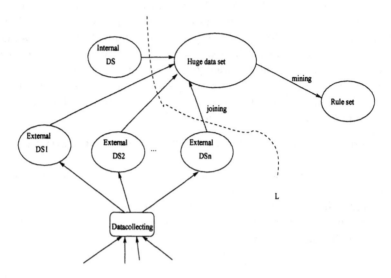

Fig. 7.1. Data collecting for a mining task

In Figure 7.1, 'InternalDS' is a set of internal data that will be mined; 'ExternalDSi' is the ith data-source collected; 'Datacollecting' is the procedure of data collecting; 'Hugedataset' is the set of all data in internal and external data-sources after joining; and 'Ruleset' is the set of rules (patterns) that are discovered from 'Hugedataset'. To the left of the cured line 'L' is data collecting. To the right of 'L', is the rest of the process of KDD.

As illustrated in Figure 7.1, joining all data together from internal and external data-sources into a single dataset for discovery leads to three main limitations.

1. Low-quality (including noisy, erroneous, ambiguous, untrustworthy, and fraudulent) data can disguise really useful patterns.
2. It is not clear which of the collected data-sources are relevant to a given mining task. In other words, data in irrelevant data-sources plays an equally important role in the mining task.
3. There is no confirmation as to which of the collected data-sources are really useful to the specific mining task.

Because of noise and related issues, external data can be impure. In particular, collected data may be fraudulent, and it can disguise really useful patterns in data. Fraudulent data can also cause applications to fail. For example, a stock investor needs to collect information from other data-sources for an investment decision. If the investor gathers fraudulent information, and the information is directly applied to investment decisions, he or she may lose money. Hence, it is very important that quality external data is selected.

Based on the above analysis, the problem for our research can be formulated as follows.

Given a mining task on a dataset DS, and n data-sources collected for the mining task, we are interested in (1) building a framework for preprocessing collected external data, and (2) improving mined patterns by using quality external data.

There are diverse techniques useful for other steps of the process of KDD, such as in [Han 2000, Liu 1998, Wu 1995]. This chapter focuses on identifying believable data-sources.

7.2.2 Our Approach

As we have seen, selecting believable data from external data is crucial when mining databases. In this chapter, we propose an approach for identifying believable external data-sources as a first step in utilizing external data, which is towards databases mining. We illustrate our approach in Figure 7.2.

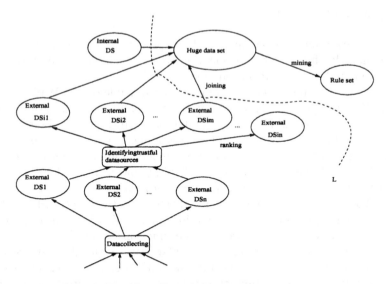

Fig. 7.2. Identifying believable collected data-sources

Figure 7.2 extends the process in Figure 7.1 by embedding a necessary procedure 'Identifyingtrustfuldatasources' for ranking collected data-sources. The data-sources are ranked $DSi1, DSi2, \cdots, DSim, \cdots, DSin$, in decreasing order of their believability. Only the data in high-belief data-sources $DSi1$, $DSi2$, $\cdots$, $DSim$ is recommended for given mining tasks. The procedure includes two steps as follows.

1. *Pre-analysis,* which is an insight into the relevant and uncontradictable data-sources collected. This is useful when we have no any other information concerning the data-sources.
2. *Post-analysis,* which is to learn the data-sources using historical data (a training set).

To improve mined patterns, a synthesis is built for utilizing collected quality external data.

7.3 External Data Collecting

In this section, we suggest a way to gather information from various sources. To mine small databases, we might use external data collected from sources such as email, the Web, journals, papers, and newspapers. To discover useful patterns in the databases, we first mine them, and then synthesize the mined association rules and collected information.

7.3.1 Available Tools

Useful information can be gathered by experts in scientific, technical, and economic fields from sources as mentioned above. The information can then be represented in the manner required.

The vast amount of relevant information available on the WWW (World Wide Web) has great potential to improve the quality of decision-making, by enhancing mined results in very small databases ([Lesser 1998, Lesser 2000]). However, data on the WWW can be undisciplined, structureless, dynamical, changeable, uncertain, and huge. Large numbers of information sources, with their different levels of accessibility, reliability and associated costs, present us with a complex information gathering coordination problem ([Lesser 1998, Lesser 2000]). Also, the information gathered must then be transformed into the required representation. Information on the WWW is usually free of charge, but selecting quality data can be time-consuming.

Email is currently a novel and popular way to quickly and effectively share and exchange information. Information via email is controllable, and representation of the information can be of an appropriate form. However, acquiring the information can cost money.

News media, such as television, radio, magazines, and newspapers can also be an important source of relevant information. From such media, we can collect news like 'If A, then B', where 'A' and 'B' are things that might have happened in some place at a certain time. The information can be easily transformed into the structure that we want.

Finally, academic forums such as books, journals, conferences, tutorials, seminars, and academic magazines are useful sources of theoretical information. Such information is generally sophisticated, well explained, and detailed. However, some information might be conjecture and will need to be verified. Information from these sources usually costs money.

Information gathered must be analyzed, tested, synthesized, and refined before it is applied, because it may be unfit for the specific purpose. Then external information can be taken as interpreted knowledge which can enhance the patterns mined in a given small database.

There have been many nice methods for information gathering from the WWW proposed in recent literature ([Etzioni 1996, Lesser 1998, Lesser 2000, Martin 2000]). We now illustrate, in a simple way, how to gather useful information from the Web using some tools available on the Web.

Using these tools, individuals and organizations can take advantage of the remarkable possibilities access to information and knowledge on the Internet provide. Web technologies such as HTTP and HTML have dramatically changed enterprise information management. Information search engines, such as Google, Yahoo, Alta Vista, Excite, offer easy ways of collecting relevant information. Moreover, an intranet relying on Internet technology and protocols enables intra-organizational communication and internal information sharing through the corporate internal network. For example, a multinational corporation can benefit from intranets and the Internet to gather, manage, distribute, and share data, inside and outside the corporation.

A company can exploit the Internet, and intranet features, in several ways. It can use internal HTML or XML pages, or external URLs containing organizational datasets, to make information accessible throughout the company. More proactive methods for creating and revising corporate datasets include integrating messages exchanged through email in the corporate dataset, extracting information from the external Web sources for technological or strategic intelligence, and using computer-supported cooperative work tools to support a complex-system of collaborative design or collaborative software development. The wide variety of organizational choices involves experts in different areas ([Martin 2000]) such as:

- human knowledge sources (experts, specialists, or operators), whose knowledge must be made explicit or who have written documents that others can access through an organizational dataset;
- knowledge engineers, who acquire and model knowledge;
- knowledge watchers, who gather, filter, analyze, and distribute knowledge elements from the external world (from external information Web sources, for example);
- organizational dataset developers, who concretely build, organize, annotate, maintain, and evolve the corporate dataset;

- a team of validating experts (for example, a reference team), who validate knowledge elements before their insertion in the organizational dataset;
- corporate dataset users, who must be able to easily access and reuse the elements in the dataset;
- organizational dataset manages, who supervise the organizational project on the dataset.

Wherever knowledge is available, it would generally be represented in the form required by applications. In this chapter, all collected knowledge is represented as rules.

7.3.2 Indexing by a Conditional Associated Semantic

Let D be the set of terms in a given document, and Q be the set of terms in a query. The prevailing methods consist of one which is based on terms of similarity, and another which is based on latent semantics. Relatively speaking, latent semantics is preferable. However, these models are considered independently. For example, the semantic distance of D and Q is the sum of the semantic distance between terms. This means, terms are used without any relationships. Generally, a term in D (or Q) has independent semantics. Previous models are based on this semantic measurement. In fact, all terms in D (or Q) have associated semantics. For example, x is a term in D (or Q), and there is a semantic set of x given D (or Q). Or, in general, for any S the subset of D (or Q), and x in S, then there is a semantic set of x, given S. In our opinion, this associated semantics of terms must be considered in semantic indexing.

We now present an approach for measuring similarity between two documents by latent semantics.

For a term t of D, the associated semantics of t is a set of all possible semantics of t given D, denoted by $AS(t|D)$. Or

$$AS(t|D) = \{s|s \text{ is a possible semantics of } t \text{ given } D\}$$

We define the distance between terms t_1 and t_2 of D based on associated semantics as follows:

$$m_{AS}(t_1, t_2) = \frac{|AS(t_1|D) \cap AS(t_2|D)|}{|AS(t_1|D) \cup AS(t_2|D)|}$$

Certainly, the larger $m_{AS}(t_1, t_2)$, the smaller the distance between terms t_1 and t_2.

Example 7.1 Let t_1, t_2 and t_3 be three terms, and $AS(t_1|D) = \{a_1, a_2, b_2, c_1\}$, $AS(t_2|D) = \{a_2, b_1, b_2, c_1\}$, and $AS(t_3|D) = \{a_1, a_2, b_2, c_1, c_2\}$. Then

$$m_{AS}(t_1, t_2) = \frac{|AS(t_1|D) \cap AS(t_2|D)|}{|AS(t_1|D) \cup AS(t_2|D)|} = \frac{3}{5} = 0.6$$

$$m_{AS}(t_1, t_3) = \frac{|AS(t_1|D) \cap AS(t_3|D)|}{|AS(t_1|D) \cup AS(t_3|D)|} = \frac{4}{5} = 0.8$$

$$m_{AS}(t_2, t_3) = \frac{|AS(t_2|D) \cap AS(t_3|D)|}{|AS(t_2|D) \cup AS(t_3|D)|} = \frac{3}{6} = 0.5$$

Also, we define the distance between a document D and a query Q based on associated semantics as follows, where $D = \{d_1, d_2, \cdots, d_n\}$ and $Q = \{q_1, q_2, \cdots, q_k\}$.

1. The simplest similarity measurement is

$$M_{AS}(D, Q) = \frac{|(AS(d_1|D) \cup \cdots \cup AS(d_n|D)) \cap (AS(q_1|Q) \cup \cdots \cup AS(q_k|Q))|}{|AS(d_1|D) \cup \cdots \cup AS(d_n|D) \cup AS(q_1|Q) \cup \cdots \cup AS(q_k|Q)|}$$

2. For a rigorous similarity measurement, and no lost generality, we assume $n \geq k$ in the above, and we construct the following distance table between terms.

Table 7.1. Mutual distances among terms given D and Q

	q_1	q_2	$\cdots$	q_k	$\emptyset$	$\cdots$	$\emptyset$
d_1	a_{11}	a_{12}	$\cdots$	a_{1k}	$a_{1(k+1)}$	$\cdots$	a_{1n}
d_2	a_{21}	a_{22}	$\cdots$	a_{2k}	$a_{2(k+1)}$	$\cdots$	a_{2n}
$\vdots$	$\vdots$	$\vdots$		$\vdots$	$\vdots$		$\vdots$
d_n	a_{n1}	a_{n2}	$\cdots$	a_{nk}	$a_{n(k+1)}$	$\cdots$	a_{nn}

In Table 7.1, $a_{ij} = m_{AS}(d_i, q_j)$ when $i = 1, 2, \cdots, n$ and $j = 1, 2, \cdots, k$; $a_{ij} = 0$, when $i = 1, 2, \cdots, n$ and $j = k + 1, \cdots, n$.
There are two means of solving the values, which are average values and weight values. We take the greatest value in the above as the distance between D and Q. Or,

$$M_{AS}(D, Q) = Max\{m_i\}_{i=1}^{N}$$

3. The Boolean OR-Query, which is a query which can be described in a standard format such as a Boolean expression. The common Boolean expression is as follows.

$$Q = (q_1 \wedge \cdots \wedge q_i) \vee (q_{i+1} \wedge \cdots \wedge q_j) \vee \cdots \vee (q_{k+1} \wedge \cdots \wedge q_n)$$

Assuming $Q_1 = \{q_1, \cdots, q_i\}$, $Q_2 = \{q_{i+1}, \cdots, q_j\}$, $\cdots$, $Q_m = \{q_{k+1}, \cdots, q_n\}$. Then the query can be expressed as

$$Q = Q_1 \vee Q_2 \vee \cdots \vee Q_m$$

The similarity measurement between D and Q is defined as

$$M_{AS}(D, Q) = Max\{M_{AS}(D, Q_1), M_{AS}(D, Q_2), \cdots M_{AS}(D, Q_m)\}$$

7.3.3 Procedures for Similarity

Because similarity using latent semantics is similar to that of associated semantics, we only present algorithms of similarity by associated semantics. Let D be a given document and Q be a query. Our algorithm for the simplest similarity by associated semantics is as follows.

Procedure 7.1 *SimpleSimMeasure*

begin
Input: *D: document, Q: a query;*
Output: $M_{AS}^{sim}(D, Q)$: *the similarity;*
(1) **for** $d \in D$ **do**
  begin
    generate $AS(d|D)$;
    let $AS_D \leftarrow AS_D \cup AS(d|D)$;
  end
  for $q \in Q$ **do**
    begin
      generate $AS(q|Q)$;
      let $AS_Q \leftarrow AS_Q \cup AS(q|Q)$;
    end
(2) **let** $M_{AS}^{sim}(D, Q) \leftarrow |AS_D \cap AS_Q|/|AS_D \cup AS_Q|$;
(3) **output** the similarity between D and Q is $M_{AS}^{sim}(D, Q)$;
  endall.
end;

The procedure *SimpleSimMeasure* estimates the similarity between two documents, D and Q, by using latent semantics.

An algorithm for rigorous similarity by associated semantics is as follows. (For simplicity, let $D = \{d_1, d_2, \cdots, d_n\}$, $Q = \{q_1, q_2, \cdots, q_k\}$, and $n = k$.)

Procedure 7.2 *RigSimMeasure*

begin
Input: *D: document, Q: a query;*
Output: $M_{AS}^{rig}(D, Q)$: *the similarity;*
(1) **input** the weight set $\{w_1, w_2, \cdots, w_n\}$;
  for $d \in D$ **do**
    generate $AS(d_1|D)$, $AS(d_2|D)$, $\cdots$, $AS(d_n|D)$;
  for $q \in Q$ **do**
    generate $AS(q_1|Q)$, $AS(q_2|Q)$, $\cdots$, $AS(q_n|Q)$;
(2) **for** $d \in D$ **do**
  for $q \in Q$ **do**
    let $a_{ij} \leftarrow m_{AS}(d_i, q_j)$;

(3) **let** $I \leftarrow$ the set of all possible reorders of $(1, 2, \cdots, n)$;
   let $M_{AS}^{rig}(D, Q) \leftarrow 0$;
   for $i = 1$ **to** n **do**
      for any $(l_1, l_2, \cdots, l_n) \in I$ **do**
         begin
            let $tem \leftarrow w_1 * a_{il_1} + w_2 * a_{il_2} + \cdots + w_n * a_{il_n}$;
            if $tem > M_{AS}^{rig}(D, Q)$ **then**
               let $M_{AS}^{rig}(D, Q) \leftarrow tem$;
         end
(4) **output** the similarity between D and Q is $M_{AS}^{rig}(D, Q)$;
   endall.

end;

The procedure *RigSimMeasure* estimates the similarity between two documents, D and Q, by using associated semantics.

7.4 A Data Preprocessing Framework

After external data is collected, we must preprocess it before it is used. This section sets up a framework for selecting quality external data.

In this framework, we propose to determine which data-sources are veridical by pre- and post-analysis. Pre-analysis develops techniques for searching, for example, relevant and uncontradictable data-sources. This is useful when we have no further information about the data-sources. Post-analysis is used to learn the veridical degrees of data-sources based upon experience (the training set). This is historical data arising from the application of external data-sources.

7.4.1 Pre-analysis: Selecting Relevant and Uncontradictable Collected Data-Sources

For a given data-source DS, and the set $DSSet$ of the collected data-sources $DS_1, DS_2, \cdots, DS_m$, we first pre-analyze the data-sources from $DSSet$ using their features and knowledge when we have no any other information about them. We do this to select those data-sources that are relevant and uncontradictable to DS.

Relevant Data-Source Selecting We define a metric similarity function to measure the relevance between pairs of data-sources. Similarity between data-sources is expressed by the closeness function, such that a high closeness corresponds to a high degree of similarity; whereas two data-sources with a very low closeness are considered to be rather dissimilar.

Let the data-sources be drawn from a set $DSSet$ of multiple data-sources, and let *sim* be a metric closeness function for pairs of data-sources. That is,

$sim : DSSet \times DSSet \rightarrow [0, 1]$. We now propose a technique for constructing a function for the similarity sim.

Let $Feature(DS_i)$ be the set of all features in DS_i $(i = 1, 2, \cdots, m)$[1]. We need to select data-sources from $DSSet = \{DS_1, DS_2, \cdots, DS_m\}$ for DS such that each data-source is relevant to a data-source DS under a measurement.

The features of data-sources can be used to measure the closeness of a pair of data-sources. We call the measurement sim, and it is defined as follows.

1. A function for the similarity between the feature sets of two data-sources DS_i and DS_j is as

$$sim(DS_i, DS_j) = \frac{|Feature(DS_i) \cap Feature(DS_j)|}{|Feature(DS_i) \cup Feature(DS_j)|}$$

where '$\cap$' denotes set intersection, '$\cup$' denotes set union, and '$|X|$' is the number of elements in the set X.

In the above definition of similarity,

$$sim : Feature(DSSet) \times Feature(DSSet) \rightarrow [0, 1]$$

we take the size of the intersection of a pair of the feature sets of data-sources to measure the closeness of the two data-sources. That is, a large intersection corresponds to a high degree of similarity, whereas two data-sources with a small intersection are considered to be rather dissimilar.

We now illustrate the use of the above similarity by an example.

Example 7.2 Let $Feature(DS_1) = \{a_1, a_2, a_3\}$ and $Feature(DS_2) = \{a_2, a_3, b_1, b_2\}$ be two sets of features of two data-sources DS_1 and DS_2, respectively. The similarity between DS_1 and DS_2 is as follows.

$$sim(DS_1, DS_2) = \frac{|Feature(DS_1) \cap Feature(DS_2)|}{|Feature(DS_1) \cup Feature(DS_2)|} = \frac{2}{5} = 0.4$$

Note that, if $sim(DS_i, DS_j) = 1$, it simply means that $Feature(DS_i) = Feature(DS_j)$, or DS_i and DS_j can be relevant under the measurement sim. It does not mean that $DS_i = DS_j$ when $sim(DS_i, DS_j) = 1$.

In this chapter, we have proposed a simple and understandable function for measuring the similarity of pairs of data-sources. We could, of course, construct more functions for similarity using, for example, the weights of features.

Using the above similarity on data-sources, we define data-sources α-relevant to DS below.

---

[1] The features of a data-source are often selected from its data. If we can only share the rules (patterns) of the data-source, the features of the data-source can be selected from the rules (patterns).

Definition 7.1 *A data-source DS_i is α-relevant to DS under the measurement sim_1 if $sim(DS_i, DS) > \alpha$, where α (> 0) is a threshold.*

For example, let $\alpha = 0.4$. Consider both the data $Feature(DS_1) = \{i_1, i_2, i_3, i_4, i_5\}$ and the data $Feature(DS) = \{i_1, i_3, i_4, i_5, i_6, i_7\}$. Because $sim(DS_1, DS) = 0.556 > \alpha = 0.4$, the data-source DS_1 is 0.4-relevant to DS.

Definition 7.2 *Let $DSSet$ be a set of m data-sources $D_1, D_2, \cdots, D_m$. The set of the selected data-sources in $DSSet$ that are α-relevant to a data-source DS under the similarity measure sim (denoted as $RDS(DS, DSSet, sim, \alpha)$) is defined as follows:*

$$RDS(DS, DSSet, sim, \alpha) = \{ds \in DSSet | ds \text{ is } \alpha\text{-relevant to } DS\}$$

Uncontradictable Data-Source Selecting The process of selecting relevant data-sources considers their features. Also, we can check the contradiction between pairs of data-sources by comparing their knowledge if we have no any other information about those data-sources. Two data-sources, DS_i and DS_j, are contradictive if there is at least one proposition A such that A holds in DS_i, and $\neg A$ holds in DS_j. Then A is called a 'contradictive proposition' in the data-sources DS_i and DS_j. We use the ratio of contradictive propositions in data-sources DS_i and DS_j to measure the contradiction between the two data-sources. We now define a function for the contradiction, *contrad*, below.

Let $Rule(DS_i)$ be the set of all propositions in DS_i ($i = 1, 2, \cdots, m$). We need to select data-sources from $DSSet = \{DS_1, DS_2, \cdots, DS_m\}$ for DS, such that each data-source is uncontradictable to a data-source DS under a measurement below.

2. We can construct the contradiction, *contrad*, by using the ratio of contradictive propositions in the data-sources DS_i and DS_j, as follows.

$$contrad(DS_i, DS_j) = \frac{\text{number of contra-propositions in } DS_i \text{ and } DS_j}{|Rule(DS_i) \cup Rule(DS_j)|}$$

In the above definition of the contradiction, $contrad : Rule(DSSet) \times Rule(DSSet) \to [0, 1]$, we take the number of contradictive propositions in the data-sources to measure the contradiction of the two data-sources. That is, a large number corresponds to a high degree of contradiction, whereas two data-sources with a small intersection are considered to be strongly uncontradiction.

We illustrate the use of the contradiction, *contrad*, by an example below.

Example 7.3 *Let* $Rule(DS_1) = \{A, B, \neg C, D\}$ *and* $Rule(DS_2) = \{A, \neg B, C, E, F\}$ *be two sets of propositions of two data-sources,* DS_1 *and* DS_2, *respectively. The contradiction between* DS_1 *and* DS_2 *is measured as follows.*

$$contrad(DS_1, DS_2) = \frac{number\ of\ contra\text{-}propositions\ in\ DS_1\ and\ DS_2}{|Rule(DS_1) \cup Rule(DS_2)|}$$

$$= \frac{2}{6} = 0.3333$$

Using the above contradiction on the data-sources, we define data-sources β-uncontradictable to DS below.

Definition 7.3 *A data-source* DS_i *is* β-*uncontradictable to a data-source* DS_j *under the measure contrad if* $1 - contrad(DS_i, DS_j) > \beta$, *where* β *(> 0) is a threshold.*

For example, let $\beta = 0.8$. Consider the data in Example 7.3. Because $1 - contrad(DS_1, DS_2) = 1 - 0.3333 = 0.6667 < \beta = 0.8$, the data-source DS_1 is not 0.8-uncontradictable to DS_2.

Definition 7.4 *Let* $DSSet$ *be the set of* m *data-sources* $D_1, D_2, \cdots, D_m$. *The set of the selected data-sources in* $DSSet$ *that are* β-*uncontradictable to a data-source* DS *under the contradiction measure contrad (denoted as* $UDS(DS, DSSet, contrad, \beta)$) *is defined as follows:*

$$UDS(DS, DSSet, contrad, \beta) = \{ds \in DSSet | ds\ is\ \beta\text{-}uncontradictable\ to\ DS\}$$

7.4.2 Post-analysis: Summarizing Historical Data

When we have information, such as in the case of applying external data-sources (or a training set), collected data can be post-analyzed. Suppose we have applied external data-sources $DS1$, $DS2$, $DS3$, and $DS4$ for ten real-world applications as shown in Table 7.2.

Table 7.2. Past data of using external knowledge

	DS1	DS2	DS3	DS4	result
a_1		1	1	1	yes
a_2	1	1	1	1	yes
a_3	1	1			no
a_4	1		1		no
a_5	1		1		no
a_6	1			1	yes
a_7		1	1	1	yes
a_8	1	1	1		yes
a_9	1	1			no
a_{10}	1	1	1	1	yes

In Table 7.2, DSi stands for the ith data-source; a_i indicates the ith application; '1' means that the knowledge in a data-source is applied to an application, and we use $DSi = 1$ to indicate that the ith data-source is applied to an application. Also, '$result$' measures the success of the applications, '$result = yes$' means that an application is successful and, '$result = no$' means that an application is a failure. For application a_1, three data-sources $DS2$, $DS3$, and $DS4$ have been applied.

After analyzing past data, we can find out which of the data-sources are veridical. The data in the above table shows

$$R1 : DS4 = 1 \rightarrow result = yes \ with \ frequency = 5$$
$$R2 : (DS1 = 1) \wedge (DS2 = 1) \wedge (DS3 = 1) \wedge (DS4 = 1)$$
$$\rightarrow result = yes \ with \ frequency = 2$$
$$R3 : (DS1 = 1) \wedge (DS2 = 1) \rightarrow result = no \ with \ frequency = 2$$
$$R4 : (DS1 = 1) \wedge (DS3 = 1) \rightarrow result = no \ with \ frequency = 2$$
$$R5 : (DS1 = 1) \wedge (DS2 = 1) \wedge (DS3 = 1)$$
$$\rightarrow result = yes \ with \ frequency = 1$$
$$R6 : (DS1 = 1) \wedge (DS4 = 1) \rightarrow result = yes \ with \ frequency = 1$$
$$R7 : (DS2 = 1) \wedge (DS3 = 1) \wedge (DS4 = 1)$$
$$\rightarrow result = yes \ with \ frequency = 2$$

where $R1$ denotes that applications are successful when the knowledge in data-source $DS4$ is used in the applications with frequency 5; $R2$ means that applications are successful when $DS1$, $DS2$, $DS3$, and $DS4$ are all applied to applications with frequency 2; and so on.

The above seven rules are considered when we determine the veridicality of data-sources. For example, the rules show that data-source $DS4$ is veridical in past applications.

Also, we can check if an external pattern is trustworthy according to the historical data of applying patterns. Let $P1$, $P2$, $\cdots$, $P6$ be six patterns. The historical data for applying patterns is listed in Table 7.3.

Table 7.3. The historical data for applying patterns

	P1	P2	P3	P4	P5	P6	result
a_1	1	1	1	1			yes
a_2	1	1			1	1	yes
a_3		1		1		1	no
a_4			1	1	1		no
a_5		1	1			1	no
a_6	1	1			1	1	yes
a_7	1	1	1	1			yes
a_8	1	1	1		1	1	yes
a_9		1	1		1	1	no
a_{10}			1	1	1	1	yes

In Table 7.3, Pi stands for the ith patterns; '1' is where a pattern is applied to an application, and we use $Pi = 1$ to indicate that the ith pattern is applied to an application. Also, 'a_i' and '*result*' are the same as in Table 7.2. For application a_1, the first four patterns, $P1$, $P2$, $P3$, and $P4$, have been applied.

Using the past data, we can discover which of the patterns are believable. For example,

$PR1 : P1 = 1 \rightarrow result = yes\ with\ frequency = 5$

$PR2 : (P1 = 1) \wedge (P2 = 1) \rightarrow result = yes\ with\ frequency = 5$

$PR3 : (P1 = 1) \wedge (P5 = 1) \rightarrow result = yes\ with\ frequency = 3$

$PR4 : (P1 = 1) \wedge (P6 = 1) \rightarrow result = yes\ with\ frequency = 3$

$PR5 : (P1 = 1) \wedge (P3 = 1) \rightarrow result = yes\ with\ frequency = 3$

$PR6 : (P1 = 1) \wedge (P4 = 1) \rightarrow result = yes\ with\ frequency = 2$

are some rules identified from Tables 7.2, where $PR1$ denotes that applications are successful when the pattern $P1$ is used in applications with frequency 5; $PR2$ means that applications are successful when both $P1$ and $P2$ are applied to applications with frequency 5; and so on.

Using historical data, such as that in Tables 7.2 and 7.3, we can post-analyze collected knowledge. And we can determine which data-sources are veridical, and which collected patterns are believable. The above instance only elucidates how possible information can be used to judge the veridicality of a data-source. If we are able to obtain more information, we can make a judgement on veridicality by synthesizing.

7.4.3 Algorithm Designing

In this subsection, we design an algorithm for preprocessing collected knowledge by means of a framework. As we have seen, the proposed framework can be taken as a basis for preprocessing collected external knowledge. Upon pre-analysis and post-analysis, we can rank all data-sources by their veridical degrees decreasingly, and we can select the first 10%, or more, as the veridical data-sources.

The purpose of ranking is to preprocess collected knowledge by determining veridical degrees of data-sources. After pre-analyzing and post analyzing the data-sources, we can make generalizations to single out the most believable candidates among the data-sources in order to compose a reference list for knowledge sharing. With the increase of information about data-sources, the reference list becomes more and more accurate and data-sources can then solely rely on it for sharing data.

At the very beginning, the historical data table (HDT) has no knowledge about the data-sources. We can only pre-analyze the data-sources using their features and knowledge to rank the data-sources. After several applications, we can also rank the data-sources by synthesizing their veridical degrees. For example, consider the data in Table 7.2. The cases for applying the four data-sources $DS1$, $DS2$, $DS3$, and $DS4$ are listed in Table 7.4.

Table 7.4. The cases of applying the four data-sources $DS1$, $DS2$, $DS3$, and $DS4$

	frequency	*success*	*fail*	success-ratio
$DS1$	8	4	4	0.5
$DS2$	7	5	2	0.714
$DS3$	7	5	2	0.714
$DS4$	4	4	0	1

In Table 7.4, *frequency* is the number of applications that use a data-source; *success* is the success times for applications when a data-source was applied; *fail* is the fail times for applications when a data-source was applied; and 'success-ratio' is *success/frequency*.

From the above table, $DS1$ was applied 8 times with success-ratio 0.5; $DS2$ was applied 7 times with success-ratio 0.714; $DS3$ was applied 7 times with success-ratio 0.714; and $DS4$ was applied 4 times with success-ratio 1.

We can now use the success-ratios to determine the veridical degrees of the data-sources. One way is to normalize the success-ratios as the veridical degrees of the data-sources as below.

$$vd_{DS1} = \frac{0.5}{0.5 + 0.714 + 0.714 + 1} = 0.167,$$

$$vd_{DS2} = \frac{0.714}{0.5 + 0.714 + 0.714 + 1} = 0.238,$$

$$vd_{DS3} = \frac{0.714}{0.5 + 0.714 + 0.714 + 1} = 0.238,$$

$$vd_{DS4} = \frac{1}{0.5 + 0.714 + 0.714 + 1} = 0.357,$$

where vd_{DSi} stands for the veridical degree of the ith data-source ($i = 1, 2, 3, 4$).

We have seen that data-source $DS4$ has the highest success-ratio, and it has the highest veridical degree; and $DS1$ has the lowest success-ratio, and it has the lowest veridical degree.

Furthermore, the veridical degree of DS_i ($i = 1, 2, \cdots, n$) can be defined as follows:

$$vd_{DS_i} = \frac{\text{success-ratio of } DS_i}{\sum_{j=1}^{n} \text{success-ratio of } DS_j}$$

However, to highlight the data-sources with high success-ratios, we can construct many methods to assign veridical degrees to data-sources. The simplest way is defined as follows.

$$vd_{DS_i} = \frac{(\text{success-ratio of } DS_i)^2}{\sum_{j=1}^{n} (\text{ success-ratio of } DS_j)^2}$$

We now check effectiveness using the above data.

$$vd_{DS1} = \frac{0.5^2}{0.5^2 + 0.714^2 + 0.714^2 + 1^2} = 0.11$$

$$vd_{DS2} = \frac{0.714^2}{0.5^2 + 0.714^2 + 0.714^2 + 1^2} = 0.225$$

$$vd_{DS3} = \frac{0.714^2}{0.5^2 + 0.714^2 + 0.714^2 + 1^2} = 0.225$$

$$vd_{DS4} = \frac{1^2}{0.5^2 + 0.714^2 + 0.714^2 + 1^2} = 0.44$$

In this formula, the data-source $DS4$ has the highest success-ratio and its veridical degree has been increased; and $DS1$ has the lowest success-ratio and its veridical degree has been decreased. In other words, the data-sources with high success-ratios are highlighted. Accordingly, the external data-sources are ranked $DS4$, $DS2$, $DS3$, $DS1$.

However, when we rank data-sources upon historical data only, if a believable data-source is utilized frequently with untrustworthy data-sources in applications, the belief of the data-source is impacted upon. We can first pre-analyze the data-sources using their features and knowledge to determine their veridical degree before the data-sources are utilized. Thus we can conduct the use of the data-sources in applications to determine their veridical degrees.

In our approach, we focus on only three factors: relevance, uncontradictability, and veridicality, when ranking data-sources. Other factors are similar to the above. To synthesize the three factors for ranking, we can use the weighting techniques proposed in [Good 1950]. We now design an algorithm for ranking external data-sources by pre- and post-analysis as follows.

Algorithm 7.1 *Data-sourcesRank*

begin
Input: *DS: data-source; DS_i: m data-sources;*
Output: *S: a set of data-sources;*
(1) **input** the collected data-sources DS_i relevant to DS;
(2) **transform** the information in each data-source into rules;
(3) **pre-analyze** the data-source $DS_1, \cdots, DS_m$;

(4) **rank** the data-sources by synthesizing the pre-analyzing results decreasingly;

(5) **post-analyze** the data-sources according to the ranking by pre-analysis;

(6) **rank** the data-sources by synthesizing the post-analyzing results decreasingly;

(7) **let** $S \leftarrow$ all high-ranking data-sources;

(8) **output** S;

end

The algorithm *Data-sourcesRank* ranks the collected m data-sources $DS_1, DS_2, \cdots, DS_m$ relevant to the data-source DS, according to the proposed framework, where S is the set of all high-ranking data-sources.

Step (1) inputs the collected data-sources $DS_1, DS_2, \cdots, DS_m$ relevant to the data-source DS.

Step (2) transforms the information in the data-sources into rules for the purpose of mining association rules in DS.

Step (3) pre-analyzes the data-sources using their features and knowledge to select data-sources that are relevant and uncontradictable to DS.

Step (4) first synthesizes the results of pre-analysis by weighting, and then ranks the external data-sources according to the decreasing synthesizing results.

Step (5) is to generate the veridical degrees of the selected data-sources in Step (4) by using historical data as follows

$$vd_{DS_i} = \frac{(\text{success-ratio of } DS_i)^2}{\sum_{j=1}^{n}(\text{ success-ratio of } DS_j)^2}$$

For convenience, Step (6) ranks the data-sources by synthesizing the pre-analysis (including relevance and uncontradictability) and post-analysis (veridical degrees) decreasingly. Step (7) selects all high-ranking data-sources and saves them into S. And the final result, S, is output in Step (8), where the data-sources in S are suggested to the user as believable data-sources.

7.5 Synthesizing Selected Rules

When we have selected some external knowledge using the techniques in the first two phases, this knowledge can be synthesized so that we can apply it to improve the results from a given database. We represent the external knowledge as rules.

To assist the exploration of small databases using the collected knowledge represented in the data-sources, we first need to synthesize all gathered rules[2].

---

[2] For description, we also regard them as of the form $X \rightarrow Y$, with a support *supp* and a confidence *conf*.

Then we apply the synthesized rules to determine which rules are of interest in small databases. In this section, we present a new model for synthesizing the collected rules[3].

Let $D_1, D_2, \cdots, D_m$ be m different data-sources, and S_i the set of rules from D_i $(i = 1, 2, \cdots, m)$. For a given rule $X \to Y$, suppose $w_1, w_2, \cdots, w_m$ are the weights of $D_1, D_2, \cdots, D_m$ respectively. The synthesizing is defined as follows.

$$supp_w(X \cup Y) = w_1 * supp_1(X \cup Y) + w_2 * supp_2(X \cup Y)$$
$$+ \cdots + w_m * supp_m(X \cup Y),$$
$$conf_w(X \to Y) = w_1 * conf_1(X \to Y) + w_2 * conf_2(X \to Y)$$
$$+ \cdots + w_m * conf_m(X \to Y)$$

7.5.1 Assigning Weights

To synthesize rules from data-sources, we need to determine a weight for each data-source. The weight of a data-source is determined by the inter-support relationship between a data-source and its rules. This means that if a data-source supports a larger number of high-belief rules, the weight of the data-source should also be higher.

In order to synthesize association rules from different data-sources, we need to determine a weight for each data-source. Let $D_1, D_2, \cdots, D_m$ be m different data-sources, S_i the set of association rules from D_i $(i = 1, 2, \cdots, m)$, and $S = \{S_1, S_2, \cdots, S_m\}$. According to Good's definition on weight ([Good 1950]), *the voting of a rule R in S* can be used to assign R a weight w_R. In practice, a company headquarters might be interested in rules that are supported, or voted for, by majority of data-sources. High-voting rules have a larger chance of becoming valid in the union of all data-sources than low-voting rules. Hence, the higher the voting rate of a rule, the larger the weight of the rule should be.

Meanwhile, the inter-support relationship between a data-source and its rules can be applied to determine the weight of the data-source. If a data-source supports a larger number of high-voting rules, the weight of the data-source should also be higher. The above idea is now illustrated by an example.

Let $minsupp = 0.2$, $minconf = 0.3$, and the following rules be mined from three data-sources.

(1) S_1 is a set of association rules from a data-source $D1$:
  $A \wedge B \to C$ with $supp = 0.4, conf = 0.72$;
  $A \to D$ with $supp = 0.3, conf = 0.64$;
  $B \to E$ with $supp = 0.34, conf = 0.7$;

---

[3] Because of data privacy and related issues, it is possible that some data-sources may share their association rules but not their original data. Therefore, this section focuses on the rules collected from data-sources.

(2) S_2 is a set of association rules from a data-source $D2$:
   $B \rightarrow C$ with $supp = 0.45, conf = 0.87$;
   $A \rightarrow D$ with $supp = 0.36, conf = 0.7$;
   $B \rightarrow E$ with $supp = 0.4, conf = 0.6$;
(3) S_3 is a set of association rules from a data-source $D3$:
   $A \wedge B \rightarrow C$ with $supp = 0.5, conf = 0.82$;
   $A \rightarrow D$ with $supp = 0.25, conf = 0.62$;

Assume $S' = \{S_1, S_2, S_3\}$. Then there are a total of four rules in S':

R_1 $A \wedge B \rightarrow C$
R_2 $A \rightarrow D$
R_3 $B \rightarrow E$
R_4 $B \rightarrow C$

From the above rules mined from different data-sources, there are 2 data-sources that support, or vote for, rule R_1[4], 3 data-sources support/vote for rule R_2, 2 data-sources support/vote rule R_3, and 1 data-source supports/votes for rule R_4. Following Good's weight of evidence ([Good 1950]), the voting of a rule in S' is used to assign a weight to that rule. After normalization, the weights are assigned as follows:

$$w_{R1} = \frac{2}{2+3+2+1} = 0.25$$

$$w_{R2} = \frac{3}{2+3+2+1} = 0.375$$

$$w_{R3} = \frac{2}{2+3+2+1} = 0.25$$

$$w_{R4} = \frac{1}{2+3+2+1} = 0.125$$

As we have seen, rule R_2 has the highest voting and the highest weight; and rule R_4 has the lowest voting and the lowest weight. Let $S = \{S_1, S_2, \cdots, S_m\}$, and $R_1, R_2, \cdots, R_n$ all be rules in S. Then the weight of R_i is defined as follows.

$$w_{Ri} = \frac{Num(R_i)}{\sum_{j=1}^{n} Num(R_j)}$$

where $i = 1, 2, \cdots, n$; and $Num(R)$ is the number of data-sources that contain rule R, or the voting of R in S.

Meanwhile, if a data-source supports, or votes for, a larger number of high-voting rules, the weight of the data-sources should also be higher. If the rules from a data-source are rarely present in other data-sources, the data-source would be assigned a lower weight. To implement this argument, the

---

[4] This support is different from the support defined in Chapter 2. The support here is the number of data-sources that vote for the rule.

sum of the multiplications of weights of rules and their voting can be used to assign weights to the data-sources. For the above rule set S', we have

$$w_{D1} = 2 * 0.25 + 3 * 0.375 + 2 * 0.25 = 2.125$$
$$w_{D2} = 1 * 0.125 + 2 * 0.25 + 3 * 0.375 = 2$$
$$w_{D3} = 2 * 0.25 + 3 * 0.375 = 1.625$$

After normalization, the weights of the three data-sources are assigned as follows:

$$w_{D1} = \frac{2.125}{2.125 + 2 + 1.625} = 0.3695$$

$$w_{D2} = \frac{2}{2.125 + 2 + 1.625} = 0.348$$

$$w_{D3} = \frac{1.625}{2.125 + 2 + 1.625} = 0.2825$$

As we have seen, data-source D_1 supports, or votes for, most rules with high weights and it has the highest weight; data-source D_3 supports, or votes for, the fewest rules with high weights, and it has the lowest weight.

Let $D_1, D_2, \cdots, D_m$ be m different data-sources; S_i the set of association rules from D_i ($i = 1, 2, \cdots, m$); $S = \{S_1, S_2, \cdots, S_m\}$; and $R_1, R_2, \cdots, R_n$ be all rules in S. Then the weight of D_i is defined as follows.

$$w_{Di} = \frac{\sum_{R_k \in S_i} Num(R_k) * w_{R_k}}{\sum_{j=1}^{m} \sum_{R_h \in S_j} Num(R_h) * w_{R_h}}$$

where, $i = 1, 2, \cdots, m$.

After all data-sources have been assigned weights, the association rules can be synthesized by the weights of the data-sources. The synthesizing process is illustrated as follows.

For rule R_1: $A \wedge B \to C$,

$$supp(A \cup B \cup C) = w_{D1} * supp_1(A \cup B \cup C) + w_{D3} * supp_3(A \cup B \cup C)$$
$$= 0.3695 * 0.4 + 0.2825 * 0.5 = 0.28905$$

$$conf(A \wedge B \to C) = w_{D1} * conf_1(A \wedge B \to C) + w_{D3} * conf_3(A \wedge B \to C)$$
$$= 0.3695 * 0.72 + 0.2825 * 0.82 = 0.49769$$

For rule R_2: $A \to D$,

$$supp(A \cup D) = w_{D1} * supp_1(A \cup D) + w_{D2} * supp_2(A \cup D) w_{D3} * supp_3(A \cup D)$$
$$= 0.3695 * 0.3 + 0.348 * 0.36 + 0.2825 * 0.25 = 0.306755$$

$$conf(A \to D) = w_{D1} * conf_1(A \to D)$$
$$+ w_{D2} * conf_2(A \to D) + w_{D3} * conf_3(A \to D)$$
$$= 0.3695 * 0.64 + 0.348 * 0.7 + 0.2825 * 0.62 = 0.68043$$

For rule R_3: $B \rightarrow E$,

$$supp(B \cup E) = w_{D1} * supp_1(B \cup E) + w_{D2} * supp_2(B \cup E)$$
$$= 0.3695 * 0.34 + 0.348 * 0.4 = 0.26483$$

$$conf(B \rightarrow E) = w_{D1} * conf_1(B \rightarrow E) + w_{D2} * conf_2(B \rightarrow E)$$
$$= 0.3695 * 0.7 + 0.348 * 0.6 = 0.46745$$

For rule R_4: $B \rightarrow C$,

$$supp(B \cup C) = w_{D2} * supp_2(B \cup C) = 0.348 * 0.45 = 0.1566$$
$$conf(B \rightarrow C) = w_{D2} * conf_2(B \rightarrow C) = 0.348 * 0.87 = 0.30276$$

The above rules are ranked by their supports as R_2, R_1, R_3, and R_4. According to this ranking, high-ranking rules can be used in applications.

Note that it is not difficult to find other methods of assigning weights to given data-sources. For example, we can use the size of data-sources to assign weights. For D_1, D_2, and D_3, let $|D_1|$, $|D_2|$, and $|D_3|$ be 30, 25, and 45, respectively. We can obtain

$$w_{D1} = \frac{|D_1|}{|D_1| + |D_2| + |D_3|} = \frac{30}{30 + 25 + 45} = 0.3$$

$$w_{D2} = \frac{|D_2|}{|D_1| + |D_2| + |D_3|} = \frac{25}{30 + 25 + 45} = 0.25$$

$$w_{D3} = \frac{|D_3|}{|D_1| + |D_2| + |D_3|} = \frac{45}{30 + 25 + 45} = 0.45$$

Also, we can consider veridical degrees to assign weights to data-sources, or we can synthesize multiple factors to assign weights.

7.5.2 Algorithm Design

Let $D_1, D_2, \cdots, D_m$ be m data-sources, S_i the set of association rules from D_i ($i = 1, 2, \cdots, m$), $supp_i$ and $conf_i$ the supports and confidences of rules in S_i, and $minsupp$ and $minconf$ the threshold values given by the user. The synthesizing algorithm for association rules in different data-sources is designed as follows.

Algorithm 7.2 *Synthesizing*
   Input: $S_1, S_2, \cdots, S_m$: *rule sets; minsupp, minconf: threshold values;*
   Output: $X \rightarrow Y$: *synthesized association rules;*

(1) **let** $S \leftarrow \{S_1 \cup S_2 \cup \cdots \cup S_m\}$;
(2) **for** each rule R in S **do**
   let $Num(R) \leftarrow$ the number of data-sources that contain rule R in S;
   let $w_R \leftarrow \dfrac{Num(R)}{\sum_{R' \in S} Num(R')}$;

(3) **for** $i = 1$ to m **do**

$$\text{let } w_i \leftarrow \frac{\sum_{R_k \in S_i} Num(R_k) * w_{R_k}}{\sum_{j=1}^{m} \sum_{R_h \in S_j} Num(R_h) * w_{R_h}};$$

(4) **for each** rule $X \rightarrow Y \in S$ **do**

let $supp_w \leftarrow w_1 * supp_1 + w_2 * supp_2 + \cdots + w_m * supp_m$;

let $conf_w \leftarrow w_1 * conf_1 + w_2 * conf_2 + \cdots + w_m * conf_m$;

(5) **rank** all rules in S by their supports;

(6) **output** the high-ranking rules in S whose support and confidence are at least $minsupp$ and $minconf$ respectively;

(7) **end all.**

The *Synthesizing* algorithm above generates high-ranking rules from the association rule sets $S_1, S_2, \cdots, S_m$, where each high-ranking rule has a high voting, support and confidence. Step (2) assigns a weight to each rule in S according to its voting. Step (3) assigns a weight to each data-source (and therefore its corresponding rule set) by the number of high-voting rules that the rule set supports. Step (4) synthesizes the support and confidence of each rule in S by the weights of different data-sources. According to the weighted supports, we rank the rules of S in Step (5). Output in Step (6) is the high-ranking rules selected by the user requirements.

7.6 Refining Rules Mined in Small Databases

In some cases, the mined association rules in small databases might not be trustworthy due to the fact that they contain too little information. On the other hand, synthesized collected rules contain a great deal of information, and high-ranking rules are generally believable. Therefore, if a mined association rule with higher confidence matches a high-ranking rule synthesized in the above method, then we can certainly extract this rule as a valid one in a small database. To demonstrate this idea, we use weighting as follows.

Let SD and D be a small database and the synthesized data-source respectively, and R_1 and R_2 the set of rules in SD and D respectively. For a given rule $X \rightarrow Y$, suppose w_1 and w_2 are the weights of SD and D, and the weighting is defined as follows.

$$supp_w(X \cup Y) = w_1 * supp_1(X \cup Y) + w_2 * supp_2(X \cup Y)$$
$$conf_w(X \rightarrow Y) = w_1 * conf_1(X \rightarrow Y) + w_2 * conf_2(X \rightarrow Y)$$

Certainly, we can determine the above weights, w_1 and w_2, by applications, experts, users and so on. Now we design the algorithm for mining small databases as follows.

Algorithm 7.3 *MiningSmallDB*

Input: *SD: small database; S_i: the set of the collected rules ($1 \leq i \leq m$), minsupp, minconf: threshold values; w_1, w_2: weights;*

Output: *$X \rightarrow Y$: valid association rules;*

(1) **mine** SD in Apriori algorithm (see Chapter 2);
    let $R_1 \leftarrow$ the association rules in SD;
(2) **collect** data-sources $\{S_1, S_2, \cdots, S_m\}$;
(3) **select** rules from the collected knowledge by the techniques in Section 7.4;
(4) **call** Synthesizing(S_i, S);
    let $R_2 \leftarrow S$;
(5) **for** each rule $X \rightarrow Y \in R_1$ **do**
    let $supp_w \leftarrow w_1 * supp_1 + w_2 * supp_2$;
    let $conf_w \leftarrow w_1 * conf_1 + w_2 * conf_2$;
(6) **rank** all rules in R_1;
(7) **output** the high-ranking rules in R_1;
(8) **end all.**

The $MiningSmallDB$ algorithm above generates high-ranking and valid rules in a small database, where each ranked rule has a high support and confidence. Step (1) is to generate all possible association rules in the given small database SD by the Apriori algorithm. And the association rules are saved in R_1. Step (2) is the same as in Procedure 7.1.

Step (3) is to select believable rules from the collected knowledge using the techniques in Section 7.4. Step (4) is to aggregate the selected rules in $S_1, S_2, \cdots$ and S_m into the set S by the procedure $Synthesizing$. And the synthesized rules in S are saved in R_2.

Step (5) is to enhance the rules in R_1 by weighting. Note that, for a rule $A \rightarrow B \in R_1$ and $A \rightarrow B \notin R_2$, the rule $A \rightarrow B$ would be labeled and not be presented in the ranked results. Step (6) is to rank the synthesized association rules. And the high-ranking rules are output in Step (7).

Obviously, we can also mine large scale databases by using $MiningSmall$-DB, and, in this case, the mined results are obviously fused with more information than in previous models for mining large scale databases.

7.7 Summary

Traditional association rule mining techniques are effective for large scale databases. However, the techniques may not be helpful for mining the small databases of certain companies or organizations, which expect to be able to apply data mining techniques to extract useful patterns from their databases in order to make their decisions. Data in databases such as the accident database of a nuclear power plant and the earthquake warning database in an earthquake bureau, may not be large enough to form sufficient patterns. Thus, current mining techniques are not adequate in these cases.

On the other hand, the advance of techniques in connection with the Internet ensures that a company can use, not only internal data, but also external data when making constructive decisions.

For this reason, we have presented techniques for mining databases by using external knowledge. The key points of this chapter are as follows.

- Proposed an approach for collecting external knowledge by associated semantics.
- Advocated a technique for synthesizing the selected rules by weighting.
- Designed an algorithm for improving the rules mined from a given database by external knowledge (rules).

8. Conclusion and Future Work

After compiling this book, we acknowledge that association rule mining is still in a stage of exploration and development. There remain some essential issues that need to be explored for identifying useful association rules. In this chapter, these issues are outlined as possible future problems to be solved. In Section 8.1, we summarize the previous seven chapters. And then, in Section 8.2, we describe four other challenging problems in association rule mining.

8.1 Conclusion

We have introduced fundamental association rule mining techniques and methods. Moving on from traditional association rule mining, we have developed new and effective fundamental techniques and methods for association rule mining. The key points are as follows.

1. The importance and challenge of association rule mining has been argued in Chapter 1.
2. Techniques for identifying hidden patterns of negative association rules of interest were proposed in Chapter 3.
3. To discover and represent causal rules among multi-value variables, we proposed techniques for mining the causality between variables X and Y by partitioning in Chapter 4. Here causality is represented in the form $X \rightarrow Y$ with conditional probability matrix $M_{Y|X}$.
4. Also in Chapter 4, the proposed techniques were applied to extract causal rules from probabilistic databases.
5. To use causal rules efficiently, we presented a causal rule analysis in Chapter 5. The causal analysis is a three-phase approach. The first phase is to merge useless (unnecessary) information in extracted causal rules. The second phase is to construct polynomial functions to approximate causality in data. The final phase is to find the approximate polynomial causality by fitting.
6. In Chapter 6, we presented some new techniques for mining association rules in very large databases, using instance selection.
7. In Chapter 7, we designed a framework for utilizing external data. It included collecting external data, selecting quality external data, and

synthesizing the selected external data to improve association rules mined from a database.

Most of the techniques and methods in this book are recent work carried out by authors. Compared to preexisting association rule mining techniques, there are four positive features proposed in this book.

(1) **Effectiveness**. Our techniques are effective in discovering hidden patterns. For example, techniques in Chapter 3 are effective in identifying negative association rules of the form $A \rightarrow \neg B$ (or $\neg A \rightarrow B$ or $\neg A \rightarrow \neg B$), which are of interest in databases. Also, the techniques are effective in mining causal rules in probabilistic databases.

(2) **Low-Cost**. Because instance selection, incremental mining and anytime techniques are used, the search costs are extremely reduced. In particular, the anytime mining algorithm can be used to serve multi-users.

(3) **Understandability and Familiarity**. Although negative association rules and causal rules are hidden in data, they are not strange to users. The techniques that are proposed, including Bayesian rules, sampling, data partition, similarity, and weighting, are all well-known techniques.

(4) **Incorporating Domain and Expert Knowledge**. To efficiently identify useful association rules, techniques from multiple principles, such as Probability, Statistics, Artificial Intelligence, and Information Retrieval, are assembled into the algorithms we have designed. For example, to measure relevance between an external data-source and a dataset, we have proposed a similarity model based on Information Retrieval.

Association rule mining is an arduous task, and this book cannot cover all problems in association rule mining. However, the book provides a practical way of understanding and applying association rule mining techniques, including attack ways to association rule mining problems.

8.2 Future Work

Association rule mining is an attractive topic of research in the field of data mining. We stress, however, that association rule mining is still in a stage of exploration and development. There are still some essential issues that need to be studied for identifying useful association rules. These issues are suggested as open problems in this section. We hope that data mining researchers can circumvent these problems as soon as possible.

Potential problems for association rule mining are suggested below:

1. establishing database-independent measurements;
2. developing efficient and effective hidden pattern mining methods and systems;
3. identifying *deep-level association rules*; and
4. exploring techniques for mining association rules in multi-databases.

Firstly, the minimal-support threshold of interesting association rules directly impacts on the automation and performance of data mining. For example, if minimal-support is too large, nothing useful can be found in a database; whereas small minimal-support leads to low-performance. However, though existing interesting measurements (such as frequency, chi-squared statistic and J-measure) are effective for identifying interesting itemsets in databases, they are actually difficult to those used in applications. For example, given a database, users or experts are required to assign the threshold (minimal-support) before interesting itemsets are searched for and extracted from the database using existing measurements. It is impossible to assign an appropriate threshold for the database if the users or experts have no knowledge of the database. This means that existing interesting measurements are database-dependent. Therefore, database-independent measurements should be developed for high-performance.

Secondly, there are many exceptional patterns hidden in databases. In real-world applications, exceptional patterns often present as more glamorous than common patterns in such areas as marketing, science discovery, and information safety. For example, intrusion detection should be focused on analyzing infrequent itemsets. This obliges us to explore efficient and effective algorithms and systems for hidden pattern mining.

Thirdly, most existing association rule mining techniques focus on effective and efficient mining algorithms. It is true that association rules are useful in real-world applications. However, these association rules can be regarded as *shallow-level rules* because they are only a simple survey or induction of data. For example, let 'if A, then a patient can recover at most 7 days' be identified from the databases of a hospital, where 'A' is an itemset. This quantitative association rule simply summarizes some of the data in the databases. This rule can be used to train student or inexperienced doctors. However, experienced doctors are often interested in more in-depth representation of the rule, which says, 'if B, then a patient may recover in 5 days', where 'B' is an itemset. This means, the in-depth representation of a rule can provide a better decision for users. Thus, it is valuable for identifying in-depth association rules.

Finally, the increasing use of multi-database technology, such as computer communication networks, distributed database systems, federated database systems, multi-database language systems, and homogeneous multi-database language systems, has led to the development of many multi-database systems in real-world applications. Many organizations need to mine multiple databases, which are distributed in their branches, for the purpose of decision-making. On the other hand, there are essential differences between mono- and multi-database mining. Because they are fascinated with mono-database mining techniques, traditional multi-database mining techniques are not adequate for discovering patterns such as '85% of the branches within a company agreed that a customer usually purchases sugar if he or she purchases coffee'.

Therefore, developing effective and efficient techniques for mining association rules in multi-databases is very important.

Although there are many other problems in the area of association rule mining, the solving of the above four problems is essential and, in our opinion, requires early attention.

References

[Aggarawal-Yu 1998] C. Aggarawal and P. Yu, A new framework for itemset generation. In: *Proceedings of Symposium on Principles of Database Systems*, 1998: 18-24.

[Agrawal-Imielinski-Swami 1993a] R. Agrawal, T. Imielinski, and A. Swami, Database mining: A performance perspective. *IEEE Trans. Knowledge and Data Eng.*, 5(6) (1993): 914-925.

[Agrawal-Imielinski-Swami 1993b] R. Agrawal, T. Imielinski, and A. Swami, Mining association rules between sets of items in large databases. In: *Proceedings of the ACM SIGMOD Conference on Management of Data*, 1993: 207-216.

[Agrawal-Srikant 1994] R. Agrawal and R. Srikant, Fast algorithms for mining association rules. In: *Proceedings of International Conference on Very Large Data Bases*, 1994: 487-499.

[Agrawal-Shafer 1996] R. Agrawal, J. Shafer: Parallel mining of association rules. *IEEE Trans. on Knowledge and Data Engg.*, 8(6) (1996): 962-969.

[Baralis-Psaila 1998] E. Baralis and G. Psaila, Incremental refinement of association rule mining. In: *Proceedings of SEBD*, 1998: 325-340.

[Bayardo 1998] B. Bayardo, Efficiently mining long patterns from databases. In: *Proceedings of the ACM SIGMOD International Conference on Management of Data International Conference on Management of Data*, 1998: 85-93.

[Berry 1994] J. Berry, Database marketing. *Business Week*. 5 September 1994: 56-62

[Brin-Motwani-Silverstein 1997] S. Brin, R. Motwani and C. Silverstein, Beyond market baskets: generalizing association rules to correlations. In: *Proceedings of the ACM SIGMOD International Conference on Management of Data*, 1997: 265-276.

[Brin-Motwani-Ullman-Tsur 1997] S. Brin, R. Motwani, J. Ullman and S. Tsur, Dynamic itemset counting and implication rules for market basket data. In: *Proceedings of the ACM SIGMOD International Conference on Management of Data*, 1997: 255-264.

[Cai-Cercone-Han 1991] Y. Cai, N. Cercone, and J. Han, Attribute-oriented induction in relational databases. In G. Piatetsky-Shapiro and W. Frawley, *Knowledge discovery in databases*, 1991: 213-228.

[Chan 1996] P. Chan, An Extensible meta-learning approach for scalable and accurate inductive learning. *PhD Dissertation*, Dept of Computer Science, Columbia University, New York, 1996.

[Chattratichat 1997] J. Chattratichat, etc., Large scale data mining: challenges and responses. In: *Proceedings of International Conference on Knowledge Discovery and Data Mining*, 1997: 143-146.

[Chen-Han-Yu 1996] M. Chen, J. Han and P. Yu, Data mining: an overview from a database perspective, *IEEE Trans. Knowledge and Data Eng.*, 8(6) (1996): 866–881.

[Chen-Park-Yu 1998] M. Chen, J. Park and P. Yu, Efficient data mining for path traversal patterns. *IEEE Trans. Knowledge and Data Eng.*, 10(2) (1998): 209-221.

[Cheung-Ng-Fu-Fu 1996] D. Cheung, V. Ng, A. Fu and Y. Fu, Efficient mining of association rules in distributed databases, *IEEE Trans. on Knowledge and Data Engg.*, 8(6) (1996): 911-922.

[Cheung-Han-Ng-Wong 1996] D. Cheung, J. Han, V. Ng and C. Wong, Maintenance of discovered association rules in large databases: an incremental updating technique. In: *Proceedings of ICDE*, 1996: 106-114.

[Clearwater-CHB 1989] S. Clearwater, T. Cheng, H. Hirsh, H., and B. Buchanan, Incremental batch learning. In: *Proceedings of the Sixth International Workshop on Machine Learning*. Morgan Kaufmann, 1989, 366-370.

[Cooper 1987] G. Cooper, Probabilistic inference using belief networks is NP-hard. *Technical Report KSL-87-27*, Medical Computer Science Group, Stanford University, Stanford, 1987.

[Cooper 1990] G. Cooper, The computational complexity probabilistic inference using belief networks, *Artificial Intelligence*, 42(1990): 393-405.

[Cooper 1997] G. Cooper, A simple constraint-based algorithm for efficiently mining observational databases for causal relationships. *Data mining and Knowledge Discovery*, 2(1997): 203-224.

[Cooper-Herskovits 1991] G. F. Cooper and E. Herskovits, A Bayesian method for constructing Bayesian belief networks from databases. In: *Proceedings of the Conference on Uncertainty in Artificial Intelligence*, 1991: 86-94.

[Cromp-Campbell 1993] R. Cromp and W. Campbell: Data mining of multidimensional remotely sensed images. *Proceedings of CIKM*. 1993: 471-480.

[Dey-Sarkar 1996] D. Dey and S. Sarkar, A probabilistic relational model and algebra, *ACM Trans. on database systems*, 21(3) (1996): 339-369.

[Dong-Li 1998] G. Dong and J. Li, Interestingness of discovered association rules in terms of neighborhood-based unexpectedness. In: *Proceedings of the second Pacific-Asia Conference on Knowledge Discovery and Data Mining*, 1998: 72-86.

[Dong 1999] G. Dong and J. Li, Efficient mining of emerging patterns: Discovering trends and differences. In: *Proccedings of International Conference on Knowledge Discovery and Data Mining*, 1999: 43-52.

[Durrett 1996] R. Durrett, *Probability: Theory and Examples*, Duxbury Press, 1996.

[Ester-Kriegel-Sander 1997] M. Ester, H. Kriegel, and J. Sander, Spatial data mining: a database approach, *Proceedings of SDD97*, 1997: 47-66.

[Etzioni-HJKMW 1996] O. Etzioni, S. Hanks, T. Jiang, R. Karp, O. Madani, and O. Waarts: efficient information gathering on the Internet. In: *Proceedings of FOCS*, 1996: 234-243

[Fayyad-Piatetsky 1996] U. M. Fayyad, G. Piatetsky-Shapiro, and P. Smyth, From data mining to knowledge discovery: an overview. In: *Advances in Knowledge Discovery and Data Mining*. AAAI Press/MIT Press, 1996: 1-36.

[Fayyad-Simoudis 1997] U. M. Fayyad and E. Simoudis, Data mining and knowledge discovery. In: *Proceedings of 1st International Conf. Prac. App. KDD& Data Mining*, 1997: 3-16.

[Fayyad-Stolorz 1997] U. Fayyad and P. Stolorz, Data mining and KDD: promise and challenges. *Future Generation Computer Systems*, 13(1997): 99-115.

[Feldman-AFLRS 1999] R. Feldman, Y. Aumann, M. Fresko, O. Liphstat, B. Rosenfeld, and Y. Schler, Text mining via information extraction. In: *Principles of Data Mining and Knowledge Discovery9*, 1999: 165-173.

[Fortin-Liu 1996] S. Fortin and L. Liu, An object-oriented approach to multi-level association rule mining. In: *Proceedings of CIKM*, 1996: 65-72.

[Frawley-Piatetsky 1992] W. Frawley, G. Piatetsky-Shapiro, and C. Matheus, Knowledge discovery in databases: an overview. *AI Magazine*, 13(3) (1992): 57-70.

[Godin-Missaoui 1994] R. Godin and R. Missaoui, An incremental concept formation approach for learning from databases. *Theoretical Computer Science*, 133(1994): 387-419.

[Goethals-Bussche 2000] B. Goethals, J. Bussche, On supporting interactive association rule mining. In: *Proceedings of DaWaK*, 2000: 307-316.

[Good 1950] I. Good, *Probability and the weighting of evidence*. Charles Griffin, London, 1950.

[Hagerup-R 1989] T. Hagerup and C. Rub, A guided tour of Chernoff bounds. *Information Processing Letters*, 33(1989): 305-308.

[Han 1999] J. Han, Data Mining. In: J. Urban and P. Dasgupta (eds.), *Encyclopedia of distributed computing*, Kluwer Academic Publishers, 1999.

[Han-Cai-ercone 1992] J. Han, Y. Cai, and N. Cercone, Knowledge discovery in databases: an attribute-oriented approach. In: *Proceedings of International Conference on Very Large Data Bases*, 1992: 547-559.

[Han-Cai-Cercone 1993] J. Han, Y. Cai and N. Cercone, Data-driven discovery of quantitative rules in relational databases. *IEEE Trans. on Knowledge and Data Engineering*, 5(1) (1993): 29-40.

[Han-Huang-Cercone-Fu 1996] J. Han, Y. Huang, N. Cercone, and Y. Fu, Intelligent query answering by knowledge discovery techniques. *IEEE Trans. on Knowledge and Data Engineering*, 8(3) (1996): 373-390.

[Han-Karypis-Kumar 1997] E. Han, G. Karypis and V. Kumar, Scalable parallel data mining for association rules. In: *Proceedings of the ACM SIGMOD International Conference on Management of Data*, 1997: 277-288.

[Han-KS 1997] K. Han, J. Koperski, and N. Stefanovic, GeoMiner: a system prototype for spatial data mining, *SIGMOD Record*, 26(2) (1997): 553-556.

[Han-Pei-Yin 2000] J. Han, J. Pei, and Y. Yin, Mining frequent patterns without candidate generation. In: *Proceedings of the ACM SIGMOD International Conference on Management of Data*, 2000: 1-12.

[Heckerman-GC 1995] D. Heckerman, D. Geiger, and D. Chickering, Learning Bayesian networks: the combinations of knowledge and statistical data, *Machine Learning*, 20(1995): 197-243.

[Hidber 1999] C. Hidber, Online association rule mining. In: *Proceedings of the ACM SIGMOD Conference on Management of Data*, 1999: 145-156.

[Hipp-GN 2000] J. Hipp, U. Gontzer, and G. Nakhaeizadeh, Algorithms for association rule mining — a general survey and comparison. *SIGKDD Explorations*, 2(1) (2000): 58-64.

[Hosking-Pednault-Sudan 1997] J. Hosking, E. Pednault and M. Sudan, A statistical perspective on data mining. *Future Generation Computer Systems*, 13 (1997): 117-134.

[Houtsma-Swami 1995] M. Houtsma and A. Swami, Set-oriented data mining in relational databases. *Data & Knowledge Engineering*, 17 (1995): 245-262.

[Hristovski-DPR 2000] D. Hristovski, S. Dzeroski, B. Peterlin, A. Rozic-Hristovski, Supporting discovery in medicine by association rule mining of bibliographic databases. In: *Proceedings of PDKK*, 2000: 446-451.

[Hussain-Liu-Suzuki-Lu 2000] F. Hussain, H. Liu, E. Suzuki, and H. Lu, Exception rule mining with a relative interestiness measure. In: *Proceedings of Pacific-Asia Conference on Knowledge Discovery and Data Mining*, 2000: 86-97.

[Jain-Murty-Flynn 1999] A. Jain, M. Murty, and P. Flynn, Data clustering: a review. *ACM Computing Surveys*, 31(3) (1999): 264-323.

[Kohavi-John 1997] R. Kohavi and G. John, Wrappers for feature subset selection. *Artificial Intelligence*, 97(1997): 273-324.

[Lakshmanan-Ng-Han-Pang 1999] L. Lakshmanan, R. Ng, J. Han and A. Pang, Optimization of constrained frequent set queries with 2-variable constraints. In: *Proceedings of the ACM SIGMOD Conference on Management of Data*, 1999: 157-168.

[Lesser-HKRWZ 1998] V. Lesser, B. Horling, F. Klassner, A. Raja, T. Wagner, and S. Zhang. A next generation information gathering agent. In: *Proceedings of the 4th International Conference on Information Systems, Analysis, and Synthesis; in conjunction with the World Multiconference on Systemics, Cybernetics, and Informatics (SCI'98)*, Orlando, FL, July 1998.

[Lesser-HKRWZ 2000] V. Lesser, B. Horling, F. Klassner, A. Raja, T. Wagner, and S. Zhang, BIG: An company for resource-bounded information gathering and decision making. *Artificial Intelligence Journal, Special Issue on Internet Information Agents*, 118(1-2) (2000): 197-244.

[Li-Shen-Topor 1999] J. Li, H. Shen and R. Topor, An adaptive method of numerical attribute merging for quantitative association rule mining. In: L. Hui and D. Lee (Eds.): *Internet Applications, 5th International Computer Science Conference*, 1999: 41-50.

[Liu-Hsu-Ma 1998] B. Liu, W. Hsu, and Y. Ma, Integrating classification and association rule mining. In: *Proceedings of International Conference on Knowledge Discovery and Data Mining*, 1998: 80-86.

[Liu-Lu-Feng-Hussain 1999] H. Liu, H. Lu, L. Feng, and F. Hussain, Efficient search of reliable exceptions. In: *Proceedings of The Third Pacific Asia Conference on Knowledge Discovery and Data Mining*, 1999: 194-204.

[Liu-Motoda 1998] H. Liu and H. Motoda *Feature selection for knowledge discovery and data mining*, Kluwer Academic Publishers, July 1998.

[Liu-Motoda 2001] H. Liu and H. Motoda, *Instance selection and construction for data mining*. Kluwer Academic Publishers, Feburary 2001.

[Liu-S 1998] H. Liu and R. Setiono, Incremental feature selection. *Applied Intelligence*, 9(1998): 217-230.

[Martin-E 2000] P. Martin and P. Eklund, Knowledge retrieval and the World Wide Web. *IEEE Intelligent Systems & Their Applications*, 15(3) (2000): 18-24.

[Massey-Newing 1994] J. Massey and R. Newing, Trouble in mind. *Computing*. May 1994: 44-45.

[Miller-Yang 1997] R. Miller and Y. Yang, Association rules over interval Data. In: *Proceedings of the ACM SIGMOD International Conference on Management of Data*, 1997: 452-461.

[Ng-H 1994] R. Ng and J. Han, Efficient and effective clustering methods for spatial data mining, *Proceedings of International Conference on Very Large Data Bases*, 1994: 144-155.

[Ng-Lakshmanan-Han-Pang 1998] R. Ng, L. Lakshmanan, J. Han and A. Pang, Exploratory mining and pruning optimizations of constrained associations rules. In: *Proceedings of the ACM SIGMOD Conference on Management of Data*, 1998: 13-24.

[Omiecinski-Savasere 1998] E. Omiecinski and A. Savasere, Efficient mining of association rules in large dynamic databases. In: *Proceedings of 16th British National Conference on Databases BNCOD 16*, 1998: 49-63.

[Park-Chen-Yu 1995] J. S. Park, M. S. Chen, and P. S. Yu, An effective hash based algorithm for mining association rules. In: *Proceedings of the ACM SIGMOD International Conference on Management of Data*, 1995: 175-186.

[Park-Chen-Yu] J. Park, M. Chen, P. Yu: Efficient parallel and data mining for association rules. In: *Proceedings of CIKM*, 1995: 31-36.

[Park-Chen-Yu 1997] J. Park, M. Chen, and P. Yu, Using a hash-based method with transaction trimming for mining association rules. *IEEE Trans. Knowledge and Data Eng.*, 9(5) (1997): 813-824.

[Parthasarathy 1998] S. Parthasarathy, M. J. Zaki, Wei Li: Memory placement techniques for parallel association mining. *Proceedings of International Conference on Knowledge Discovery and Data Mining*, 1998: 304-308.

[Pearl 1988] Pearl J., *Probabilistic reasoning in intelligent systems: networks of plausible inference*, Morgan Kaufmann Publishers, 1988.

[Piatetsky 1991] G. Piatetsky-Shapiro, Discovery, analysis, and presentation of strong rules. In: *Knowledge discovery in Databases*, G. Piatetsky-Shapiro and W. Frawley (Eds.), AAAI Press/MIT Press, 1991: 229-248.

[Piatetsky-Matheus 1992] G. Piatetsky-Shapiro and C. Matheus, Knowledge discovery workbench for exploring business databases. *International Journal of Intelligent Systems*, 7(1992): 675-686.

[Pramudiono-STK 1999] I. Pramudiono, T. Shintani, T. Tamura, M. Kitsuregawa, Parallel SQL based association rule mining on large scale PC cluster: performance comparison with directly coded C implementation. In: *Principles of Data Mining and Knowledge Discovery*, 1999: 94-98.

[Prodromidis-S 1998] A. Prodromidis, S. Stolfo. Pruning meta-classifiers in a distributed data mining system. In: *Proceedings of the First National Conference on New Information Technologies*, Athens, Greece, October 1998: 151-160.

[Prodromidis-Chan-Stolfo 2000] A. Prodromidis, P. Chan, and S. Stolfo, Meta-learning in distributed data mining systems: issues and approaches, In: *Advances in Distributed and Parallel Knowledge Discovery*, H. Kargupta and P. Chan (eds), AAAI/MIT Press, 2000.

[Provost-Kolluri 1999] F. Provost and V. Kolluri, A survey of methods for scaling up inductive algorithms. *Data Mining and Knowledge Discovery*, 3(2) (1999): 131–169.

[Rasmussen-Yager 1997] D. Rasmussen and R. Yager, Induction of fuzzy characteristic rules. In: *Principles of Data Mining and Knowledge discovery*, 1997: 123-133.

[Ribeiro-Kaufman-Kerschberg 1995] J. Ribeiro, K. Kaufman, and L. Kerschberg, Knowledge discovery from multiple databases. In: *Proceedings of International Conference on Knowledge Discovery and Data Mining*. 1995: 240-245.

[Santos 1996] JR. E. Santos, On linear potential functions for approximating Bayesian computations, *Journal of The ACM*, 43(1996): 399-430.

[Sarawagi-Thomas-Agrawal 2000] S. Sarawagi, S. Thomas, and R. Agrawal, Integrating association rule mining with relational database systems: alternatives and implications. *Data Mining and Knowledge Discovery*, 4(2/3) (2000): 89-125.

[Savasere-Omiecinski-Navathe 1995] A. Savasere, E. Omiecinski, and S. Navathe, An efficient algorithm for mining association rules in large databases. In: *Proceedings of International Conference on Very Large Data Bases*. 1995: 688-692.

[Savasere-Omiecinski-Navathe 1998] A. Savasere, E. Omiecinski, and S. Navathe, Mining for strong negative associations in a large database of customer transactions. In: *Proceedings of the International Conference on Data Engineering*. 1998: 494-502.

[Seshadri-WS 1995] V. Seshadri, S. Weiss and R. Sasisekharan, Feature extraction for massive data mining. In: *The First International Conference on Knowledge Discovery & Data Mining*, 1995: 258-262.

[Shafer 1976] G. Shafer, *A mathematical theory of evidence*. Princeton University Press, Princeton, 1976.

[Shimony-Charniak 1990] S. Shimony and E. Charniak, A new algorithm for finding map assignments to belief networks. In: *Proceedings of the Conference on Uncertainty in Artificial Intelligence*, Morgan Kaufmann, 1990.

[Shimony 1993] S. Shimony, The role of relevance in explanation, I: irrelevance as statistical independence, *Int. J. Approx. Reasoning*, 1993.6.

[Shintani-Kitsuregawa 1998] T. Shintani and M. Kitsuregawa, Parallel mining algorithms for generalized association rules with classification hierarchy. In: *Proceedings of the ACM SIGMOD International Conference on Management of Data*, 1998: 25-36.

[Shintani-Kitsuregawa 1999] T. Shintani and M. Kitsuregawa, Parallel generalized association rule mining on large scale PC cluster. In: M. Zaki and C. Ho (Eds.): *Large-Scale Parallel Data Mining, Workshop on Large-Scale Parallel KDD Systems, SIGKDD*, 1999: 145-160.

[Shortliffe 1976] E. Shortliffe, *Computer based medical consultations: MYCIN.* Elsevier, New York, 1976.

[Shyu-Chen-Kashyap 2001] M. Shyu, S. Chen, and R. Kashyap, Generalized affinity-based association rule mining for multimedia database queries. *Knowledge and Information Systems*, 3(3) (2001): 319-337.

[Silverstein-BMU 1998] C. Silverstein, S. Brin, R. Motwani and J. Ullman, Scalable techniques for mining causal structures. In: *Proceedings of ACM SIGMOD Workshop on Research Issues in Data Mining and Knowledge Discovery*, 1998: 51-57.

[Smyth-Goodman 1991] P. Smyth and R. Goodman, Rule induction using information theory. In: *Knowledge Discovery in Databases*, AAAI/MIT Press, 1991: 159-176.

[Smyth-Goodman 1992] P. Smyth and R. Goodman, An information theoretic approach to rule induction from databases. *IEEE Trans. on Knowledge and Data Engg.*, 4(4) (1992): 652-669.

[Srikant-Agrawal 1996] R. Srikant and R. Agrawal, Mining Quantitative Association Rules in Large Relational Tables. In: *Proceedings of the ACM SIGMOD International Conference on Management of Data*, 1996: 1-12.

[Srikant-Agrawal 1997] R. Srikant and R. Agrawal, Mining generalized association rules. *Future Generation Computer Systems*, 13(1997): 161-180.

[Srivastava-CDT 2000] J. Srivastava, R. Cooley, M. Deshpande, and P. Tan: web usage mining: discovery and applications of usage patterns from web data. *SIGKDD Explorations*. 1(2) (2000): 12-23.

[Tsai-Lee-Chen 1999] P. Tsai, C. Lee and A. Chen, An efficient approach for incremental association rule mining. In: *Principles of Data Mining and Knowledge Discovery* , 1999: 74-83.

[Ting-Witten 1997] K. Ting and I. Witten, Stacked generalization: when does it work? In: *Proceedings of IJCAI-97*, 1997: 866–871.

[Toivonen 1996] H. Toivonen, Sampling large databases for association rules. In: *Proceedings of International Conference on Very Large Data Bases*, 1996: 134-145.

[Tsumoto 1999] S. Tsumoto, Rule discovery in large time-series medical databases. In: *Principles of Data Mining and Knowledge Discovery*, 1999: 23-31.

[Tsur-Ullman-Abiteboul-Clifton 1998] D. Tsur, J. Ullman, S. Abiteboul, C. Clifton, R. Motwani, S. Nestorov and A. Rosenthal, Query flocks: a generalization of association-rule mining. In: *Proceedings of the ACM SIGMOD International Conference on Management of Data*, 1998: 1-12.

[Tung-Han-Lakshmanan-Ng 2001] A. Tung, J. Han, L. Lakshmanan, and R. Ng, Constraint-based clustering in large databases. In: *Proceedings of International Conference on Database Theory*, Jan. 2001.

[Webb 2000] G. Webb, Efficient search for association rules. In: *Proceedings of International Conference on Knowledge Discovery and Data Mining*, 2000: 99-107.

[Wolpert 1992] D.H. Wolpert, Stacked generalization. *Neural Networks*, 5(1992): 241-259.

[Wu 1995] X. Wu, *Knowledge acquisition from databases*, Ablex Publishing Corp., U.S.A., 1995.

[Wu 2000] X. Wu, Building intelligent learning database systems, *AI Magazine*, 21(3) (2000): 59-65.

[Wu-Lo 1998] X. Wu and W. Lo, Multi-layer incremental induction. In: *Proceedings of the 5th Pacific Rim International Conference on Artificial Intelligence*, 1998: 24-32.

[Wu-Zhang 2002] X. Wu and S. Zhang, Synthesizing high-frequency rules from different data sources. *IEEE Transactions on Knowledge and Data Engineering*, accepted, forthcoming.

[Yao-Liu 1997] J. Yao and H. Liu, Searching multiple databases for interesting complexes. In: *Proceedings of Pacific-Asia Conference on Knowledge Discovery and Data Mining*, 1997: 198-210.

[Yip-LKCC 1999] C. Yip, K. Loo, B. Kao, D. Cheung and C. Cheng, LGen - a lattice-based candidate set generation algorithm for I/O efficient association rule mining. In: *Principles of Data Mining and Knowledge Discovery* , 1999: 54-63.

[Zhang 1996] N. Zhang, Irrelevance and parameter learning in Bayesian networks. *Artificial Intelligence*, 88(1996): 359-373.

[Zhang 1989] S. Zhang, Discovering knowledge from databases. In: *Proceedings of National Conference on Artificial Intelligence and Its Applications*, 1989: 161-164.

[Zhang 1993] S. Zhang, Premonitory dependency based on historical data. *Chinese Journal of Computing Technology*, 20 (3) (1993): 50-54

[Zhang 1999] S. Zhang, Aggregation and maintenance for databases mining. *Intelligent Data Analysis: An international journal*, 3(6) (1999): 475-490.

[Zhang 2000] S. Zhang, A nearest neighborhood algebra for probabilistic databases. *Intelligent Data Analysis: an international journal*, 4(1) 2000.

[Zhang-Liu 2002] S. Zhang and L. Liu, Causality discovery in databases. In: *Proceedings of ICAIS'2002*, 2002.

[Zhang-Luo-Zhang 1998c] S. Zhang, X. Luo and C. Zhang, A model of integrating statistical and probabilistic techniques to uncertainty reasoning. In: *The Proceedings of International Symposium on Intelligent Data Engineering and Learning*, 1998: 14-16.

[Zhang-Qin 1997] S. Zhang and Z. Qin, A robust learning model. *Computer Sciences*, 24(4) (1997): 34-37.

[Zhang-Qiu-Luo 1999] S. Zhang, Y. Qiu, and X. Luo, Weighted values acquisition from applications. In: *Proceedings of 8th International Conference on Intelligent Systems*, 1999: 24-26.

[Zhang-Wu 2001] S. Zhang and X. Wu, Large scale data mining based on data partitioning. *Applied Artificial Intelligence*, 15(2) (2001): 129-139.

[Zhang-Yan 1992] S. Zhang and X. Yan, CTRCC: an analogical forecast model. In: *Proceedings of ICYCS'91*, 1991: 553-556.

[Zhang-Zhang 2001] C Zhang and S. Zhang, Collecting quality data for database mining. In: *Proceedings of The 14th Australian Joint Conference on Artificial Intelligence*, 2001: 593-604.

[Zhang-Zhang 2002] C. Zhang and S. Zhang, Identifying quality association rules by external data. In: *Proceedings of ICAIS'2002*, Feb. 2002.

[Zhang-Zhang 1998] S. Zhang and C. Zhang, A method of learning probabilities in Bayesian networks. In: *Proceedings of ICCIMA'98*, Australia, 1998: 119 - 124.

[Zhang-Zhang 2000] S. Zhang and C. Zhang, Tractable problems in Bayesian networks. *Information*: an international journal, 3(3) (2000): 361-378.

[Zhang-Zhang 2001] S. Zhang and C. Zhang, Mining small databases by collecting knowledge. In: *Proceedings of DASFAA01*, 2001: 174-175.

[Zhang-Zhang 2001a] S. Zhang and C. Zhang, Estimating itemsets of interest by sampling. In: *Proceedings of the 10th IEEE International Conference on Fuzzy Systems*, 2001.

[Zhang-Zhang 2001b] S. Zhang and C. Zhang, Discovering causality in large databases. *Applied Artificial Intelligence*, to appear in 2002.

[Zhang-Zhang 2001c] S. Zhang and C. Zhang, Pattern discovery in probabilistic databases. In: *Proceedings of The 14th Australian Joint Conference on Artificial Intelligence*, 2001: 619-630.

[Zhang-Zhang 2002a] . Zhang and C. Zhang, Anytime Mining for Multi-User Applications, *IEEE Transactions on Systems, Man and Cybernetics (Part B)*, accepted, forthcoming in 2002.

[Zilberstein 1987] S. Zilberstein, Using anytime algorithms in intelligent systems. *AI Magazine*, 17(3) (1996): 73-83.

[Zhong-Yao-Ohsuga 1999] N. Zhong, Y. Yao, and S. Ohsuga, Peculiarity oriented multi-database mining. In: *Principles of Data Mining and Knowledge Discovery*, 1999: 136-146.

Subject Index

Lecture Notes in Artificial Intelligence (LNAI)

Lecture Notes in Computer Science